General Editors: J. R. MULRYNE
and J. C. BULMAN
Associate Editor: Margaret Shewring

The Merchant of Venice

Already published in the series

J. L. Styan *All's Well that Ends Well*
Jill Levenson *Romeo and Juliet*
Roger Warren *Cymbeline*
Graham Holderness *The Taming of the Shrew*
Hugh Richmond *Richard II*
Alan Dessen *Titus Andronicus*

Volumes on most other plays in preparation

Of related interest
J. L. Halio *Understanding Shakespeare's plays in performance*

The Merchant of Venice

JAMES C. BULMAN

Manchester
University Press

Manchester and New York
Distributed exclusively in the USA and Canada by St. Martin's Press

Copyright © JAMES C. BULMAN 1991

Published by
Manchester University Press
Oxford Road, Manchester M13 9PL, UK
and Room 400, 175 Fifth Avenue,
New York, NY 10010, USA

*Distributed exclusively in the USA and Canada
by* St. Martin's Press, Inc.,175 Fifth Avenue,
New York, NY10010, USA

British Library cataloguing in publication data
Bulman, James C. *1947–*
  The Merchant of Venice. – (Shakespeare in performance).
  I. Title   II Series
  822.33

Library of Congress cataloging in publication data
Bulman, James C., 1947
    The Merchant of Venice / James C. Bulman.
      p.   cm. – (Shakespeare in performance)
    Includes bibliographical references and index.
    ISBN 0-7190-2745-4 – ISBN 0-7190-2746-2 (pbk.)
    1. Shakespeare, William, 1564-1616. Merchant of
  Venice.
  2. Shakespeare, William, 1564-1616 – Stage history.
  I. Title II. Series.
  PR2825.B78   1990
  822.3'3—dc20   90-39971

ISBN 0 7190 2745 4 *hardback*
0 7190 2746 2 *paperback*

Typeset by
Koinonia Limited, Manchester
Printed in Great Britain
by Bell & Bain Limited, Glasgow

CONTENTS

	Series editors' preface	vi
	Prefatory note	vii
Chapter I	An Elizabethan *Merchant*: performance and context	1
Chapter II	Henry Irving and the great tradition	28
Chapter III	Wayward genius in the high temple of bardolatry: Theodore Komisarjevsky	53
Chapter IV	Aesthetes in a rugger club: Jonathan Miller and Laurence Olivier	75
Chapter V	The BBC *Merchant*: diminishing returns	101
Chapter VI	Cultural stereotyping and audience response: Bill Alexander and Antony Sher	117
Chapter VII	Shylock and the pressures of history	143
	Bibliography	154
	Appendix	159
	Index	162

The illustrations appear between chapters II and III, pp. 52, 53

SERIES EDITORS' PREFACE

The study of Shakespeare's plays as scripts for performance in the theatre has grown in recent years to become a major interest for many university, college and secondary-school students and their teachers. The aim of the present series is to assist this study by describing how certain of Shakespeare's texts have been realised in production.

The series is not concerned to provide theatre histories. Rather, each contributor has selected a small number of productions of a particular play and studied them comparatively. The productions, often from different periods, countries and media, have been chosen because they are significant interpretations in their own right, but also because they represent something of the range and variety of possible interpretations of the play in hand. We hope that students and theatregoers, by reading these accounts of Shakespeare in performance, may enlarge their understanding of the text and begin, too, to appreciate some of the ways in which practical considerations influence the meanings a production incorporates: the stage the actor plays on, the acting company, the player's own physique and abilities, stage-design and theatre-tradition, as well as the political, social and economic conditions of performance and the expectations of a particular audience.

Any study of a Shakespeare text will reveal only a small proportion of the text's potential meaning. We hope that the effect of this series will be to encourage a kind of reading that is receptive to the ever-varying discoveries theatre interpretation provides.

J. R. Mulryne
J. C. Bulman
Margaret Shewring

PREFATORY NOTE

The theatre is a wonderful teacher. The many productions of *The Merchant of Venice* I have seen during the past twenty years have taught me more about the play than countless readings, and some of what I learned from them I hope to share with readers in the following pages. My responses to those productions, however, have not gone untested: they have been challenged, sharpened and enriched by friends who have read the manuscript in whole or in part. I am especially grateful to my colleagues Doug Lanier, Jim Ogden and Brian Rosenberg, three of the most generous readers one could hope to find; to my meticulous editors, Ronnie Mulryne and Margaret Shewring; to Miriam Gilbert and Bob King, who shared their production notes with me; and to Werner Habicht, whose knowledge of Shakespearian production in Germany helped me to flesh out the final chapter.

I am grateful, too, to the librarians at the Shakespeare Centre in Stratford-upon-Avon – Marian Pringle, Sylvia Morris and Mary White – whose patience and good humour are legendary; to Andrew Kirk at the British Theatre Museum and Bob Taylor at the Museum of the City of New York for their kind co-operation; to Liz Page in the Script Department of the National Theatre for allowing me to use Jonathan Miller's prompt book and other production materials; and to the staffs of the Lincoln Center Library, the Folger Shakespeare Library, the Senate House Library at the University of London, the British Library and the Pelletier Library.

I am deeply indebted to Dan Sullivan, Andy Ford and the Faculty Development Committee of Allegheny College for their unstinting support of this project; to the National Endowment for the Humanities for a fellowship which allowed me to undertake the research for it; and to the University College of Wales for providing me with an office – and the comforts of home – while I wrote the final draft. To all, my thanks.

J. C. B.
March 1990

All references, unless otherwise noted, are to the New Cambridge edition of *The Merchant of Venice*, ed. M. M. Mahood (Cambridge, 1987).

CHAPTER I

An Elizabethan *Merchant*: performance and context

If history is any judge, the crucial problem in staging *The Merchant of Venice* is how to balance its two distinct and seemingly unrelated plots. Although both ultimately derive from folk tales, Shakespeare dramatised them in such disparate styles that they seem to compete with rather than to complement one another. The casket plot, involving the winning of Portia by a lottery, is romantic, even at times Lyly-like: the scenes of wooing are witty; their pace, leisurely; their ethos, courtly. Above all, they are dominated by the comic resourcefulness of an aristocratic woman. The sordid bond plot, on the other hand, betrays its origins in darker legend. Dominated by men of business, the Venetian scenes have an urgency at odds with the leisure of Belmont: their prosaic idiom contrasts with the poetic formality of the wooing scenes, and their mercantile ethos calls into question the aristocratic assumptions of comic romance. By working such a tonal division between the two plots, Shakespeare made it difficult to bring them into an effective theatrical balance with one another. Venice and Belmont seem to belong to different plays.

To compound this difficulty, Shakespeare allowed the bond plot, to which he actually allots less stage time, to keep subverting the romance plot. The juxtaposition of the play's twin climaxes illustrates this subversion. Bassanio's winning of the lottery and Portia in III.ii, a scene full of romantic hyperbole, is immediately preceded by the passionately colloquial scene in which Shylock vows to take revenge on Antonio. Our knowledge of this sober turn of events invariably colours our response to Bassanio's victory, just as the

[1]

power of Shylock's idiolect, with its unconventional rhythms and Biblical repetitions – 'no ill luck stirring but what lights o'my shoulders, no sighs but o'my breathing, no tears but o'my shedding' (III.i.74-6) – sets in arch relief the artifice of the verse spoken by Portia and Bassanio. When, therefore, a letter from Antonio interrupts the festivities in III.ii, it recalls us to Venice and to the bond plot. The nuptials are effectively broken, or at least postponed, by the obligation Bassanio feels to assist his friend; and in the eyes of many, a latent rivalry between Antonio and Portia for Bassanio's love here becomes overt (Kahn, pp. 104-12). In this scene, the bond plot intrudes on and threatens to overwhelm the comic romance.

Harley Granville-Barker, a pioneer in twentieth-century Shakespeare production, identified the rivalry between these plots as symptomatic of a problem in the play's design:

> How to blend two such disparate themes into a dramatically organic whole; that was [Shakespeare's] real problem. The stories, linked in the first scene, will, of themselves, soon part company. Shakespeare has them run neck and neck till he is ready to join them again in the scene of the trial. But the difficulty is less that they will not match each other by the clock than that their whole gait so differs, their very nature. (p. 71)

At the time Granville-Barker made this observation, *The Merchant* had virtually become Shylock's play, a vehicle for star actors. Belmont, as a result, had been butchered, and on occasion performances even concluded with Shylock's exit from the court, leaving the lovers' plot unresolved – and, one assumes, of little consequence. Given this history, it is no wonder Granville-Barker thought that the problem was inherent in the text: 'How,' he asked, 'is the flimsy theme of the caskets to be kept in countenance beside its grimly powerful rival?'

It is a question any director of the play must ask. Most have found a true balance impossible to achieve. For reasons I shall discuss later, a growing fascination with Shylock as a symbol of oppression, representative of all Jews, has lent a cultural resonance to the bond plot that has made the lottery seem insubstantial, if not frivolous, in comparison. Those directors who *have* achieved a balance usually have done so by denying that resonance, insisting that both plots be taken on their own terms as folk tales, unencumbered by social and political history. After all, a Jew bargaining for a pound of Christian flesh is no more real than an heiress winning a husband by lottery or a condemned man being saved by a cross-dressing lawyer; all such absurdities require a willing suspension of disbelief. In such productions, *The Merchant* becomes a fairy tale wherein characters are types, action is allegorical, and Belmont proves as theatrically credible as Venice.

Certainly this was true of Terry Hands' production for the Royal Shakespeare Company in 1971, which, more than any other in recent memory, attempted to honour both plots as playful fictions. His intention was clear in the opening scene, where fantastically dressed merchants rolled giant dice and pushed 'enchanting toy galleons' (*Daily Telegraph*, 31 March 1971), replicas of Antonio's argosies, across a stage floor that was a mosaic of azure oceans and golden continents. Here, in miniature, was a model of life: the serious busi-ness of trade was encoded as a game of Ludo. Hands thus introduced a metaphor for all the 'games, gambles, wagers, bonds' that were to follow in both Venice and Belmont (*Birmingham Post*, 31 March 1971). Understood in this way, Bassanio's hazarding for Portia became just as significant as Antonio's gambling with his ships: its magnitude was signified by the giant caskets of gold, silver and lead from which he had to choose, the last of which contained a life-size effigy of Portia herself. Such romantic fictions, of course, work against any notion of bourgeois realism in this most money-oriented play; and Hands tried to solve the problem, as one critic observed, by 'siting the play in no place at all – or perhaps I should simply say in a theatre' (*Financial Times*, 31 March 1971). Such self-reflexive theatricality was reinforced by groups of spectators who from time to time stood at the rear of the stage looking on, as an audience at a play.

Shylock, too, was appropriately fantasticated. An extravagantly theatrical villain who spoke with a Yiddish accent tinged with the native Welsh of actor Emrys James, he bared his teeth at his enemies, bayed like a dog for Christian blood, and even barked at Antonio on the line, 'But since I am a dog, beware my fangs!' (Prompt book III.iii.7). As several critics noted, James conceived of Shylock as an actor and stole shamelessly from the bag of tricks of Shylocks past – 'a stage villain,' according to John Barber, 'barefoot, robed in old curtains, with a mouthful of spittle and plenty of "oi-yoi-yoi"' (*Daily Telegraph*, 31 March 1971). An exotic among other exotics, he was not so much an outcast of any recognisable Western society as the ogre of a fairy tale. One could readily believe that he wanted his pound of flesh because, in fairy tales, ogres eat people.

Within the assumptions of such implausible fictions, Shylock's villainy at the trial was strikingly credible. He flourished his props – knife and scales in either hand – like an allegorical figure of Justice untempered by Mercy (Slater, p. 177). As his moral opposite, the Portia of Judi Dench proved equally credible: charmingly boyish, confident, authoritative. When her pleas for mercy met deaf ears, however, she became visibly uneasy. Then, in the nick of time, just as Shylock moved behind the flinching Antonio and placed the dagger on his bare chest (see cover photograph), Portia screamed 'Tarry a little' (IV.i.301), surprising even herself with the sudden inspiration to save the day with a legal quibble. Hands' staging of the trial, by critical consensus, thrillingly dramatised the allegorical oppositions inherent in the play: the victory of Mercy over Justice, of the New Law over the Old, of Charity over Greed, of Belmont over Venice.

There are consequences for staging *The Merchant* in this way, however, for fantastication suppresses the individuality and psycho-logical subtlety with which Shakespeare invested his characters. As B. A. Young observed, Hands so deliberately under-emphasised the personalities of the characters that their performances were 'externalised', every point made by some simple visible means (*Financial Times*, 31 March 1971); and Jonathan Raban concurred that characters were 'dehumanised ... stereotypes' serving what he took to be Hands' moral theme (*New Statesman*, 9 April 1971). Romantic comedy, however, despite the implausibility of its plots, is deeply concerned with the plausibility of human behaviour; and in the modern theatre, its success depends on the ability of actors to get an audience to respond to them as real people. This may not have been entirely true of the Elizabethan theatre, in which actors submerged the individual in the type: they strove not to create particular 'identities' or 'inner selves' for their characters as actors do in naturalist theatre, but rather to imitate behaviour that would be understood as appropriately and recognisably general (Hattaway, pp. 72-9). Today, however, to make their performances convincing, actors must seek humanly explicable motives for the things they say and do. It is not sufficient for them simply to think of their characters as moral abstractions. Characters in *The Merchant*, however fanciful, may be seen to act in ways so complex and ambiguous as to cast doubt on any simple allegorical assumptions.

Antonio, for example, the most enigmatic character in the play, is willing to sacrifice himself for his friend. Some critics posit that he embodies the ideals of platonic friendship or Christian *caritas*. But this does not explain *why* he acts as he does, nor why audiences sense in him a languor and a self-deprecation – 'I am the tainted wether of the flock,/ Meetest for death' (IV.i.114-15) – that lead him to want to martyr himself and, by doing so, to bind Bassanio to him for life. 'Commend me to your honourable wife,' he tells Bassanio;

> Tell her the process of Antonio's end,
> Say how I loved you, speak me fair in death,
> And when the tale is told, bid her judge
> Whether Bassanio had not once a love. (269-73)

Actors would have difficulty understanding an abstract motivation for such lines: can *caritas* explain the emotional burden Antonio now places on his friend? Rather, these sentiments have suggested to actors that Antonio may feel an unfulfilled, possibly homosexual longing for Bassanio: even the comic matter of the rings wherein Portia tests Bassanio's fidelity to her often becomes, at Antonio's insistence, a test of Bassanio's love for *him* instead (Tennenhouse, p. 62). Psychoanalytic explanations are usually more useful to actors than allegory.

Nor are Portia's motives free from question. Allegorically, she may be the embodiment of mercy, functioning like the Virgin Mary of medieval miracle plays who, as Molly Mahood reminds us (p. 9), interceded with divine grace on behalf of the hero. By saving Antonio's life, furthermore, she frees her husband from a guilt that might forever burden him, and thus spares their marriage into the bargain. More realistically, however, Portia, as a woman in a patriarchal society, may betray a desire to usurp male prerogatives. She has no power herself: her fate has been dictated by her father's will, and all she inherits is won in an instant by Bassanio. Is she sensible of this disempowerment? And if so, does she go to Venice in male disguise more to test her mettle in a man's world than to administer divine mercy? Such questions lead one to examine the nature of her 'inspiration' in saving Antonio. Has the quibble occurred to her on the spot, or does her knowledge of the law – gained perhaps from consulting Doctor Bellario, and demonstrated when she lists the penalties for an alien's seeking the life of a citizen – suggest that she has plotted her strategy well in advance? We may reasonably conclude that she arrives at court with her trump up her sleeve: 'no jot of blood' (302). But if this is true, why does she wait so long to play it? Does she want to allow Shylock sufficient opportunity to show mercy, knowing that the law will come down on him hard if he does not? Or, less charitably, does she simply allow him rope enough to hang himself? Furthermore, does she realise that by saving her trump to the last possible moment, she brings extraordinary anguish to Antonio and to her husband? Or might that be – as psychoanalytic studies have suggested – precisely her intention?

This potential for dramatising relationships in *The Merchant* as shifting and unpredictable defies the neat schematisation towards which allegory tends. *How* audiences view the play thus depends on how directors adjust the balance between psychological realism and the play's deep allegorical structure. Directors usually find that the play resists any attempt to strait-jacket it with one particular concept. Hands certainly found this to be true. Despite his uses of enchantment, the actors' search for credible motivation kept disrupting the fantasy, with Portia so sensitive to her rivalry with Antonio that she became, in the words of the actress who played her, a most unpleasantly 'neurotic' heroine (Biggs, pp. 153-9). Conversely, directors who privilege the play's realism often do so at the expense of the allegorical constructs that give the play its moral grounding. They tend to foreground the plight of Shylock, who in many ways is the least conventional, most believably idiosyncratic of all the characters, and relegate the romantic artifices of Belmont to a subordinate role. This happened in Jonathan Miller's famous 'Victorian' *Merchant* for the National Theatre in 1970. His Venice was so authentically detailed, so rich in social nuance, that Belmont simply could not provide a credible alternative to it: thus Miller satirised the casket plot as a patently insincere fiction by which the bourgeoisie disguised their avarice. Such choices suggest that we, in our century, conceive of drama more categorically than Shakespeare could have anticipated. One reason for this may be that the nature of theatre itself has changed. *The Merchant* is a play whose potential to be various things at once – allegory and folk tale, romantic comedy and problem play – may have been realisable only on the Elizabethan stage.

✽

Shakespeare's theatre was unlike our own. Audiences stood or sat very close to a bare, thrust stage, and such intimacy fostered a participatory pact between actors and audience in which actors relied on the audience to piece out a performance's imperfections with their thoughts. The participation of the audience was necessary to foster any illusion of reality because the bare stage itself did not. Props were few; costuming, most of it Elizabethan, was eclectic; and plays were performed during the afternoon, in broad daylight. Such conditions, far from a liability, were in fact liberating: they attested to the Elizabethan audience's capacity for multi-consciousness, for adjusting imaginatively to a complex mixture of formal and realistic elements, and for losing themselves in the play while remaining aware of its artifice (Styan, pp. 164-5).

On such a stage, actors could move in and out of their roles more easily than actors do today. They could speak in character yet at the same time signal to the audience their conventionality, thereby preserving their fictive credibility while acknowledging their status as players. As Michael Hattaway has argued, the conception of acting as 'personation' paradoxically involved not only a quest for authenticity of character, but also an element of feigning or self-conscious role-play – as the etymology (from the Latin *persona*, mask) suggests – at odds with the modern notion of personality (pp. 78-9). Actors would use mimicry and stand 'apart' from the characters they played to achieve the desired response from the audience. Such flexibility may best be seen among those low comedians who played the clowns, such as Lancelot Gobbo, whose debate with his conscience over whether to leave Shylock's service owes a debt to the psychomachia of Morality plays. Drawing on a primitive theatrical tradition, Lance's comic monologue often proves a stumbling block in modern productions: it is not comfortably contained within the frame of naturalistic theatre. Its effect on the Elizabethan stage, however, would have been different, the actor performing much as a stand-up comedian would perform today, addressing the audience directly, at once in and out of character, and, by eliciting their response, making the scene a participatory experience. By all accounts clowns like Will Kempe, who probably played Lancelot Gobbo, exploited this potential for give-and-take, altering material at each performance, extemporising, milking an audience for laughs. As Peter Thomson suggests, Hamlet's complaint about clowns – 'Let those that play your clowns speak no more than is set down for them ...' (*Hamlet*, III.ii.43-51) – may have been Shakespeare's *ad hominem* attack on Kempe (p. 35). The idea of ad-libbing, of course, may offend our notion of the sacredness of Shakespeare's text; but in fact, as recent scholarship has shown, texts of his plays were unstable (see Honigmann; also Goldberg). As part of a rapidly changing repertory, they were modified to suit theatrical exigencies – what actors were available, and how many – and no doubt were unwittingly altered by actors who, pressed by the demands of a gruelling schedule and little rehearsal time, had to depend on their ability to extemporise simply to get through a performance. Clowns like Kempe, therefore, only did by design (and perhaps to excess) what was common practice among actors.

Direct address to the audience may have characterised the acting of Shylock as well. We cannot know whether the actor who first essayed the role exploited its comic potential (doubtful tradition has it that young Richard Burbage played Shylock in a red wig), but certain devices suggest that he may have bid for audience response in a way comic villains since the days of the Vice had done. In his first scene, for example, Shylock acknowledges his intention to catch Antonio on the hip in an aside that is disarmingly direct: 'I hate him for he is a Christian' (I.iii.34). Later, the scene affords the actor an opportunity for mimicry in the comic vein of Lancelot Gobbo, as when Shylock feigns the role of humble supplicant before Antonio:

> Shall I bend low, and in a bondman's key,
> With bated breath and whisp'ring humbleness,
> Say this:
> 'Fair sir, you spat on me on Wednesday last,
> You spurned me such a day, another time
> You called me dog ...' (115-20)

This is very much an actor's turn, a flamboyant appeal to the audience. And when, after he has been ridiculed for crying in the streets over the loss of his ducats and his daughter, he delivers his vehement self-defence as a Jew, he again may speak both in and out of character. On the one hand, he attempts in the speech to justify an odious revenge against Antonio, something he has already confessed to the audience he hungers for. Yet the series of rhetorical questions he asks – 'Hath not a Jew eyes? Hath not a Jew hands, organs, dimensions, senses, affections, passions?' (III.i.46-7) – extends beyond the immediate context of the play to become an overarching plea for toleration; and it is quite possible that the actor delivered this speech directly to the audience, as a soliloquy, rather than to Solanio and Salarino.

The same may have been true of Portia's eloquent plea for mercy. Certainly this rhetorically sophisticated speech would seem a bit out of character for the mere youth she pretends to be: it stands as a set piece, an expression of Christian values at once *of* the play and beyond it. Its original delivery would have been complicated by another convention of Elizabethan theatre, that of male disguise.

Shakespeare's audience accepted disguise as an artifice far less alien to reality than we regard it today. It suggested a conception of character more ludic than our demands for naturalism will allow. Further, the trying-on of roles signified the potential for one character to have a multiplicity of selves: it revealed that Portia, like other disguised Shakespearean heroines, understood how to think and act like a man. Her anticipation of cross-dressing prompts a satiric evaluation of the masculine behaviour she will imitate:

> [I will] speak of 'frays
> Like a fine bragging youth; and tell quaint lies
> How honourable ladies sought my love,
> Which I denying, they fell sick and died –(III.iv.68-71)

Yet in court, Portia's 'worthy doctor' outwits men at a more serious game. Her knowledge of the law, a male preserve, is greater than theirs, her eloquence more persuasive, her authority surer. And by maintaining her authority throughout the charade with the rings in Act V, Portia differs from other heroines such as Rosalind who relinquish control when they shed their male disguises.

The Elizabethan practice of boy actors playing women's roles complicated matters further. No doubt boys did a creditable job of impersonating women, and audiences readily accepted them as such. Such acceptance, however, does not imply the same thing as our contemporary notion of suspended disbelief, for, as we have seen, certain signals reminded the Elizabethan audience of theatre's essential artifice: the audience would have accepted a boy as Portia and yet remained fully cognisant that Portia was a boy. This multi-consciousness made particularly playful the scenes of cross-dressing in which onstage 'women' assumed male 'disguises', which paradoxically allowed the boy actors to resume their male identity – to drop their dresses, put on pants, and speak and act *as* boys. In *The Merchant* Shakespeare provides three cross-dressings, Jessica's, Nerissa's, and Portia's, the compound effect of which is to insist on the artificiality of the convention (Shapiro, *Boy Heroines*, p. 110). Jessica's disguise would have been most familiar to Elizabethan audiences, because it drew on Italian comedy for the resourceful, headstrong daughter determined to deceive her father by escaping his house in male attire. This conventional use of disguise, however, barely anticipated the more intricate effect of Portia's cross-dressing at the trial.

It has been argued that on the Elizabethan stage, Shakespeare submerged Portia's gender identity so completely in the fusion of

Balthasar with the boy actor that the audience would have perceived her *only* as male (Geary, p. 58). Indeed, unlike other disguised heroines who keep us aware of their gender through periodic asides and soliloquies, Portia never breaks her cross-gender concealment. Yet in subtler ways, as Michael Shapiro points out in his study of *Boy Heroines in Male Disguise* (pp. 117-20), Shakespeare insists on the presence of 'Portia' throughout the trial and thereby keeps the dynamic of sexual transformation before the audience. When Bassanio, for example, generously offers Shylock twice, even ten times the money owed him – Portia's money – it is 'Balthasar' who disallows the offer. In the theatre, this confrontation often brings Bassanio face to face with Portia, a situation which, by hinting at the risk she runs of being discovered, comically heightens our awareness of her identity. Later, when Antonio's 'Commend me to your honourable wife' (IV.i.269) prompts Bassanio to profess that he would sacrifice that wife to free his friend, he is not aware, as we are, that his wife is within earshot. Portia's reply – 'Your wife would give you little thanks for that/ If she were by to hear you make the offer' (284-5) – may be delivered directly to him by 'Balthasar', or as an aside to the audience; in either case, Portia's voice is heard. Gratiano's similar offer meets a like response from Nerissa, an echo which compounds the effect of the comedy. And when, at last, Portia asks for Bassanio's wedding ring as tribute, the layering of sexual identities yields a humorous irony. 'Balthasar' challenges Bassanio to break an oath to his wife by accusing him of ungenerosity, yet the audience simultaneously sees Portia playing mercilessly on her husband's divided loyalties. Her wry admonition, 'I pray you know me when we meet again' (415), is directed as much to the audience as to him; for who is the 'me' the audience is to know? The boy actor has been playing games with them as well as with the court. As Balthasar, he has played both a heroine in disguise and, no doubt more convincingly, himself. When he is next seen at Belmont, he will have resumed his 'real' identity as Portia, yet the audience would recognise that identity as no more than conventional transvestism. Such ironies are lost in the modern theatre, where actresses have difficulty establishing their credibility as young men and thus make of the trial a more absurd fiction than it ever would have been for the Elizabethans.

Other Elizabethan staging practices would have enhanced the audience's appreciation of the play's design. The minimal use of props in a neutral space, for example, allowed Shakespeare to establish a rhythm of scenic juxtapositions that both confirmed and challenged the oppositions between Venice and Belmont. Allegorically, of course, the casket plot and the bond plot represent antithetical values: Belmont and Venice are poles apart. Yet on a bare stage, every place is here, every moment is now. Belmont and Venice are the same place because they are undifferentiated by representational sets: the neutral playing space ensures fluid transitions from scene to scene and makes correspondences readily apparent. The first two scenes of the play, for instance – one in Venice, the other in Belmont – are stikingly similar in design. Portia's opening line, 'By my troth, Nerissa, my little body is aweary of this great world' (I.ii.1-2), echoes Antonio's opening line, 'In sooth I know not why I am so sad' (I.i.1). Both characters, in a sense, surfeit with too much. Antonio's friends proffer reasons for his sadness, all of which he dismisses, just as Nerissa lists the suitors who account for Portia's weariness, all of whom she dismisses. The parallel structure is clear; and though differences are obvious – the merchants are concerned with money, the women with marriage – the parallelism indicates that the women of Belmont are as much *like* the men of Venice as *unlike* them. Furthermore, Shakespeare works a remarkably fluid transition between these scenes. At the end of the first scene, Bassanio launches into a lyric paean to Portia which anticipates her arrival on stage; and by mentioning the Jasons who come in quest of her, he introduces the subject of Portia's conversation with Nerissa. He in effect summons them up: a Venetian can create the Lady of Belmont through words alone, and no sooner do we imagine her than she appears. Bassanio thus serves as a link between the casket plot and the bond plot: loved by both Antonio and Portia, he becomes the agency for bringing them together.

The mirroring of scenes in a neutral space was Shakespeare's favourite device for establishing a rhythm of correspondences. Perhaps the overriding correspondence in *The Merchant* is between those who sue for money and those who sue for love. Like Portia's suitors, Bassanio and Antonio are suitors to Shylock – and for money, which is a tacit goal of Portia's suitors as well. The succession of suits early in the play demonstrates how effectively Elizabethan stagecraft could create a network of relationships among scenes (Overton, pp. 29-30). The line in which Portia caps her dispara-gement of her suitors, for example – 'Whiles we shut the gate upon one wooer, another knocks at the door' (I.ii.110-11) – provides an apt transition to the next scene, which opens on

Shylock's rehearsal of Bassanio's request for three thousand ducats; for as Shylock notes, Bassanio is a wooer too: 'Monies is your suit' (I.iii.111). This successful suit is followed immediately by the entrance of Morocco who, to sue for Portia's hand, must agree to the hard condition never to marry if he chooses wrong. The rhythm hereby established culminates in Bassanio's hazarding for Portia, a scene in which she metamorphoses the mercantile vocabulary by which Venetians 'sue' into something of transcendent value:

> for you
> I would be trebled twenty times myself,
> A thousand times more fair, ten thousand times
> More rich, that only to stand high in your account
> I might in virtues, beauties, livings, friends,
> Exceed account. (III.ii.152-7)

The speech is no sooner spoken, however, than word arrives that Antonio must pay a mortal price for having incurred a debt to Shylock. Such fluid dramatic configurations as these preserve a fine balance between the two plots, a balance forfeited when staging becomes too representational.

The bare stage would also have lent more dramatic weight to Act V, which in 'realistic' productions is sometimes scanted as an embarrassing excrescence, a contrived return to the artifices of Belmont to ensure a happy ending. Granted, the trial is a hard act to follow; but the contrivance of Act V might have had more point on the Elizabethan stage than it has today. In it, Shakespeare cleverly recapitulates the bond plot that has threatened to upset the comedy in Act IV. Using Bassanio's and Gratiano's loss of their rings as a ploy, Portia vows to break off the nuptials (just as they were broken before) until Antonio stakes his life upon the loyalty of his friend (much as he has done before). Now, however, we perceive no risk in Antonio's doing so, for we know that Portia will pull strings – or rings – to get these men off the hook, just as she has done at the trial. An Elizabethan audience would have been aware of yet another level of meaning; for throughout the scene, Shakespeare kept them alert to the fact that Portia and Nerissa were really males who now, paradoxically, had resumed their female disguises. The audience's awareness of the boy actors inside the dresses, as Shapiro observes (*Boy Heroines*, pp. 125-6), is repeatedly piqued by references to male identity –

Nerissa	The clerk will ne'er wear hair on's face that had it [the ring].
Gratiano	He will, and if he live to be a man.
Nerissa	Ay, if a woman live to be a man.
Gratiano	Now by this hand, I gave it to a youth, A kind of boy, a little scrubbed boy No higher than thyself ... (V.i.158-63)

Portia, furthermore, uses legal jargon one last time, probably with a wry smile, to remind us of her appearance in the courtroom as Balthasar (Mahood, p. 166 n.):

> Let us go in,
> And charge us there upon inter'gatories,
> And we will answer all things faithfully. (297-9)

This final evocation of the trial would have had particular point on the Elizabethan stage, where locations were undifferentiated; for here, in this very space and only minutes earlier, Antonio came within a hair's breadth of being killed, Bassanio nearly lost a friend, and Portia, quite possibly, a happy marriage. The bare stage thus would have reinforced the correspondences between Acts IV and V by serving simultaneously as Belmont and, through imaginative recall, as the court of Venice. The comic artifices by which Act V recreates and resolves the tensions of the trial attest to the suggestive neutrality of Elizabethan staging and to the capacity of Elizabethan audiences to perceive a play on different levels.

✽

One cannot, of course, be certain how *The Merchant* was staged in Shakespeare's theatre, and it would be presumptuous to speculate how an Elizabethan audience might have responded to it. At most, using social history to provide a context, one may hazard a guess. Apparently *The Merchant* was a popular play. The Lord Chamberlain's Men acted it *'diuers times'*, according to the quarto text of 1600; and as the King's Men, they performed it twice at court in 1605. The popularity of any play, of course, is determined in part by how successfully it captures the mood of its audience: their attitudes, their *mores*. Few plays were so successful in doing this as *The Merchant*. By dramatising the tensions inherent in a nascent capitalist society – the acquisition of wealth weighed against the perils of trade, class antagonisms, the changing role of women, prejudice against minorities – it held a mirror up to London of the 1590s. That Shakespeare grafted such contemporary concerns on to the material of folk tale may seem surprising; but folk tales themselves enshrine the myths of the cultures from which they emerge, and Shakespeare's play does much the same thing. Like the society for which it was written, it has money at its heart.

The Merchant spoke to its first audience in complex ways. English trade had grown enormously during the final decades of the sixteenth century: a burgeoning merchant class had accumulated considerable wealth and, inevitably, wished to share power with those aristocrats who had traditionally held it. Class tensions thus arose between city entrepreneurs who, having made their fortunes, were in a position to buy what they could not take, and the landed gentry who, having inherited theirs, sought to maintain a hierarchy of privilege. Venice appealed to the Elizabethan imagination as a place where mercantile interests and social privilege were not mutually exclusive. An opulent centre of world trade and banking, founded in liberty and famous for toleration, Venice represented a vigorous fusion of cultures where those on the margins of society – Jews especially – did business daily with those at the centre (Grubb, pp. 43-4). In the eyes of Shakespeare's audience, therefore, Antonio and his companions were engaged in typically Venetian activities.

Their class attitudes, however, were decidedly English. One hears in their opening conversation a distinction between the noble 'signor' or 'rich burgher', Antonio (I.i.10), whose argosies are the envy of Venice, and those lesser men of trade – Solanio, Salarino[1] – whose business calls on them. Although Venice had been in decline as a maritime commercial power since the mid sixteenth century and few shipping magnates had the social standing of Antonio (Pullen, pp. 379-408; Mahood, p. 13), Shakespeare chose to perpetuate the Myth of Venice because it served his purpose: English merchants were aggressively acquiring the wealth, confidence, and social privilege that their Venetian counterparts were fearful of losing. In 1596, one might have found more Antonios in London than in Venice.

Elizabethans might have heard in this scene, too, some class tension between the lesser merchants and Antonio's 'worthier friends' (61) – Bassanio, Gratiano, Lorenzo – fashionable young men who apparently have the leisure (or idleness) not to work at all.

---

[1] For an explanation of why the three Venetians named in Q1 – Salanio, Salarino, and Salerio – are usually, and probably mistakenly, reduced to two – Solanio, Salerio – in editions and in performance, see Mahood, pp. 179-83.

'We'll make our leisures to attend on yours,' Salarino pointedly tells them on departing (68). Bassanio, we learn, has taken the usual course for the son of an aristocratic house: 'a scholar and a soldier', he has served 'in the company of the Marquis of Montferrat' (I.ii.93-4), returned home, and gambled away his father's estate. He thus depends on a rich friend, as impecunious aristocrats often did, to supply his wants. In an emergent capitalist economy like England's, there was plenty of room for opportunists, and it is feasible that the audience would have recognised Bassanio as one. His explanation of how he plans to pay back his debts by further speculation is suspect: clearly he intends to exploit his friendship with Antonio and, if possible, exploit the heiress of Belmont as well. 'In Belmont is a lady richly left ...' (I.i.160).

The view of Belmont as a green world, a society based on inherited wealth and removed from the anxieties of commerce, is not necessarily at odds with this Venetian concern with capital. For the 'imaginative space' of Belmont, as J. R. Mulryne rightly suggests (p. 7), 'is that of the great house' which increasingly, in England as in Venice, was purchased and sustained with the profits of commercial enterprise. Shakespeare may have found an analogue for Belmont in the lavish estates on the Veneto, where the Venetian patriciate, having turned away from trade, were enjoying the fruits of their success: 'the journey to Belmont represents for the former merchants of Venice ... the acceptance of an aristocratic life-style that without abandoning Venetian wealth contrasts in a marked way with the style of their former existence' (Mulryne, p. 8). Even if one defines Belmont in more traditionally English terms as an estate of the landed gentry, the same would hold true; for the maintenance of aristocratic values paradoxically eschewed, yet was predicated on, abundant capital.

Such values inform the casket lottery, wherein any suitor worthy of Portia should by nature recognise the difference between outward show – gold and silver, the media of commercial exchange – and inner merit. Winning the lottery presupposes that the victor have *sprezzatura*, which Castiglione defines in *The Courtier* as the means by which aristocrats recognise in one another an inherent worth that upstarts cannot buy. Bassanio shares this aristocratic assumption with Portia. His eloquent speech bears witness to it–

> So may the outward shows be least themselves:
> The world is still deceived with ornament. (III.ii.73-4)

– and proves thereby that however tainted he may be with Venetian opportunism, he nevertheless is to the manor born. Alone among the suitors, he recognises the value of meagre lead; as a reward, he earns Portia and, with her, her father's place in the hierarchy. Having lost his own estate, he comes to govern hers.

This is a capitalist fairy tale indeed. In it, Shakespeare bridges the worlds of commerce and inherited wealth by allowing Belmont to incorporate Venice, to subsume new-gotten gain under a conservative vision of aristocratic privilege. This adds a powerful social dimension to the romantic affirmations of Act V that would not have been lost on Shakespeare's audience; for once Portia has intervened at the trial to ensure victory by her innately superior values, the victors are free to move with her to Belmont, a green world *sustained* by money but not consumed with the *getting* of it.

※

Some, however, are excluded from this world. Among them are Portia's erstwhile suitors who, despite their noble breeding, do not fit into her particular version of aristocratic privilege. The list includes worthies from Naples, France, Germany, Scotland and England, all of whom she summarily dismisses with xenophobic barbs about their national characters. More pointedly dismissed are the two suitors who venture to choose: the black Prince of Morocco, whose bravado recalls the Marlovian excesses of Tamburlaine, and the Prince of Arragon, whose elegant self-absorption glances at those Spaniards who were the butt of English jokes. Nowadays, the suitors are commonly played for laughs, but such playing invalidates the dramatic premise of the lottery by making them too clearly unworthy of Portia. Although Arragon is more comically stereotypical than Morocco, neither suitor is necessarily ridiculous: each in his own way is eligible, articulate and worthy of marrying a woman of Portia's class. The reason she rejects them is that she harbours prejudices which a majority of Elizabethans would have shared: Morocco is the wrong race, and Arragon the wrong nationality. Therefore, when she tartly bids them farewell, calling Arragon a 'deliberate fool' (II.ix.79) and saying of Morroco, 'Let all of his complexion choose me so' (II.vii.79), her xenophobia would not have been reprehensible to the audience. Indeed, it might have won her their approval.

Most notably excluded from Portia's community, and most victimised by its prejudices, is Shylock. In him, Shakespeare created a character who conformed in many ways to the anti-Semitic stereotype prevalent in Elizabethan England. On numerous occasions characters attest to his villainy: Solanio and Salarino mock him as a miser who cares more for his ducats than his daughter; Antonio damns him as a figure from a Mystery play –

> The devil can cite Scripture for his purpose.
> An evil soul producing holy witness
> Is like a villain with a smiling cheek ... (I.iii.90-2);

Lancelot Gobbo, who famishes in his service, proclaims the Jew 'the very devil incarnation' (II.ii.20-1); and even his daughter Jessica calls his house a 'hell' (II.iii.2) and plots to escape it. Shylock's behaviour, furthermore, would seem to justify these bad opinions. He openly admits to the audience,

> I hate [Antonio] for he is a Christian;
> But more, for that in low simplicity
> He lends out money gratis, and brings down
> The rate of usance here with us in Venice. (I.iii.34-7)

Significantly, his two reasons for hating Antonio are not causally connected: the one invokes an age-old antipathy which Jews, as Christ-killers, supposedly felt towards Christians; the other invokes the stereotype of Jewish greed. Shylock's barbarism is confirmed by Jessica when she confides to her Christian hosts that she has 'heard him swear/ ... That he would rather have Antonio's flesh/Than twenty times the value' of the bond (III.ii.283-6). Shylock uses ironic humour to lure Antonio into agreeing to this bond as 'a merry sport' (I.iii.138); but once it appears the argosies are lost, he turns deadly earnest:

> Go, Tubal, fee me an officer ... I will have the heart of him if he forfeit, for were he out of Venice I can make what merchandise I will. (III.i.99-102)

That Shylock's revenge is apparently sanctioned by Venetian law does not make it any less barbaric: in fact, his insistence on law without mercy represents a Pauline distortion of Judaism that went largely unchallenged in the Renaissance (J. Cooper, pp. 117-24; Glassman, pp. 14-83). Little wonder, then, that Shylock's forced conversion to Christianity, often so repugnant to modern audiences, was welcomed as a just retribution by Elizabethans, who commonly regarded the soul of a Jew 'as already forfeit in so far as he, like his forbears, refused to acknowledge the Christian Messiah. Baptism alone, it was believed, could put a Jew in the way of salvation' (Mahood, p. 19).

Some knowledge of the history of anti-Semitism in England is critical to an understanding of the stereotype with which Shakespeare appealed to his audience's prejudices. Jews first came to England after the Norman Conquest. Operating out of a special Exchequer of Jews, they financed the needs of court, aristocracy and clergy during a period of national expansion: in effect, they were tolerated only to the degree they were willing to be extorted. During the Crusades, however, persecution of Jews erupted on a large scale throughout Europe, and England was not exempt; riots, pillage and killing grew more and more frequent. The arrival of mendicant Dominican friars may have contributed to the expulsion of the Jews in 1290, yet the primary reason was economic. For by the thirteenth century, taxes were exceeding Jewish resources, the Jews' money-lending monopoly had been broken by the Lombards, and Edward I could safely expel them without incurring financial hardship. Jews were not officially readmitted until 1655, under Cromwell, though a few hundred real or pretended converts to Christianity did remain. Some of them were attached to the court; others were prosperous merchants; none conformed to the anti-Semitic stereotype (Sanders, pp. 339-51; Sinsheimer, *passim*).

When *The Merchant* was first performed in late 1596 or 1597, therefore, Jews had not lived in England for over three hundred years, and anti-Semitic myths had been able to grow and prosper unimpeded by the presence of Jews to refute them. Most widespread was the myth of child murder: Jews were said to steal Christian children, crucify them, and use the blood in the Passover ritual. One hundred and fifty such cases were reported, the most notorious being the death of young Hugh of Lincoln, recounted in the tale told by Chaucer's Prioress. Jews' daughters, furthermore, always beautiful, were believed to act as decoys for these children. Another popular myth was that Jews caused the black death by poisoning wells and such like. The fact that many Jews were doctors perpetuated the myth, and it contributed even as late as 1594 to the frenzy surrounding the case of Ruy Lopez, a Portuguese Jew who, as physician to the Queen, was accused of attempting to poison her.

The early English stage reinforced the stereotype by dressing villains of the Corpus Christi plays in Jewish cloaks and horned hats, often completing the identification with a circle of yellow cloth on the arm, which since 1215 had been the badge of European Jewry (Fisch, pp. 13-18). Judas in particular was said to have looked very much like the devil with his red wig, hook nose, and usurer's bag. This tradition may have carried over to the Elizabethan stage as well, if one believes the following description of Shylock's appearance in a ballad written by an actor in the 1630s (and published in *The Royal Arbor of Loyal Poesie*, 1664):

> His beard was red; his face was made
>   Not much unlike a witches.
> His habit was a Jewish gown
>   That would defend all weather;
> His chin turn'd up, his nose hung down,
>   And both ends met together. (Thomas Jordan, 'The Forfeiture')

The most immediate source for Shakespeare, Marlowe's *The Jew of Malta*, first performed c.1590, revived in 1594 to capitalise on the Lopez affair and again in 1596, just prior to *The Merchant*, provided a contemporary dramatic inspiration for Shylock. A wealthy Maltese Jew, Barabas is a miser – in love with his ducats more than his daughter – who conspires to undermine the ostensibly 'Christian' government that has levelled taxes on him and his fellow Jews to finance its wars. Through him, Marlowe attacks Christian hypocrisy much as Shakespeare may be said to do through Shylock (Dessen, pp. 231-45). Yet the differences between Shylock and Barabas are significant. Barabas without remorse poisons his daughter along with the nuns with whom she has sought refuge; Shylock's anger over Jessica's defection is altogether more familial. Barabas plots treachery on the authority of Machiavelli; Shylock seeks revenge through the course of law. Ultimately, they are products of different societies. Barabas is like those Jews who, in medieval England, were expected to finance – through taxation and extortion – the activities of a government that barely tolerated them. Shylock, on the other hand, does business in the more tolerant climate of the Venetian Republic. He is a usurer; and it is in this capacity that he raises some of the play's most vexing questions about the relationship of the outsider to those in power.

In the view of many Elizabethans, usury and Judaism were virtually synonymous. The advent of a money economy, the decay of the old aristocratic houses, chronic borrowing, and thrift sapped by the availability of easy credit all produced tensions within Elizabethan society. The money-lender, according to Wilbur Sanders, 'though merely the economic instrument of new desires, had all the resultant tensions and crises laid to his door; and the money-lender was, by an ineradicable popular association, the Jew' (pp. 345-6).

Historical circumstances explain this association. Jews had been allowed to lend money at interest because Christians were forbidden to do so: the Gospels taught that it was wrong to lend for gain, and people still assented to Aristotle's belief that it was unnatural for money to breed more money. This belief underlies Antonio's attack on Shylock for taking 'a breed of barren metal' (I.iii.126). 'Is your gold and silver ewes and rams?' he asks, implicitly pointing out the disparity between natural and unnatural increase, to which Shylock wryly replies, 'I cannot tell, I make it breed as fast' (87-8).

Like Antonio, Elizabethans commonly condemned usurers as wolves, devils, and heretics: they were 'greedie cormoraunte wolfes in deede, that rauyn vp both beaste and man' according to *A Discourse upon Usury* (1572); their 'houses were called the devils houses, his fields the devils croppe', according to *The Death of Usury, or, The Disgrace of Usurers* (1594). Behind such virulence lay the fear that capitalism itself might be ungodly. Were the old religion and the new mercantilism fully compatible? Was the 'thrifty' pursuit of trade distinguishable from the 'prodigal' indulgence of greed? (Moisan, p. 189). As an emergent economic power, England of course placed a great value on her merchants, and usury was necessary to ensure that their ventures could thrive. Furthermore, not only merchants, but Parliament and the Queen herself sought the resources of usurers – virtually none of whom in fact were Jews (Draper, pp. 39-45); and the Queen, by putting a ceiling of 10 per cent on lending rates, officially condoned the practice. Usury and trade thus existed in an embarrassing symbiotic relationship that no tract against usury could suppress.

The Merchant reflects this anxiety over how best to accommodate the new mercantile ethic. Although the play formally reconciles the monied classes under the dominant aristocratic ideology at Belmont (W. Cohen, p. 772), performance history reveals that it resists such easy closure; for Shylock, whose usury is necessary to effect this reconciliation, is not so casually dismissed by the audience as he is by the ducal court. Economic necessity may turn him into the kind of wolf or devil condemned in anti-usury tracts, but he also may be seen to serve as a scapegoat for the Christians, bearing the burden of their guilt, mythologising an evil – greed – from which they would like to dissociate themselves (Girard, pp. 100-19). Shakespeare seems to acknowledge as much when he has Shylock plead his own humanity – 'I am a Jew' – at the very moment he is being most savagely mocked. This speech has so powerfully bid audiences to understand him as a victim of Christian bigotry that it has taken on a life of its own outside the play.

Shakespeare offers audiences other reasons to sympathise with Shylock as well. His first exchange with Antonio establishes that his malice is not without cause: he accuses Antonio of berating him on the Rialto, calling him misbeliever and cut-throat dog, spitting on his Jewish gaberdine, and kicking him across his threshold like a stranger cur – provocation enough, one would think, for anyone to rebel. Yet Antonio is unrepentant:

> I am as like to call thee so again,
> To spit on thee, to spurn thee too.
> If thou wilt lend this money, lend it not
> As to thy friends ... (122-5)

Shakespeare's audience may have thought that Antonio was in the right: if one condemns usury as a diabolical practice, as Elizabethans were told to do, then of course one would not expect him hypocritically to flatter Shylock, even if he was suing for a loan. But, alternatively, they might have found his speech surprisingly angry, for as many of them no doubt realised, usury was a necessary evil; and on the stage, no matter what Shylock may allegorically signify, it is difficult *not* to see him as a human being victimised by a smug community of merchants who tolerate him only when, as now, he proves useful to them.

The Christianity of the Venetian community is thus very much at issue. At the trial, Portia's plea for Shylock to have mercy is counterpoised with Gratiano's vindictive – and familiarly anti-Semitic – attacks on his character: 'O be thou damned, inexecrable dog' (IV.i.128); 'Thy currish spirit/ Governed a wolf' (133-4); 'thy desires/ Are wolfish, bloody, starved, and ravenous' (137-8). And when the law turns against Shylock to protect the interests of those in power, the Christians administer mercy most strangely: they strip him of his money and his religion, the very things for which, as a Jew, he lives. 'You take my life/ When you do take the means whereby I live,' he cries (372-3); and historically he is right, for usury was one of the only ways in which Jews were allowed to earn a living. Twice before Christians have contributed to his financial undoing: Antonio by forfeiting the bond, and Lorenzo by stealing his ducat-laden daughter. Here, his undoing is completed. If one regards Shylock as evil, then of course this turn of events must seem good: the devil is exorcised, the Jew turns Christian. Yet Shakespeare endows Shylock with enough integrity to complicate our response to his defeat. This interplay between the individual and the type is interestingly reflected, as Bill Overton observes (pp. 28-9), in variations of speech prefixes in the Quarto, where *Jew* precedes those speeches that tend to characterise Shylock as a traditional villain – his nasty aside in I.iii, his harassment of Antonio and the Jailer, and that portion of the trial where he exults in his apparent victory – and *Shylock* precedes those in which he deviates from the type: his domestic conversation with Jessica and Lancelot, his explosions of grief and anger in III.i, and all his speeches at the trial after Portia has defeated him. If these variations originated in Shakespeare's manuscript (and a scribe, compositor, or theatre official is unlikely to have introduced them), they afford us a glimpse of how consciously Shakespeare sought to revise the stage Jew as a credibly complex human being. His success in doing so is proven by four hundred years of stage history.

*

That seventeenth-century audiences may have found Shylock the play's most absorbing character is evidenced by George Granville's adaptation of 1701. Called *The Jew of Venice*, thereby awarding Shylock a titular prominence that may reveal how he had come to be regarded (and which, in fact, the Stationers' Register records as the play's alternate title on 22 July 1598), Granville's adaptation responded to the demands of a 'refined' age to make Shakespeare conform to the dictates of generic decorum, as if the products of his untutored genius needed to be purged of those anarchic pressures which our own age regards as their chief glory. In brazen testimony to the arrogance of the age, Bevill Higgons provided a Prologue in which Shakespeare's ghost praises Granville's improvements:

> *These Scenes in their rough Native Dress were mine;*
> *But now improv'd with nobler Lustre shine;*
> *The first rude Sketches* Shakespear's *Pencil drew,*
> *But all the shining Master-stroaks are new.* (35-8)

By briefly examining what Granville excised and revised in order to accommodate the play to the requirements of his stage and audience, we may learn what features of the original were deemed indecorous, or at least problematic, for performance in the early eighteenth century.

To exploit the new theatre technology, with its painted flats and more representational scenery, Granville drastically reduced the number of scenes from twenty to nine. This reduction of course retarded the quick transitions and juxtapositions characteristic of Elizabethan staging. Granville also eliminated many secondary characters as either superfluous to the action or too lowly comic to be appropriate for it. The Gobbos were first to go; they were followed by Solanio and Salarino, by Tubal, and even by Portia's unsuccessful suitors. Thus began an exodus that would be imitated in later, more spectacular productions, the effect of which was to throw a greater emphasis on the 'big' scenes – Bassanio's choice of the lead casket, Antonio's trial – and to jeopardise the network of correspondences that had made Shakespeare's original so compelling.

In his Advertisement for the play, Granville promises that the reader 'will observe so many Manly and Moral Graces in the Characters and Sentiments, that he may excuse the Story' (Spencer, p. 347). Such graces particularly inform the friendship between Antonio and Bassanio, the latter played by Thomas Betterton, for whose heroic acting style the play served as a vehicle. Granville filled their scenes with chivalric protestations of love, honour, fame, and self-sacrifice, such as these with which Antonio concludes the first act:

> There is not the least Danger, nor can be,
> Or if there were, what is a Pound of Flesh,
> What my whole Body, every Drop of Blood,
> To purchase my Friend's Quiet! Heav'n still is good
> To those who seek the Good of others. Come, *Bassanio*,
> Be chearful, for 'tis lucky Gold we borrow:
> Of all the Joys that generous Minds receive,
> The noblest is, the God-like Power to give. (I.iii.163-70)

There is no mercantile talk in Granville's Venice: the text is purged of the capital concerns that made Shakespeare's Venice seem authentic. Instead, its manners and speeches are modelled on the ideals of a precapitalist age which English Augustans were attempting, through art, to appropriate as their own.

Like other dramatists of the period, Granville sacrificed psychological credibility to the 'interests of moral clarity' (Spencer, p. 12), so that his characters were generalised and their motivation easily understood. Bassanio is a case in point: what motivates his quest for Portia is not a desire for her wealth, but love alone. Thus, when Portia dedicates herself to him after he has chosen right, her speech is shorn of the ambiguous mercantile vocabulary that made it so allusive in Shakespeare's play; and Bassanio's response to her emphasises love's magnanimity – a concept from heroic drama – instead of love's 'worth'. Such magnanimity ennobles the trial as well, which Granville was careful to purge of its potential rivalry between Antonio and Portia for Bassanio's love. In place of Bassanio's vow that he would sacrifice his wife to deliver Antonio – a remark that carries moral, if not sexual, ambiguity – Granville inserted conventional testimonials to the value of friendship. Intent on idealising the Venetians as courtiers, he suppressed the questionable motives that made them recognisably human.

The most notable suppressions occurred in the role of Shylock. Thomas Doggett, an actor noted for low comedy, played him as a caricature miser who, according to the Prologue, is punished as a '*Stock-jobbing Jew*' (29), possibly modelled on disreputable sharpers of the London Exchange. In keeping with the aristocratic prejudices of Granville (later Lord Lansdowne) and his audience, Shylock lost the individuality with which Shakespeare had imbued him. His richly colloquial speeches to Antonio are conflated and vulgarised:

>   Be this
> The Forfeiture.
> Let me see, What think you of your Nose,
> Or of an Eye – or of – a Pound of Flesh
> To be cut off, and taken from what Part
> Of your Body – I shall think fit to name.
> Thou art too portly, Christian! (I.iii.124-30)

At the supper to which he is bid forth – a scene Shakespeare chose not to write – Shylock follows the Christians' toasts to Love and Friendship with a toast of his own to his Mistress Money. And robbed of the opportunity to defend himself against the goading of Solanio and Salarino and to express anguish over his losses to Tubal, he becomes simply an abstracted figure of revenge, as clear in his villainy as his antagonists are in their virtue (Zimbardo, p. 224). Shylock's behaviour at the trial is thus predictably diabolical. Refusing Bassanio's generous offer to die in place of his friend, he reveals a motive more sinister than any Shakespeare ascribed to him; for, he gloats,

> When [Antonio] has paid the Forfeit of his Bond,
> Thou canst not chuse but hang thy self for being
> The Cause: And so my ends are serv'd on both. (206-8)

Given such transparent allegory, it is odd that Granville omitted Shylock's forced conversion to Christianity – evidence, perhaps, that this harsh condition had proven distasteful even to early audiences. Its omission would have been consistent with Granville's aim of suppressing the problematic nature of Shakespeare's text and offering in its place the decorous comedy Shakespeare *should* have written.

Yet there were objections to his adaptation. Nicholas Rowe in 1709 protested the reduction of Shylock to a comic turn: 'tho' we have seen the Play Receiv'd and Acted as a Comedy, and the Part of the *Jew* perform'd by an excellent Comedian, yet I cannot but think that it was design'd Tragically by the Author' (`Life', p. 9). Rowe here argues for the potential of Shylock to turn the play from comedy to its opposite. Indeed, the focus returned to a more fully fleshed Shylock when, in 1741, Charles Macklin persuaded the management of Drury Lane to restore Shakespeare's play in a text that included Portia's suitors, both Gobbos, and Tubal. Macklin was renowned as a comedian, famous for roles such as Osric, Touchstone and Trinculo, so that, according to John Russell Brown, 'his Shylock cannot have been "tragic", but all witnesses affirm that he gave full vent to the Jew's contrasted passions' (p. xxxiii). Macklin's interpretation would have satisfied Rowe's call for 'a savage Fierceness and Fellness' of purpose: he apparently terrified audiences by his ferocity in III.i and his portentous silences at the trial. In its menacing power, Macklin's portrayal drew attention away from the Venetians and even from the Portia of Kitty Clive who, as Balthasar, comically aped the mannerisms of well-known lawyers of the day. His Shylock held the stage to the end of the century, for a total of 316 performances; and despite its anti-Semitic appeal, his portrayal so altered audiences' perception of the play that one commentator imagined a future adaptation, written by a Jew, in which Shylock would become the wronged hero, his opponents overwhelmed by remorse (Hole, p. 566).

Clearly the potential of Shylock to disrupt the comedy had seized the popular imagination. Before long Belmont began to be trivialised: the suitors were (once again) eliminated, songs and dances were added, and although such notable actresses as Sarah Siddons and Peg Woffington played Portia, 'there is every indication that *The Merchant* had become Shylock's play' (Brown, p. xxxiii). This was even more the case in the nineteenth century, when, in a line beginning with Edmund Kean, productions in England, America and Germany transformed the play into the history of a tormented Jew who, when injured, would fight his oppressors with a terrible, contemptuous scorn. Donning a black wig, Kean broke with the traditional red-bearded, hook-nosed Shylock by infusing 'credibly human qualities into ... a mythical figure' (see Lelyveld, pp. 39-60). Passionate and sober by turn, he played Shylock, in the words of Coleridge, 'by flashes of lightning', and III.i became for Kean, as it had been for Macklin, the lightning rod that grounded his performance. In that scene, one spectator wrote, Kean's 'voice swells and deepens at the mention of his sacred tribe and ancient law' (*Examiner*, 16 March 1828). In his exchange with Tubal, he rivetted audiences with instantaneous shifts of grief and rage; and by delivering asides as if they were soliloquies, he bid for sympathy. His bid was most successful, apparently, when, wishing his daughter dead at his foot with the jewels in her ear, Kean recoiled in revulsion at his own unnaturalness and, with his face buried in his hands, murmured 'No, no, no.'

William Hazlitt, who was in the audience on the opening night in 1814, wrote that Kean's 'Jew is more than half a Christian. Certainly, our sympathies are much oftener with him than with his enemies. He is honest in his vices; they are hypocrites in their virtues' (*The Chronicle*, 6 March 1816). Shylock's claim to moral superiority over the Christians turned the trial into a painful ordeal rather than a celebration. In the words of one recent editor, 'the collapse of this intelligent and vulnerable man was horrible to watch; the reaction of the spectator who, in Heine's hearing, exclaimed "the poor man is wronged" was only a little more extreme than that of the audience as a whole' (Mahood, p. 44). Shylock's exit from the court thus came to be regarded as a fitting conclusion to the play, and Act V was often omitted.

These changes were in keeping with the sensibility of the early nineteenth century. Just as Granville had revised *The Merchant* to accommodate the expectations of his decorous age, so Kean and his followers found that the play spoke, through Shylock, to a Romantic age whose fascination with passionate individuality and exotic difference made Shakespeare's tragedies more popular than his comedies. Tellingly, measured by the number of performances, *The Merchant* was second only to *Hamlet* in popularity during the century. It was embraced by such great tragic actors as William Macready in England and Edwin Booth in America, whose performances are copiously documented by Toby Lelyveld in *Shylock on the Stage*. Furthermore, *The Merchant* grew grander as stage technology advanced. Throughout the Victorian period an increasing emphasis on spectacle, on the splendour of painted and then architecturally representational scenery, tended to focus audiences' attention on the play's most picturesque character, Shylock, in his authentic Venetian context. Charles Kean's production in 1858 was celebrated for recreating the Rialto with remarkable fidelity, and the Bancrofts took pains to reproduce such specific locales as the Sala della Bussola for their production in 1875 (Shewring, pp. 89-94). Depictions of Belmont were far less evocative; the fantastic goings-on at Portia's palace evidently inspired the Victorians less than the more credible events occurring at the Doge's. Their preference for Venice over Belmont revealed an even deeper preference for psychological and historical realism over the comic artifice with which Shakespeare had carefully balanced his two plots. This tradition reached its apogee in Henry Irving's production at the Lyceum Theatre in 1879, which firmly established *The Merchant* as one of Shakespeare's great tragedies.

Not long ago, an American critic argued that *The Merchant* 'dramatises not the triumph of one set of values over another, but the transformation of conflicts into harmonies that incorporate what at the same time they transcend' (W. Cohen, p. 766, on Danson). The history of performance would suggest otherwise. The anarchic pressures of the text have usually resisted such harmony: it has been difficult, if not impossible, for directors to balance the dramatic, ideological, and aesthetic alternatives Shakespeare offers. As a result, *The Merchant* has invited more tampering and revision than any other of his plays. What follows are accounts of how, in the past hundred years, *The Merchant* has been adapted not only to the prevailing theatrical technology and taste, but to ever-changing social and political contexts as well. Something in the mythology of the play has appealed so fundamentally to an audience's sense of cultural identity that each age has used *The Merchant* as a mirror to reflect its own face. That the play is capable of revealing so many faces may help to explain its enduring fascination.

CHAPTER II

Henry Irving and the great tradition

If the test of a good production is that it bring new insight into a play and prompt audiences to return to the text, then Henry Irving's *Merchant* was triumphant. Opening in 1879 to almost universal acclaim, it 'naturalised' the emotionally volatile, theatrically vengeful Shylocks popularised by Macklin and Kean while at the same time, in its quest for historical verisimilitude, epitomising Victorian values in staging. It became the most influential *Merchant* ever produced, running for 250 performances during its first season alone and, over the course of twenty-five years, a total of a thousand performances both in England and on tour – eight times – in America (L. Irving, p. 708). It helped to make Irving a legend and cast the mould for *Merchants* well into the twentieth century.

Irving was the foremost actor-manager of the nineteenth century. This implies a number of things about the organisation of his theatre that were instrumental in his production of *The Merchant*. The actor-manager system revolved around a single authority figure who planned the repertory, cast and directed each play, and usually star-red in it. Primary focus, therefore, was on the talents of one individual, not on an entire company as in Shakespeare's theatre: there were no 'sharers' at Irving's Lyceum. The artistic hegemony inherent in this system reflected the patriarchal structure of Victorian culture in general – the submission of all members of a family to the will of the father. At best, such authoritarianism resulted in a stylistic co-herence and ensemble playing that achieved a marvellous unity of effect; and it is for such effects that Irving is best known. At worst, the divided duties of actor and director clashed, and the actor-manager's desire to perform a role distorted the design of the whole by subordinating all facets of production to his overbearing ego.

Both the strengths and the weaknesses of the system may be observed in Irving's *Merchant*. His company was still in its formative stages: he had taken control of the Lyceum from the Batemans only a year earlier, in 1878, inaugurating his management with a production of *Hamlet*, and had begun slowly to replace the Batemans' mediocre actors with better ones, most notably Ellen Terry. *The Merchant* thus became a test case for his managerial discipline. He selected the play to showcase his own talents, and reasonably so, since audiences would come to see him act, and as a manager he had to be concerned with box-office revenue. Irving was noted for idiosyncratic portrayals. He had a towering stage presence – an ungainly carriage and a stride that caricaturists loved. According to his contemporary William Winter, his 'stilted and angular' way of moving resulted from a 'nervous excitement' that made him compelling to watch; his range of facial expressions was 'weird, eccentric, saturnine, mystical'; and his voice, 'neither copious nor resonant', was alternately tender, piercing, and vibrant – 'the flute and not the trumpet' (or in the words of those less charitable, forced and nasal). Although these characteristics rendered him capable of 'erratic and dazzling excursions into the domain of grim or grotesque ... humour', he nevertheless demonstrated through them 'a soul and mind rich in the capacity to feel and to translate the tragic aspects of humanity' (pp. 8-10). Irving had won instant fame when he used these mannerisms to magnetic effect as Mathias in *The Bells*, and it is likely that he was attracted to the role of Shylock because it offered him similar opportunities to display eccentric pathos.

Irving's account of how he came to do *The Merchant* is instructive. He had accepted an invitation from the Baroness Burdett-Coutes to accompany her and her friends on a cruise to the Mediterranean in the summer of 1879, with perhaps nothing more in mind than collecting a few prints in Venice to inspire designs for a revival of *Othello* or *Venice Preserved* (Brereton, 1:295). He could not have anticipated that, in Tunis, his imagination would be sparked by the picturesque figure of a Levantine Jew 'whose romantic appearance and patriarchal dignity against the background of his native landscape was so much at variance with the popular conception of his race which was held by Western Europeans' (L. Irving,

p. 333). Irving returned home determined to recreate that dignity in *The Merchant*, telling his acting manager Bram Stoker, 'I never contemplated doing the piece which did not appeal very much to me until we were down in Morocco and the Levant. You know the *Walrus* ... put into all sorts of places. When I saw the Jew in what seemed his own land and in his own dress, Shylock became a very different creature. I began to understand him; and now I want to play the part – as soon as I can' (Stoker, 1:84).

This narrative reveals two things: first, the Victorians' fascination with historical accuracy in their stage productions, and second, their attempt to bring a realistic awareness of cultural difference to the portrayal of 'the other'. The nineteenth century had firmly ensconced Shakespeare behind the proscenium arch, inhibiting the fluidity of action for which his plays were known: thus removed from their audiences, productions depended more and more heavily on spectacle – on lavishly representational illusions of 'reality' – to please the public, and often the sets earned the loudest applause, just as they do on the stages of London and New York today. The elaborate realisations of specific locales, so alien to the neutral space of the Elizabethan theatre, may have been an inevitable cultural by-product of British imperialism, resonant of the material wealth which conquest had brought; certainly, as Richard Foulkes suggests, they were reinforced by the Victorian appetite for historical exhibitions of all kinds (*Victorian Stage*, pp. 5-6). Irving, I should note, for the most part used only painted canvas in his sets for *The Merchant*; and though his decision to do so may have been dictated by the constraints of time, he claimed thereby to 'have endeavoured to avoid hampering the natural action of the piece with any unnecessary embellishment' (preface to his acting edition of *The Merchant of Venice*). His sets, executed by designer Hawes Craven, nonetheless were praised for their rich and sombre colours and for their archaeological detail in depicting Renaissance Venice (Moore, pp. 205-6). His sumptuous costumes, too, were clearly patterned on those of Renaissance painters. As one spectator observed, 'The pictures of Moroni and Titian had been studied for the dove-coloured cloaks and jerkins, the violet merchant's gown of Antonio, the short hats ... and the frills. The general tone was that of one of Paolo Veronese's pictures' (Fitzgerald, p. 103). Irving's trip to Venice, therefore, powerfully inspired his imagination with images of an earlier, vastly wealthy commercial empire whose culture the Victorians had in many ways tried to emulate.

More importantly, the narrative reveals Irving's fascination with the Jew. He was inspired to play a role, not to mount a historical pageant, and everything would be subordinated to his playing of that role (Foulkes, 'Trial Scene', p. 313). His attraction to the Levantine Jew sprang in part from a Victorian interest in what we now call the Third World, those peoples whom the English had subjugated to their imperial will and whom they now were refashioning in their own image. The English prided themselves on their toleration: after centuries of blatant anti-Semitism, Jews, albeit few, were becoming assimilated into the highest ranks of society and were gaining access to political power; a Rothschild was elected to Parliament in 1847, and Benjamin Disraeli, who according to one observer resembled Irving in manner and speech, was Prime Minister when Irving first staged *The Merchant* (Fraser, pp. 313-14; also Craig, p. 191). Irving thus focused attention on questions of social morality raised by Shylock – the rights accorded to aliens, the prejudices of those in power – which he regarded as central to Shakespeare's art. For him, Shakespeare was an eminent Victorian and the stage a forum to advance the moral agenda of a nation, as these remarks made in 1881 suggest: 'If you uphold the theatre honestly, liberally, frankly, and with discrimination, the stage will uphold in the future, as it has in the past, the literature, the manners, the morals, the fame, and the genius of our country.'(Irving, *The Drama*, p. 31.)

These are the words of a man confident of his own national values; and indeed, everything about his conception of Shylock reflected this cultural imperialism. What struck Irving most about the Levantine Jew was not his exotic difference so much as his inherent dignity and patriarchal nobility. Years later he recalled his impression of that Jew: 'I saw a Jew once, in Tunis, tear his hair and raiment, fling himself in the sand, and writhe in a rage, about a question of money – beside himself with passion.' This much would seem to conform to the anti-Semitic caricature of the previous age; but Irving insisted that the Jew quickly regained his composure: 'he was old, but erect, even stately, and full of resource. As he walked behind his team of mules he carried himself with the lofty air of a king' (Hatton, p. 269). By conceiving Shylock in this regal image, Irving transformed him from a seething, malevolent Semite into a natural aristocrat, 'almost the only gentleman in the play'. If he rejected the demeaning stereotype of Shylock as 'a mere Houndsditch usurer', he replaced it with another, nobler stereotype which betrayed an impulse to universalise Shylock as strong as that of actors who had once sought to reduce him to comic villainy: 'Shakespeare's Jew,' Irving claimed, 'was ... not a mere individual ... [but] a type of the great, grand race ... a man famous on the Rialto; probably a foremost man in his synagogue – proud of his descent – conscious of his moral superiority to many of the Christians who scoffed at him, and fanatic enough, as a religionist, to believe that his vengeance had in it the element of godlike justice' (Hatton, p. 269).

It is one thing to argue this in theory, quite another to put it in practice. Irving of course realised that Shylock *was* an individual and had to be played as such, and that his decision to play Shylock as a gentleman therefore demanded more specific justification. Interviewed while on tour in America in 1884, he provided such justification in terms that sound like special pleading. Shylock, he argued, 'is a merchant, who trades in the Rialto, and Bassanio and Antonio are not ashamed to borrow money of him, nor to carry off his daughter. The position of the daughter is, more or less, a key to his own. She is the friend of Portia' (Hatton, p. 265). This is a wilful misreading of the text: there is no evidence Shylock was himself a merchant, Bassanio and Antonio do indeed have qualms about borrowing from Shylock, and the suggestion that Jessica's 'friendship' with Portia (when they have never met before) attests to her father's gentility borders on the absurd. Nevertheless, Victorians were prepared to accept this as a perfectly reasonable defence of Shylock and, with it, to dismiss the conception of him as a usurer:

> Shylock was well-to-do – a Bible-read man, as his readiness at quotations shows; and there is nothing in his language, at any time, that indicates the snuffling *usurer* which some persons regard him, and certainly nothing to justify the use the early actors made of the part for the low comedian. He was a religious Jew; learned, for he conducted his case with masterly skilfulness, and his speech is always lofty and full of dignity. Is there a finer language in Shakespeare than Shylock's defence of his race? (Hatton, p. 266)

Shylock's sentiments, of course, are not always lofty; some do indeed expose him as a snuffling usurer (though Irving purged the most blatant of them to preserve his decorous image); and to argue that Shylock's quotation of the Bible identifies him as a learned man falls little short of perverse, for 'The devil can cite Scripture for his purpose' (I.iii.90). Most revealing of all, however, is Irving's celebration of Shylock's 'I am a Jew' as a defence of his race. This speech, as we have seen, builds inexorably towards Shylock's justification of revenge – a loathsome end, no matter what the provocation – and in the past it had been delivered as such. But Irving passed over its immediate dramatic function to universalise it as a plea for racial tolerance. Perhaps nothing better indicates the Victorians' willingness to redeem the Jew in light of their own cultural values.

Irving's Shylock, therefore, was very much the product of his age, a man marked by an intense pathos and a keen sense of injury that bespoke the refined sensibilities of his race, a businessman whose dignity and intelligence, to the outrage of some, rivalled those of a Rothschild (L. Irving, p. 355). However distorted, this interpretation of Shylock came as a revelation to audiences. Yet it smacked of a cultural solipsism masquerading as moral enlightenment, for in fact Irving seemed unable to imagine refinement and dignity in anyone whose manners did not ape those of the Victorians themselves. A review of his performance in the *Chicago Tribune* cited in *Mr. Henry Irving and Miss Ellen Terry in America* confirms this suspicion with its myopic self-righteousness: 'It is a nineteenth century Shylock ... a creation only possible to our age, which has pronounced its verdict against medieval cruelty and medieval blindness.'

※

Irving's sense of historical verisimilitude, therefore, both in the design of his production and in his portrayal of Shylock, was more anachronistic, idealised, and even operatic than his audiences realised. Always compellingly believable, his *Merchant* tended to romanticise Shakespeare's play by heightening its pathos and striving for grand theatrical effects. Yet these effects, seldom simple, demonstrated the subtle psychological nuances of which Irving's naturalistic acting (as it was then conceived) was capable. They were in evidence the very first time Shylock appeared. The set, 'A Public Place in Venice', occupied the full depth of the stage (Hughes, 'Shylock', p. 252). Behind the wall of a quay, which spanned the entire upstage area, ran a canal in which a small ship was moored: it was outlined against a backcloth depicting the imposing colonnade of the Doge's Palace in the distance. Steps at stage centre led from a rostrum down to the quay, littered with bales left there by coolies in Scene i, and it was down these steps that Irving made his memorable entrance.

Given the priorities of the Victorian theatre and the relative immaturity of Irving's company, it is not surprising that reviewers described Irving's entrance in detail while virtually ignoring how others in the cast essayed their roles. Salanio and Salarino were dismissed as 'skipping, featherbrained fops' (*Blackwood's Edinburgh Magazine*, December 1879, p. 650); the middle-aged Antonio of Henry Forrester impressed critics as dull and weak (*The Times*, 3 November 1879); and Bassanio, played by the company's juvenile lead, proved so innocuous that he was soon replaced by another. None of them could match the richly textured performance of Irving's Shylock. The tapping of his walking stick could be heard before he appeared; it hinted that he was old and infirm enough to need the support of a cane. A glimpse of Shylock proved this to be so: he was a man near sixty, a bit stooped, with an iron-grey wisp of beard (*The Spectator*, 8 November 1879). He was dressed soberly, not unlike the other men doing business on the Rialto: his fur-trimmed brown gaberdine, faced with black, and a short robe underneath it were relieved by a multi-coloured sash; and on his head he wore a cap with a yellow stripe, an historical emblem of Jewish oppression (see photo-graph 1). In the opinion of Percy Fitzgerald, he was 'not the conven-tional Hebrew usurer with patriarchal beard and flowing robe, dirty and hook-nosed, but a picturesque and refined Italianised Jew, genteelly dressed, a dealer in money in the country of Lorenzo de' Medici' (p. 131).

An anonymous account of Irving's performance in the British Theatre Museum entitled *Critical Notes on Shylock as Played by Sir Henry Irving*, handwritten by a contemporary who must have seen the play on numerous occasions, provides a wealth of detail. Shylock descended the steps to the quay slowly, looking suspiciously at Bassanio as he muttered 'Three thousand ducats, well' (I.iii.1), drawing figures on the floor with his walking stick as if debating the sum, and pausing after each line to let Bassanio linger in uncertainty. Irving used pauses and hesitations as a strategy to suggest that he was revolving the advantages of the bargain in his mind; but on 'I will be assured I may' (24) he became suddenly defiant. Thereafter his acting grew compulsively unpredictable. The 'deadly rancour' with which he 'hissed out' his scorn of Antonio – 'I hate him for he is a Christian' (34) – dramatically contrasted with the 'affected courtesy' with which he greeted him. He delivered his account of Jacob with patriarchal reverence, but that reverence soon yielded to bitterness as he upbraided his old enemy for past injustices – 'Signor Antonio, many a time and oft ...' (98) – bending low in mock humility to recite 'Fair sir, you spat on me on Wednesday last' (118) and delivering with particular fervour 'Hath a dog money?' (113), a line which, according to the anonymous account, 'revealed a whole chapter in the history of the Jews, as Shylock, the individual was, for the nonce, Shylock the representative of the whole tribe of Israel'. The alacrity with which reviewers saw in Shylock's performance a whole 'history of the Jews' indicates how snugly Irving had fitted his interpretation to prevailing cultural biases.

This speech became the psychological cornerstone of Irving's portrayal. Throughout it he stood apart, a strange and gaunt figure, varying his gestures, first rigid with scorn, then low with studied humility. Its passion carried over to his next speech as well – 'Why look you how you storm!' (130) – which a note in Irving's acting edition suggests made Shylock aware that he, not Antonio, had lost control. Suddenly conscious of his error, he craftily drew himself in, adopting a propitiating manner on 'I would be friends with you' (131) and assuming an injured innocence in order to further his plot. Half cringing, half mocking, with his arms outspread, shoulders raised and head bowed, he sought to soothe Antonio. On 'This kindness will I show' (136), a stage direction in Irving's prompt book indicates that he 'Places his hand upon him, at which Antonio draws back resentfully. At this Shylock draws a foot apart, showing (aside) his enmity, although he assumes friendship' (Mellish prompt book, p. 39). Several reviewers commented on this moment, noting that Shylock's contempt was finely etched when 'he touched the Christian merchant, and, seeing the action resented, bowed deprecatingly with an affectation of deep humility' (*Saturday Review*, 8 November 1879).

Antonio's shrinking from Shylock spoke worlds about the social ostracism the Jew had suffered and elicited great sympathy for him, even to the point of justifying (for some) his nomination of a pound of flesh in the bond. Irving later spoke about his playing of the scene:

> One of the interesting things for an actor to do is to try to show when Shylock is inspired with the idea of this bargain, and to work out by impersonation the Jew's thought in his actions. My view is, that from the moment Antonio turns upon him, declaring he is 'like to spit upon him again,' and invites him scornfully to lend the money, not as to a friend, but rather to his enemy ... from that moment I imagine Shylock resolving to propose his pound of flesh, perhaps without any hope of getting it. Then he puts on that hypocritical show of pleasantry which so far deceives them as to elicit from Antonio the remark that 'The Hebrew will turn Christian; he grows kind.' (Hatton, p. 267)

According to the anonymous account, the intensity of Shylock's hatred reached a climax when, after Bassanio and Antonio had exited laughing, he walked slowly to the steps, ascended two, paused, then turned to the audience 'as shaking with rage he raised his stick above his head and uttered an inarticulate curse in his throat three times'.

Such potent stage images help to explain how Irving transformed Shylock into his finest tragic role, a vengeful victim of racial intolerance. Yet performances do not remain static during the run of a play; they change according to audience response, or the actor's mood, or circumstance, and Irving was not immune to such things. His Shylock perceptibly coarsened over the years, growing more adamant in his lust for Antonio's flesh (Lelyveld, pp. 91-5). A stage direction in a prompt book used for an American tour in 1895 and copied by Fuller Mellish, who played Lorenzo, calls for 'a cry of fiendish and cruel exultation' from Shylock at the end of I.iii. as his hand reaches out in a grasping manner, like a tiger to seize his prey (pp. 26-7). The scene with Tubal in particular afforded Irving an opportunity for big emotional effects. Although his playing of the scene originally was restrained, reviewers within a few years began to comment on the ferocity he displayed on hearing news of Antonio's losses. A critic in the *Manchester Guardian* noted in 1881 that in contrast to his performance two years earlier, Irving 'kindles very rapidly into flame ... there is, indeed, something animal in the Jew's entire loss of self-control, and Mr. Irving spares us no detail of the wild eyes, wolfish teeth, and foaming mouth – but it is consummately played' (Brereton, 1:346). Audiences apparently liked such unrestraint, and Irving offered them more of it. He delivered his lament beginning 'Why there, there, there, there!' (III.i.66) with a strange 'mixture of rapacity, pathetic despair and stunned abstraction', according to the anonymous account, cutting refer-ences to his ducats in order to focus attention on the loss of his daughter (Moore, p. 202). And to compound the agony of 'loss upon loss', he opened his robe and repeatedly smote himself on the breast, slowly and heavily, perhaps in the manner of the Jew he had once seen in Tunis (Winter, pp. 139, 190). Such histrionics might have alienated audiences from a lesser actor, but Irving never lost their sympathy. Indeed, for all one knows, he might have deliberately coarsened his performance with an actor's sense of daring to see whether he could snatch tragic pathos from the jaws of excess.

However histrionic, these effects at least were validated by the text. But Irving occasionally embellished his tragic portrayal with stage business that went beyond the text. In II.iii, for example, a conflation of Shakespeare's II.v and II.vi, he staged a spectacle contrasting Shylock's sobriety with the festive abduction of Jessica that, for effect, rivalled grand opera. The set, designated 'Shylock's house by a bridge', was extravagant – one hundred stage hands were required to set it up – for against the Venetian backdrop Irving had constructed a practicable bridge over the canal (Hughes, 'Shylock', pp. 254-5). This idea was not new: Charles Kean had included such a bridge in his production of 1858, but it had not been put to such dramatic use as Irving was to put it (see photograph 2). Over that bridge Shylock left to dine with the Christians. No longer drab, he was now attired in a robe of rich design with a bright scarf to cover his head, 'flaunt[ing] his wealth in the Christian dogs' faces', in the opinion of Ellen Terry (*Memoirs*, p. 147). After a silent leave-taking of Jessica, he slowly wound his way up the steps of the bridge, leaning heavily on his stick, lantern in hand, and murmuring to himself, 'Fast bind, fast find ... ' (II.v.52). Pausing at the top, he glanced once more at the home he was loath to leave; then, keeping his eyes fixed on his daughter, he slowly ambled off.

What followed was an interlude of Irving's own invention that grew increasingly elaborate over the years, as a comparison of prompt books shows. In the original production, which used a prompt book now located in the British Theatre Museum, a gondola carrying a lady and a zither-playing noble passed along the canal while masquers – three ladies, two gentlemen – entered laughing and climbed the steps in order to catch a glimpse of the gondola. Gratiano, Solanio and Salarino, wearing masks and dominoes, passed them as they entered and conversed for thirteen lines, decorously omitting Gratiano's references to 'the strumpet wind', at which point another gondola, festooned with lanterns and full of revellers, moved on slowly and stopped before Jessica's window, where she was serenaded with a barcarolle (p. 34). Lorenzo entered; he and Jessica played their brief scene together with much humour as Lorenzo pretended to lose the box of ducats she had thrown to him, and they eloped amid a whirl of masquers with tabors and pipes. Antonio was written out of the scene. Mellish, in his prompt book of some years later, described a more lavish conclusion to the scene. The Belmont-bound party, while making their escape, was met on the bridge by masquers who engaged them in playful mime: Gratiano and Salarino doffed their hats and kissed the ladies, whose escorts feigned to draw swords. Four pierrots then bounded over the bridge and formed a ring on the stage; they were soon joined by more masquers who, preceded by boys and girls strewing flowers, formed a larger ring around them; and together they danced a whirligig of time, pierrots whirling one way, masquers the other (pp. 46-53). When their dance was done, reported *Harper's New Monthly Magazine*, the 'masked revellers, merrily singing, passed in the cold moonlight across the bridge over the canal, while a lighted gondola, with throbbing guitars and blended voices, glided below' (cited in *Mr. Henry Irving and Miss Ellen Terry in America*).

The stage emptied; ripples of laughter died away; one heard the tapping of Shylock's walking stick. Then, in an interpolated scene illustrative of Irving's genius, Shylock entered carrying his lantern, slowly wending his way home from dinner. He crossed the bridge, descended the steps, and crossed stage left to his house. He knocked at the door three times, slowly. There was no answer. He paused: the silence disturbed him. With greater deliberation he knocked again, three times. Then, 'raising his lantern to search the darkened upper windows, across his features came a look of dumb and complete despair' (anonymous account). The curtain fell on this picture of 'unrelieved simplicity' (Lelyveld, pp. 85-6), 'the image of the father convulsed with grief' (Winter, p. 182).

Nothing in the production elicited sympathy for Shylock so much as this scene. It provided a moment of calm after the chaos of carnival, of restraint after youthful abandon. Furthermore, by so poignantly portraying a man betrayed by his own flesh and blood, Irving appealed to the sacred Victorian belief in the obedience of children, a belief here violated by a rebellious daughter who, in the opinion of *The Spectator*, 'amply justifies his plain distrust of her, an odious, immodest, dishonest creature, than whom Shakespeare drew no more unpleasant character' (8 November 1879). No one objected that this scene was not Shakespeare's or that it cheapened with sentiment Shakespeare's more rigorous conception of Shylock. And few, if any, recognised its source in the scene where Rigoletto entered his house to discover, with horror, that his daughter had been abducted by masked men who had duped him into holding the ladder for them, his cries of 'Gilda, Gilda!' echoing throughout the opera houses of Europe (Moore, p. 202). This was a time when great composers and librettists, by extracting vivid emotional effects from Shakespeare's plays, were managing to transform them into grand opera. Irving simply reversed the process by importing an effect from Verdi; and in so doing, he made Shylock into a figure whose anguish over his daughter and whose tragic pathos as a freak tricked by his social superiors rivalled those of his great operatic progenitor, the hunchback jester of Mantua.

*

Irving's penchant for archaeological realism, for creating detailed illusions of place, had inevitable consequences for the shape of the play. As had been the case with other nineteenth-century productions of *The Merchant*, his elaborate staging forced him to compress and rearrange scenes to minimise the number of set changes required: by alternating 'big' scenes with smaller 'front' scenes played before a painted cloth, and by conflating scenes that might reasonably be played together such as II.v and II.vi discussed above, he reduced the number of set changes from nineteen to twelve (Hughes, 'Shylock', p. 251) and, more significantly, reduced the number of alternations between Venice and Belmont by four (Moore, p. 203). For the first two acts the Venetian scenes were played in sequence, broken only by I.ii, which was staged as a front scene; similarly, the wooing scenes at Belmont were conflated and postponed until Act III, where they were played together with only one interruption (a conflation of II.viii and III.i, also staged as a front scene). As a result of such changes, the quick alternation of scenes which Elizabethan staging had facilitated, with the attendant juxtaposition of ideas and values, was replaced by a simpler and structurally damaging isolation of the Venetian (here, tragic) scenes from the Belmont (comic) scenes. This drastically upset the balance that Shakespeare had striven to create and led, eventually, to Granville-Barker's observation that the play's two distinct plots may be irreconcilable.

By giving pride of place to the tragedy of Shylock, Irving in effect suppressed the plot of the three caskets and relegated Belmont to a position inferior to Venice. His displacement of the women's sphere of action further indicated the hegemony of the actor-manager system and, indeed, of the Victorian patriarchy; for although Irving was praised by his contemporaries for restoring a relatively complete text of *The Merchant*, he in fact used less of the text than his two most scenically lavish predecessors, Charles Kean and the Bancrofts, and was particularly brutal in cutting the Belmont scenes (Moore, p. 203). As might be expected, he omitted passages that disparaged Shylock: Solanio and Salarino's derogatory remarks about him – 'his stones, his daughter, and his ducats' – in II.viii and their mockery of him – 'Out upon it, old carrion' – in III.i;

the whole of Lancelot Gobbo's spirited exchange with Jessica about her father's tyranny in II.iii; and their similar banter in III.v. Such omissions helped to preserve Shylock's decorum as a tragic figure by denying his affinity with earlier comic stage Jews. Deeper cuts, however, were made in the casket plot: the Prince of Arragon disappeared altogether (thus, presumably, leaving the audience in the dark as to which was the casket when Bassanio made his choice), and Morocco's two scenes were compressed into one, II.i serving as an introduction to his selection of the gold casket in II.vii. As a result, the thematic significance of hazarding all one has – a pursuit Portia's suitors have in common with the venture capitalists in Venice – was markedly weakened, for the audience could not readily weigh events in Belmont against those in Venice.

Other cuts were made to avoid offending Victorian sensibilities. Shylock, for instance, was not allowed to speak of urine, nor Gratiano of cuckoldry. Portia's wit was the chief victim of Irving's scalpel; as Alan Hughes notes (p. 252), she 'has a bawdy streak in her character which was mercilessly eradicated.' Irving did not allow her to be so bold as to suggest that a hot temper may leap o'er a cold decree (I.ii.17-20) nor so worldly as to speculate that the Neapolitan prince's mother might have played false with a smith (41-3). She was too decorous to insult the English and the Scots (54-79), too prudent to risk saying that she would do anything rather than marry a sponge (94-5), too obedient to entertain the idea of circumventing her father's will (99-104). The impulse to transform Portia into a Victorian lady determined cuts in her later scenes as well: she was not allowed to mention hell (III.ii.18-21, III.iv.11-21), nor to take delight in a male disguise that might suggest she is 'accomplished with that [she] lacks' (III.iv.60-1), nor to taunt Bassanio that she would deny neither her body nor her bed to the learned doctor (V.i.227-33). Irving may not have realised that by trying to make Portia conform to the manners of his own sexually repressed society, he was robbing her of a wit and earthiness that had once made her a credible antagonist for Shylock.

Or perhaps he did; for some cuts blatantly demonstrate Irving's will to suppress the romance of the casket plot in favour of the bond plot. He was most ruthless in III.ii, from which he pruned nearly seventy lines, eviscerating Bassanio's role and reducing Portia's considerably as well. Gone is Portia's apostrophe to 'these naughty times' that 'puts bars between the owners and their rights' (18-19); gone, the charming lines in which she banters with Bassanio about being 'upon the rack' (25-7). Gone is the lyrical effusion in which she compares him first to a new-crowned monarch, then to Alcides – 'He may win, and what is music then?' (47-62); gone, too, his Petrarchan praise of her eyes, the most ornately romantic passage in the play (115-29). Gone, his comparison of himself to an athlete who still stands in doubt of the prize (141-6); gone, his confession of a wild feeling of joy when he is no longer in doubt (177-83). The effect of these cuts is to streamline the scene, to eliminate lyrical expressions of passion in order to get right to the heart of the matter: Bassanio's choice of the lead casket, his claiming Portia as his prize, and her dedication of herself and her wealth to him. The fundamentals of the plot remain, but much of what invests them with romantic beauty is lost. Clearly Irving wished to stage the scene with dispatch in order to get on with the trial, and Shylock's apotheosis.

Paradoxically, however, this scenic arrangement allowed Act III – which, in Irving's script, included all the Belmont scenes from Morocco's entrance to Bassanio's departure for Venice – to unfold at its own pace and to find its own rhythm. Belmont, as a consequence, emerged as a world morally and aesthetically at odds with Venice, resistant to the correspondences one might have discovered on the Elizabethan stage. Here, Ellen Terry was free to indulge herself by playing the wooing scenes as drawing-room comedy. In her, Irving had found a master-mistress of comic art. She had played Portia before, opposite Coughlin in the Bancrofts' unsuccessful production a few years earlier; Irving's production thus afforded her an opportunity to draw on her earlier conception of the role and, over the next twenty years, to refine it. An emotional actress whose 'tears follow[ed] quickly upon her laughter' (Winter, p. 69), she captivated critics with her natural grace, her charm, her gaiety, her intelligence. The *Chicago Daily News* found 'her comedy exquisite, her pathos touching, and her elocution round as a middle-age madrigal in the mouths of cathedral chorister boys' (cited in *Mr. Henry Irving and Miss Ellen Terry in America*). William Winter concurred: 'Her voice is perfect music. Her clear, bell-like execution is more than a refreshment – it is a luxury ... Her simple manner, always large and adequate, with nothing puny or mincing about it, is a great beauty of the art which it so deftly conceals' (p. 36). Perhaps this was the key to Terry's popularity: she had a generosity that concealed art.

Her playing of the scene with Bassanio amply displayed that generosity. The curtain rose to reveal a formal drawing room graced with elegant furniture and potted palms – more Victorian than it was Venetian. Portia and Nerissa were discovered on a settee; a page stood behind them, three women attendants upstage. Portia was 'radiantly beautiful in her Venetian robes of gold-coloured brocaded satin, with the look of a picture by Giorgione' (Brereton, 1:306); her hair, too, was gold. In fact, Michael Booth suggests that Terry appealed to audiences *as* a work of art who, by combining the images of both maiden and temptress, became a cultural icon for Victorian womanhood: she was an enchantress of gold mixed with virginal beauty – a twinning not unfamiliar to the Pre-Raphaelites (p. 83). Such aesthetic appeal was reinforced by the charm of her acting, at once chaste and coy. When Bassanio entered – handsomely attired in rose-coloured silken hose, a golden doublet, and a long rose cloak slung over one shoulder – she greeted him eagerly, unafraid to show her love but a bit coquettish. She caressed his hand rather forwardly while urging him to tarry (*Blackwood's*, December 1879, p. 653), but on 'Beshrew your eyes!' (III.ii.14) she turned blushingly away, holding a fan between their faces as if to hide her embarrassment. When he moved to the caskets, *The Times* reported that she seemed sorely tempted to break her vow; anxiety could be 'seen in her face, in her eyes, in her twitching fingers' (3 November 1879); and while he made his choice, she engaged in romantic byplay with him that many reviewers commented on: her 'surging love ... ever and anon would vent itself in ejaculations more eloquent than words' (*The Referee*, 2 November 1879). Nevertheless, when Bassanio touched the casket of lead, 'she did not fly to him, she let him open the casket, find the picture, read the legend, and sat there looking at him, smiling and quoting the legend ahead of his reading' (San Francisco *Chronicle*, 6 September 1893). Her restraint fled, however, when he knelt before her to claim the prize: she gave him her hand, he rose to embrace her; as she spoke to him of 'the full sum of me' (157) she allowed him to place her hands on his breast; and at the conclusion of her speech 'she submissively and tenderly hid her face upon his breast' as well (Mellish, pp. 72-3).

Such behaviour may seem tame enough to a modern audience, but for a few Victorian critics it proved unacceptably demonstrative. An anonymous review in *Blackwood's* not only found her too forward to preserve the essential modesty of Portia, but found that forwardness the more offensive for being *public*. The reviewer complained that 'too much of what Rosalind calls "a coming-on disposition" in Miss Terry's bearing towards her love ... might tempt her to break her father's will' (p. 653); and here, as in the matter of

Jessica's elopement, we tread on the sacred Victorian ground of family obligation, especially that of the child to her father. Terry, the reviewer observed, 'fails especially to suggest the Portia that, as Shakespeare most carefully makes us aware, would have sacrificed even her love for Bassanio, deep as it is, had he failed to win her by the process appointed by her father'. In reviews of this production, as in Irving's own remarks, Shakespeare keeps resurfacing as an eminent Victorian.

It was an open secret that this critic was none other than Theodore Martin, husband of Helen Faucit, who had been the great Portia of the preceding generation. Faucit's Portia had epitomised traditional Victorian womanhood – mature, not at all girlish, 'a woman of strong character and high intellectual culture' according to Martin's biography of his wife (p. 324; also Foulkes, 'Helen Faucit', pp. 27-37). Her portrayal had emphasised such values as self-sacrifice in love, obedience to the father's will, and righteousness in pleading the Christian cause – such emphases as made her acting in the trial scene more convincing than in the wooing scenes. That some professional jealousy may have crept into her husband's appraisal of Terry's more spirited performance should not surprise us; but he was not alone in his criticism. John Ruskin, in a famous letter, censured Terry for failing to achieve the 'majestic humility' he thought was owed Portia (L. Irving, p. 346); Henry James likewise objected that she was 'too free and familiar, too osculatory in her relations with Bassanio' (James, p. 143); and in his introduction to the play in *The Henry Irving Shakespeare*, F. A. Marshall concurred, though less censoriously, that 'one cannot help thinking that, if her father's absurd legacy of the caskets had resulted in the choice of an uncongenial husband, Portia would not have found it difficult to set aside the parental injunction in spirit if not in letter' (3:252).

Such carping was perhaps an inevitable response to a Portia who was an original – a young, impulsive, blithe spirit, as original in her way as Irving's Shylock was in his. Terry herself admitted that her Portia was more wilful and independent than audiences were accustomed to: where Helen Faucit had invoked the bonds of family loyalty to defend submission to her father's will, Terry struck a liberationist stance as the 'new woman' who used her wits to get her way and thereby challenged traditional Victorian expectations of female behaviour. In a lecture entitled 'The Triumphant Women', she noted that she had found the commentary of Danish critic Georg Brandes useful to her conception of Portia as 'independent, almost masculine in her attitude towards life'. 'This orphan heiress,' she explained, 'has been in a position of authority from childhood. She is used to acting on her own authority ... She is the spoiled child of fortune, or would be if she were not so generous' (*Four Lectures*, p. 117). How, then, does Terry justify Portia's surrendering all she has to Bassanio? 'It is clear that Portia's gracious surrender is a "beau geste", and little more. The proof is that she retains her independence of thought and action' (p. 118). Here is a new reading of the text indeed. As further proof that she regarded Portia as self-determined, Terry commented in her *Memoirs* that she had been persuaded by an Italian essay to believe that Portia chose the song 'Tell me where is fancy bred' deliberately to tip off Bassanio as to which casket contained her picture. 'And why shouldn't Portia sing the song herself?', she asked. 'She could make the four rhymes, "bred, head, nourished, fed" set the word "lead" ringing in Bassanio's ears. A woman of Portia's sort couldn't possibly remain passive in such a crisis in her life' (p. 152).

What Terry thought in 1908, of course, may not be what she thought in 1879. She grew in her roles and, as the years passed, grew also in her feminist convictions. Martin was the only critic of her original performance who had accused her of actually violating the spirit of her father's will; others had noted only her *potential* for doing so. Her Portia was unconventional but not, finally, subversive. As Terry put it, Portia was 'the fruit of the Renaissance, the child of the period of beautiful clothes, beautiful cities, beautiful houses, beautiful ideas' (*Four Lectures*, p. 116). Although Terry attributed these things to the Renaissance, her conception of the role was clearly anachronistic; for what she portrayed was a young woman of Victorian London whose manners might grace a drawing room in Mayfair (Boston *Evening Transcript*, 13 December 1883). As such, her Portia happily sacrificed dignity – even modesty – for the new spirit of the age. After all, one critic asked, how much dignity could there be in a Portia who 'lounges idly on the sofa as Nerissa describes her lovers?' (Scott, p. 169).

Ironically, Faucit's Portia might have been tonally more consistent with Irving's Shylock than Terry's was: her high seriousness, maturity and sense of decorum would have made her a more appropriate antagonist for him at the trial and truer to the moral dimension he tried to bring to the play. Yet paradoxically, by allowing the casket and bond plots to develop almost independently of one another, each in its own style, Irving's production realised the play's potential to be both moral tragedy *and* romantic comedy – two plays in one; and in doing so, it honoured the text's competing generic claims more fully than Irving may have recognised, or wished.

※

In the trial scene the two styles clashed – and the male hegemony of the actor-manager system asserted itself– most royally. This was to be the climax of Irving's tragic performance, and Ellen Terry was expected to accommodate her style of acting to his. The evocation of the ducal palace itself seemed to favour the heightened realism at which Irving was so skilled. According to Percy Fitzgerald, the set, 'with its ceiling painted in the Verrio style, its portraits of Doges, the crimson walls with gilt carvings, and the admirable arrangements of the throne, etc., surely for taste, contrivance, and effect has never been matched' (p. 130; also Foulkes, 'Trial Scene', pp. 313-16). But his description does not do justice to the operatic spectacle to which the audience was treated. The stage was crowded with spectators – nobles, guards, and clerks. With a flourish of trumpets, eight Magnificoes in black velvet caps and gowns, followed by the Doge 'habited in a rich crimson cap and robe' with pages holding his train, entered and marched to their places on the dais (Boston *Herald*, 13 December 1879). This much was similar to Charles Kean's staging. But among the spectators in the rear, Irving included Tubal and a small gathering of Jews (*Athenaeum*, 8 November 1879, p. 605); and the use to which he put them attested to the universality of racism and once again distinguished his production from its predecessors.

The prompt book transcribed by Mellish details how the scene began. Part of the crowd of spectators

> point and jeer as two Jews enter. One of the Jews brushes against Gratiano who angrily resents it. Solanio and Salarino interpose and the Jew retires upstage right, joining the other Jew. While this has been going on, some of the crowd at the back – all of whom have been watching the foregoing – take the opportunity to jeer at three Jews who are amongst them; the guards interpose across the barrier, and with their halberds, gently force the three Jews into a corner by themselves right. The rest of the crowd now keep apart from them. (p.89)

By opening the scene in this way, Irving conditioned his audience to sympathise with these Jews before a line of dialogue was spoken. When he entered, looking gaunt and older in the short gown for which he had exchanged his gaberdine, he scanned the crowd for a friendly face, spotted one of the Jews upstage right, went to him, then gently and fervently pressed his hand (Mellish, p. 90): Irving clearly wanted Shylock to be regarded not as a solitary victim, but as belonging to a whole persecuted race.

Furthermore, he used these Jews as a silent chorus to direct the audience's responses to Shylock. They provided a kind of cheering section, 'laughing at his mordant jests' and cueing the audience to laugh as well (Odell, 2:423). Those jests were made with an irony that suggested the theatrical control of which this Shylock was capable: the 'grotesque touch of humour' when he suddenly produced the scales from the folds of his garment, for example, 'never failed to cause amusement'; nor did his mock surprise at Portia's request that he have a surgeon ready: 'Without a word Shylock came to her side, peered over her shoulder with short sighted eyes at the document in her hands, and pointing at the various items with his knife as if to find it there inscribed, his face all the while expressing a bland simplicity mingled with cunning, said "Is it so nominated in the bond?"' (Fitz-gerald, p. 107). He maintained control of the scene in other ways as well, tempering his malice with tones of subdued scorn, refusing to raise his voice, remaining calmly indifferent to Portia's pleas, Gratiano's gibes, and Bassanio's offers of gold. Here was none of the melodramatic exultation or 'fiendish eagerness' that had charac-terised the performances of Macklin and Kean at the trial: the fixed purpose of Irving's more naturalistic Shylock was better communi-cated through the controlled emphasis with which he spoke four key lines, underscored and rewritten in the interleafings of one of his prompt books, now at the Folger Shakespeare Library (Lelyveld, p. 88): *I would have my bond, I stand for judgement, I stand here for law,* and *I stay here on my bond* (IV.i.87, 103, 142, 238).

Nor did Shylock lose control in defeat. When the judgement came, it appeared to strike him 'like lightning' (*Saturday Review*, 8 November 1879); crushed, he dropped his knife and his scales and stood as though mesmerised, his lips murmuring incoherent words (Scott, p. 70). The provision that he become a Christian hit him particularly hard, and its force was registered in the shock of the Jews who looked on, 'among whom the sentence condemning Shylock to deny his religion falls like a thunderbolt' (*The Theatre*, November 1879, p. 274). Yet this was but a prelude to the heroic performance that followed when, like the Tunisian Jew who had once so impressed Irving, Shylock regained his composure and 'left the court with a dignity that seemed the true expression of his belief in his nation and himself' (*Saturday Review*, 8 November 1879). This exit, for which Irving used the whole width of the stage, has been most fully described by Irving's grandson, who gleaned details from many contemporary accounts:

> When Shylock grasped the severity of his sentence, his eyelids became heavy as though he was hardly able to lift them and his eyes became lustreless and vacant. The words 'I am not well ...' were the plea of a doomed man to be allowed to leave the court and to die in utter loneliness. But Gratiano's ill-timed jibe governed Shylock's exit. He turned. [Bram Stoker recalls that Irving 'dropped his shoulder and shrank from the touch of Gratiano', 2:296.] Slowly and steadily the Jew scanned his tormentor from head to foot, his eyes resting on the Italian's face with concentrated scorn. The proud rejection of insult and injustice lit up his face for a moment, enough for the audience to feel a strange relief in knowing that, in that glance, Shylock had triumphed ... As he reached the door and put out his hand towards it, he was seized with a crumpling convulsion. It was but a momentary weakness indicated with great subtlety. Then, drawing himself up to his full height once more, Shylock bent his gaze defiantly upon the court and stalked out. (L. Irving, pp. 343-4)

At the last, Irving's Shylock was intensely human. As Lelyveld concludes, 'overshadowing his threefold role of usurer, outraged father and vengeful creditor, is the haunting figure of a retreating, broken old man' (pp. 90-1). Ellen Terry's engaging young doctor of laws could not compete with such tragic pathos. She was a figure from a different play, and though reviewers praised her refined delivery of 'The quality of mercy', no one regarded her as an opponent worthy of Shylock. In a scene where Portia's victory traditionally had been thought to represent the triumph of mercy over mean-spirited legalism, Irving muted the allegory and made Portia the agent of Shylock's tragic downfall instead. Terry recognised that she and Irving were working at artistic cross-purposes. 'I found that H I's Shylock necessitated an entire revision of my conception of Portia,' she complained in her *Memoirs*, 'especially in the trial scene, but here there was no point of honour involved. I had considered, and still am of the same mind, that Portia in the trial scene ought to be very *quiet*. I saw an extraordinary effect in this quietness. But as Henry's Shylock was quiet, I had to give it up. His heroic saint was splendid, but it wasn't good for Portia' (p. 128).

Here, apparently, was yet another instance of the actor-manager imposing his will on a text and expecting others in his company to gauge their performances accordingly. But Terry was as strong-willed as Irving; and if she couldn't play Portia as she wished in this scene, she nevertheless resisted playing the role *his* way. Instead of the naturalism he strove for, which would have required her to make her male disguise as credible as possible, she acted 'Balthasar' in a charmingly romantic style appropriate for light Victorian comedy and consistent with her playing of the wooing scenes. In other words, she played Portia still, and *Blackwood's* understandably found her too 'little in earnest' to convince either the audience of her masculinity or the court of her serious purpose (December 1879, p. 653). *The Spectator*, which elsewhere praised Terry's performance, complained of 'the absence of all pretence at incognito' and 'the absurdity of a quantity of curling hair under the beretta of a lawyer in a piece costumed with such elaborate accuracy in other respects' (8 November 1879). In fact, she used her black silk lawyer's gown (later replaced by an ornate gown of crimson) more to flaunt her femininity than to hide it, and she fooled no one when she archly pretended to shield her face from her husband (*The Theatre*, 1 January 1880). Indeed, observed the aptly named *Truth*, 'she has disguised herself so badly that her husband and anyone else must, unless they were blind, have seen in a moment who she is' (6 November 1879); yet the lines that might best have justified a suspension of her male disguise – 'Your wife would give you little thanks for that ... ' (284-5) – were cut (Foulkes, 'Helen Faucit', p. 32). Years later, in response to such criticism, Terry herself maintained that 'the impenetrableness of a disguise is a dramatic convention' that wins instant acceptance in the theatre (*Four Lectures*, p. 119); and however wrong she may have been in this case – however miscalculated the effect of her feminine 'Balthasar' on audiences – her remark nevertheless points to a crucial difference between her conception of how Elizabethan comedy should be played and Irving's. Terry would not for a minute have *expected* to be taken for a male. Her understanding of conventional disguise assumed a ludic element – a sense of play shared with the audience – that by its very nature eschewed naturalism. This, of course, is a defensible way to interpret Portia's role at the trial, but it contradicted and, as the critical comments above suggest, was ultimately swallowed up by the detailed authenticity of Irving's performance.

Irving's bid for tragic pathos also made it difficult for Terry to keep the moral allegiance of the audience, especially at the crucial moment when she stopped him cold with 'no jot of blood'(302). One spectator confessed to being 'distinctly disappointed when, by means of a miserable legal quibble, Shylock was cheated of his pound of Antonio's flesh' (Hiatt, p. 172). This response, of course, suggests how powerfully the emotional appeal of Irving's performance inhibited the ethical appeal of Portia's; and others objected to the staging of the trial precisely because it led to such distortion. Graham Robertson, for instance, argued that Irving's 'heroic martyr upset the balance of the play and ruined Portia's trial scene'. His allocation of the trial scene to Portia reveals a bias grounded in ethos rather than pathos.

> How small and mean sounded her quibbling tricky speeches when addressed to a being who united the soul of Savonarola and the bearing of Charles I with just a touch of Lord Beaconsfield that made for mystery. After her best effect, we momentarily expected the Doge to rise, exclaiming: 'My dear sir, pray accept the apology of the Court for any annoyance that this young person has caused you. By all means take as much of Antonio as you think proper, and if we may throw in a prime cut of Bassanio, and the whole of Gratiano, we shall regard your acceptance of the same as a favour. (pp. 54-6)

As if in defiance of the naturalism that led to such distortion, Terry insisted that Portia's behaviour, even at the trial, was motivated not by logic, but by romantic inspiration. Unlike Helen Faucit, who maintained that Portia must have plotted legal strategy with Dr Bellario beforehand and left nothing to chance, not even the quibble, Terry argued that the quibble had sprung spontaneously from Portia's female intuition and had nothing at all to do with Bellario. Taking a liberal stand for the power of woman's intellect, she speculated that Bellario had probably told Portia that the law had no remedy in such cases: 'He advised her to try an appeal to Shylock's mercy, and if that failed, to try another to his cupidity. If *that* failed, well then I fancy the learned Bellario may have suggested trying a threat.' One hears in these remarks some disparagement of male reason, provoked perhaps by Terry's frustration over Irving's refusal to accommodate her style of play.

> To my mind, and I have always tried to *show* this in the trial scene, Portia is acting on a preconcerted plan up to the moment of pronouncing sentence: then she has an inspiration, and acts on that. Hence her 'Tarry a little: there is something else.' There has flashed through her brain suddenly the thought that a pound of flesh is not quite the same as a pound of flesh and blood ... I am convinced that this bit of casuistry was not conceived by Shakespeare as being carefully planned. It strikes me as a lightning-like inspiration – just such an inspiration as a woman might have when she is at her wit's end, and is willing to try anything to avoid defeat. (*Four Lectures*, pp. 120-1).

Though to a late-twentieth-century ear her analysis may sound like sexual stereotyping, attributing to women an intuition at odds with male rationality, her argument by Victorian standards was decidedly feminist; for by drawing the distinction in favour of women and by speaking of Portia's inspiration in laudatory terms (it is, after all, what saved the men from themselves at the trial), she revealed a strong commitment to what was then regarded as manifestations of the feminine – to intuitive reason, to comic artifice, to romance – in the face of a masculine logic that was always ready to dismiss such things as irrelevant.

To his credit, Irving restored Act V – an act traditionally dropped by actor-managers intent on ending the play with Shylock's downfall. Although he cut all the bawdy from it and, a worse offence, cut some of the loveliest verse in the play, such as Portia and Nerissa's exchange about moonlight and music (92-110), the act nevertheless revived the feminine artifices that had been sacrificed to the cause of naturalism in Act IV and rounded out the play as romantic comedy. The set itself depicted a scene of 'summer luxury' far airier than the heavy interior of the court (Winter, p. 74) – a terraced garden bathed in moonlight against a backdrop of Portia's Palladian villa. Irving achieved the effect of moonlight through new gaslight techniques he had developed, and reviewers were quick to appreciate it: 'The moon rose from the lagune, through the level bars of vapor, over the lighted palace of Belmont', rhapsodised *Harper's*, while 'in the garden, on a seat of marble, Jessica and Lorenzo told their love' (cited in *Mr. Henry Irving and Miss Ellen Terry in America*). Portia entered dressed in 'a train of deep tint of purple silk, bordered with gold embroidery, worn over a petticoat of dull gold' (Indianapolis *Daily Journal*, 9 February 1884) – a costume in which, as the Victorians' golden girl, she could fittingly resume her sparkling style of play. She was, again, charmingly in her element, good-humouredly chiding Bassanio for the loss of his ring and magnanimously welcoming all her visitors to the nuptial festivities. A stage direction in Mellish's prompt book illustrates her generosity of spirit: after the couples move to enter her house and Portia has spoken the final line of the play, promising to 'answer all things faithfully' (299) – Gratiano's bawdy last speech has of course been cut – she 'suddenly remembers Antonio, and conveys in pantomime how selfish it was of them to have forgotten him. She turns round, graciously smiles, extends her hand' (p. 125). This resumption of comic values after the tragic sobriety of the trial scene struck a few reviewers as 'an ironic post mortem in which the villains of the

Erinyes dance upon the hero's grave' (Hughes, 'Shylock', p. 263), but most were untroubled by the tonal disjunctions caused by the return to Belmont.

Nevertheless, in late May of 1880 the production again fell victim to Irving's agenda as actor-manager. He decided to drop Act V and replace it with Wills's *Iolanthe*, a light vehicle well suited, he thought, to the talents of Ellen Terry. True, its omission was not his last word: he did reinstate the act from time to time. But clearly he had come to regard the play as a vehicle for himself, 'and from this time on he was able to do with or without the fifth act, as mood or policy prompted him' (Lelyveld, pp. 92-3). Certain assumptions were implicit in his decision: first, that it was legitimate to think of Shakespeare's plays, as Victorians were wont to do, as character studies more than total works of art; second, that *The Merchant* belonged to Shylock, not to Portia; third, that as a consequence, the play was tragic rather than comic, and the tone of moral gravity in Shylock's defeat ought not to be jeopardised by a return to comic harmony in the fifth act; fourth, and most condescendingly, that Ellen Terry's more 'artificial' acting style could be better employed in Victorian comedy than in Shakespeare.

These assumptions, largely unchallenged by his contemporaries, suggest how successfully Irving's *Merchant* captured the spirit of the age. It held the stage until 1905 – a quarter of a century– and spawned a host of imitators. In fact, most productions of the play for the next fifty years paid homage to Irving, directly or indirectly, and his celebrated stage effects were often carried to absurd lengths, as when the Shylock of Beerbohm Tree, having returned home from dining with the Christians, first knocked at the door of his house, then, in a rage, entered, ran to all the windows calling frantically for Jessica, and finally rushed back through the door, flung himself on the ground, tore his garments and sprinkled ashes on his head (Lelyveld, p. 100). The best clones of Irving's production were more temperate, featuring tastefully representational sets and restrained, dignified Shylocks; but none dimmed the memory of Irving's incomparable achievement. Scant attention was paid to William Poel's attempts in 1898 and 1907 to return to Elizabethan staging practices and to play Shylock as the comic, red-wigged, hook-nosed villain he assumed Shakespeare had intended. Even in the decades between the world wars, audiences persisted in regarding *The Merchant* with Victorian high seriousness and expected their Shylocks to be tragically sympathetic. Winthrop Ames's production of 1928, for which the Mellish prompt book was used, epitomised how Irving's conception had evolved: in it, George Arliss played the most patrician of all Shylocks, a suave, rich, well-tailored broker who made no concessions to comedy, responded stoically to the loss of his daughter and his ducats, and plotted with the poise and intellectual cunning of a Disraeli. Shylock by this time had become 'merely a dignified British gentleman who happened to be playing Shylock' (Lelyveld, p. 110), the logical extension of Irving's attempt to transform the Tunisian Jew into his own countryman. This conception was not effectively challenged until 1932 when, in Stratford-upon-Avon – that bastion of bardolatry – a Russian *émigré* named Komisarjevsky overturned Victorian stage traditions like a bear in an English china shop.

this page and facing
- I Henry Irving as Shylock at the Lyceum Theatre, 1879. Courtesy of The Mansell Collection Ltd.
- II Setting by William Telbin for Act II of Charles Kean's production, 1858. Courtesy of the Shakespeare Centre Library, Stratford-upon-Avon.
- III The Venetian set for Theodore Komisarjevsky's production of 1932, designed by Komisarjevsky and Lesley Blanch. Courtesy of the Shakespeare Centre Library, Stratford-upon-Avon.

overleaf
- IV Joan Plowright as Portia and Laurence Olivier as Shylock in the trial scene of the National Theatre production directed by Jonathan Miller, 1970. Courtesy of The Kobal Collection.
- V Bassanio (John Nettles) makes his choice: Oliver Bayldon's set for Belmot in the BBC production directed by Jack Gold, 1980. Courtesy of BBC Enterprises Ltd.
- VI Gemma Jones as Portia and Warren Mitchell as Shylock in the trial scene of the BBC production, 1980. Courtesy of BBC Enterprises Ltd.
- VII Antonio (John Carlisle) bullying Shylock (Antony Sher) in I. iii of the RSC production directed by Bill Alexander, 1987. Courtesy of Joe Cocks Studio.
- VIII 'What demi-god / Hath come so near creation?' Bassanio (Nicholas Farrell) to Portia (Deborah Findlay) in the RSC production of 1987. Courtesy of Joe Cocks Studio.

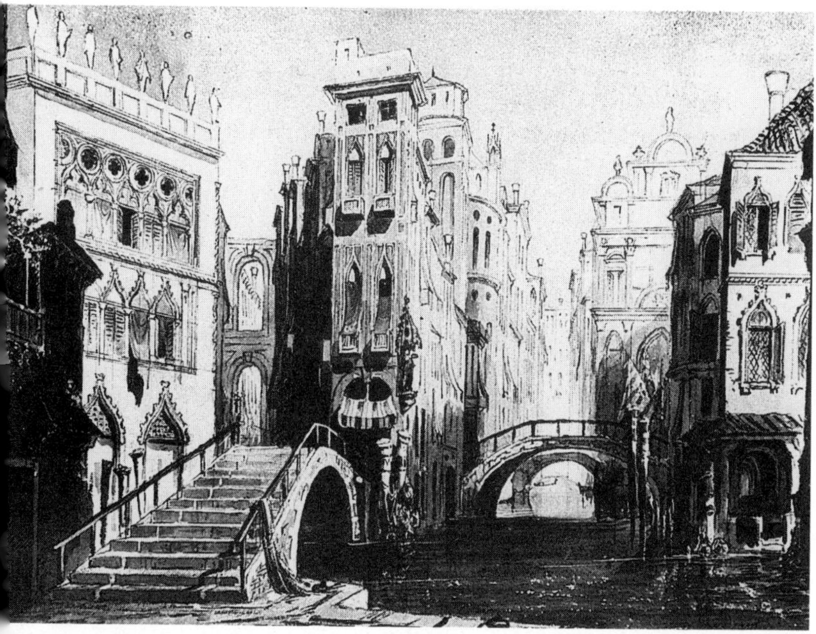

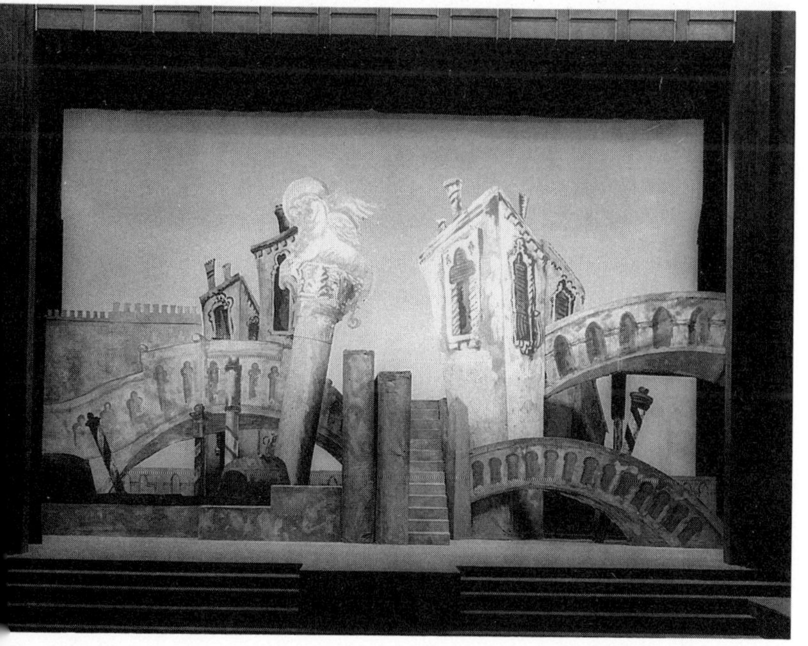

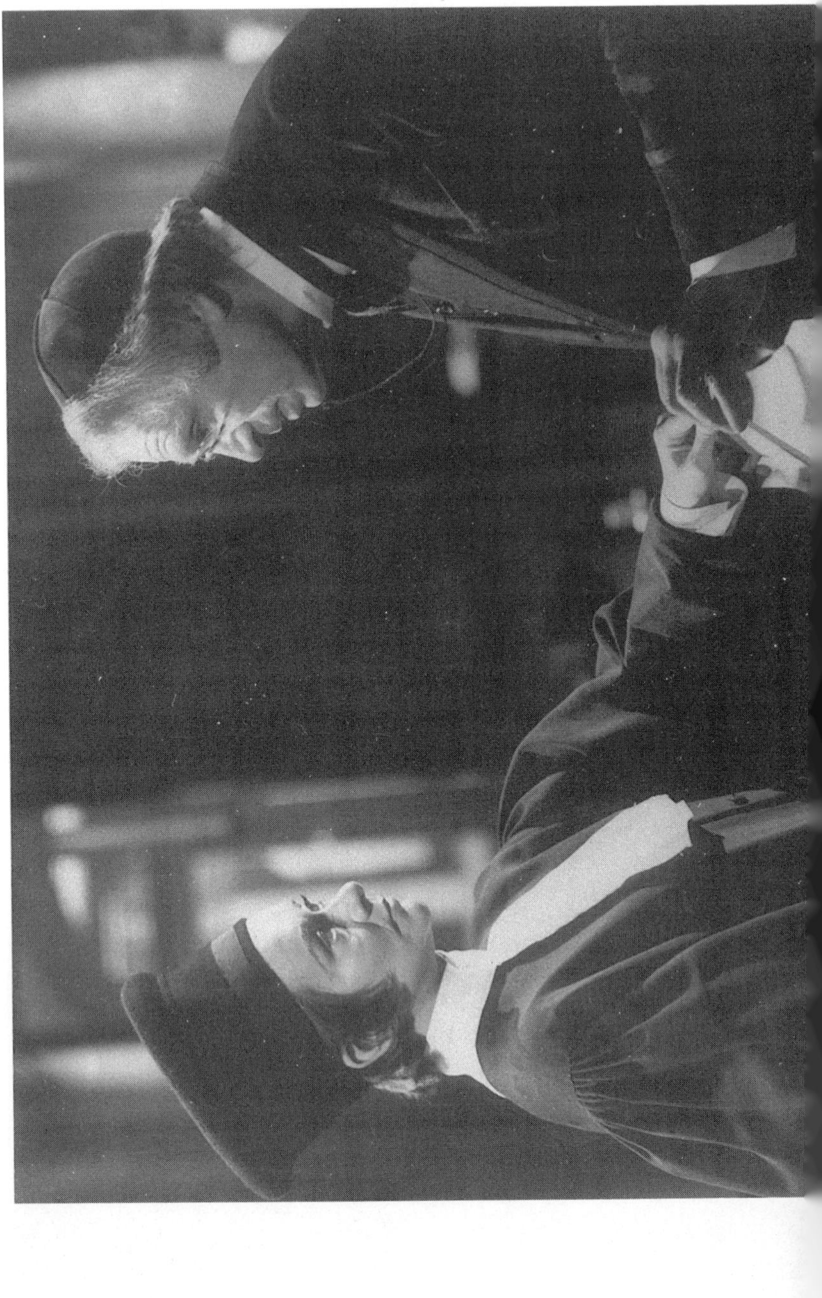

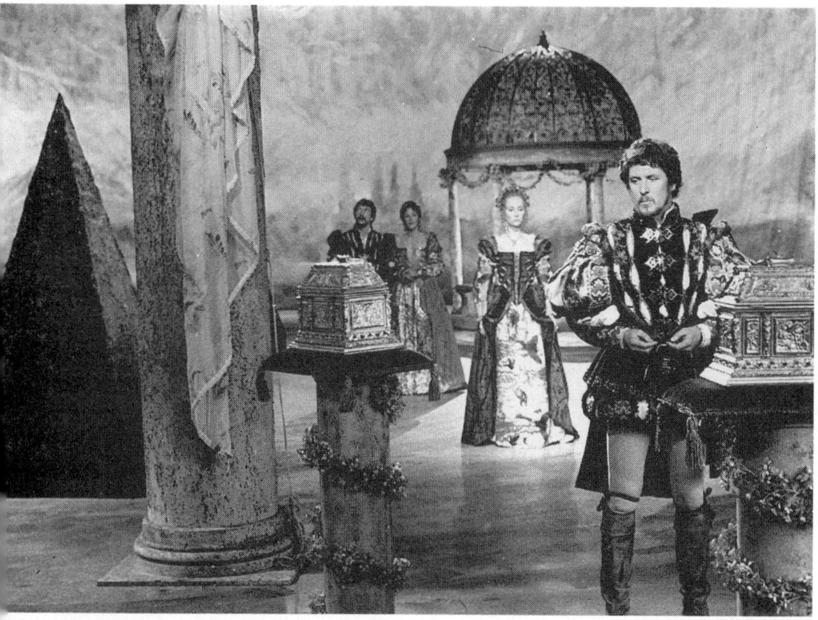

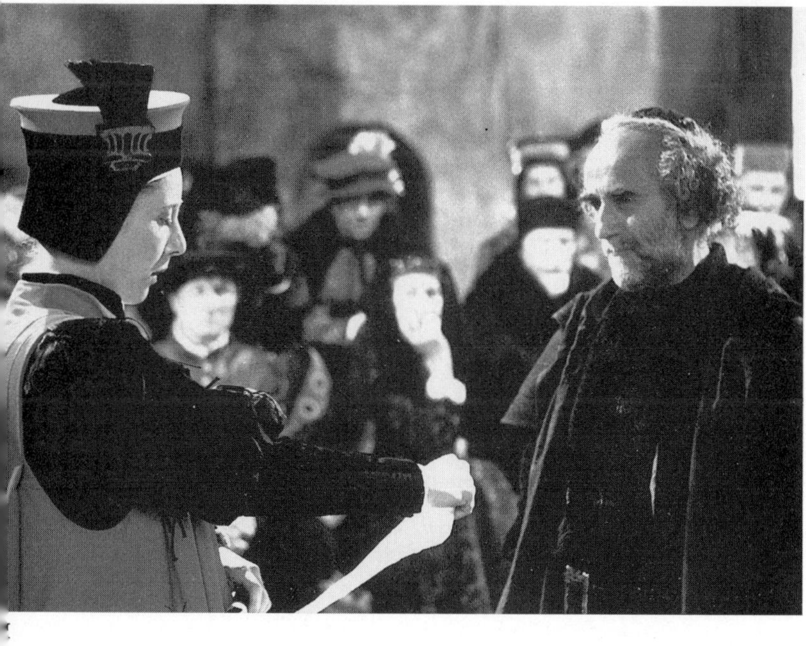

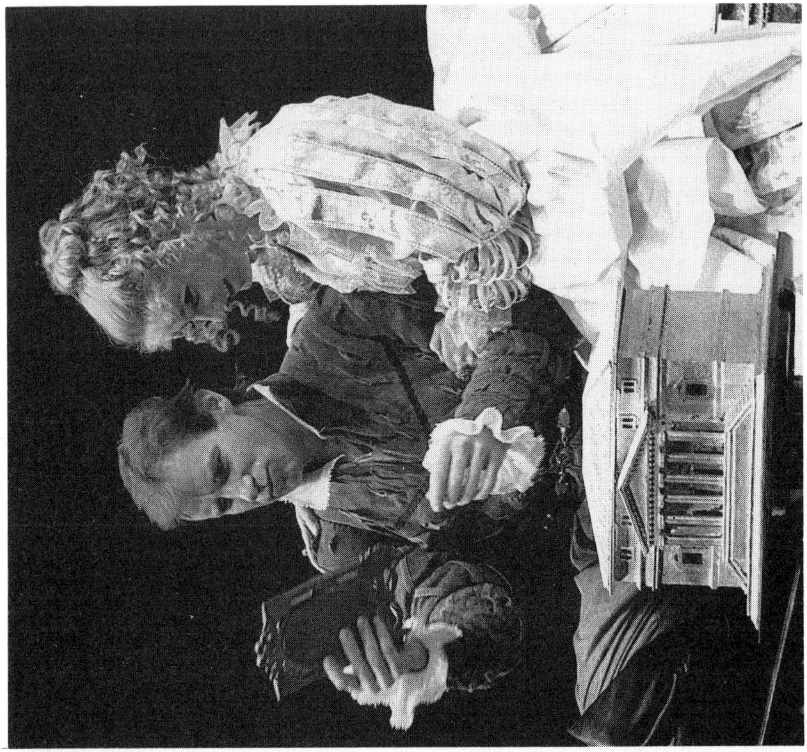

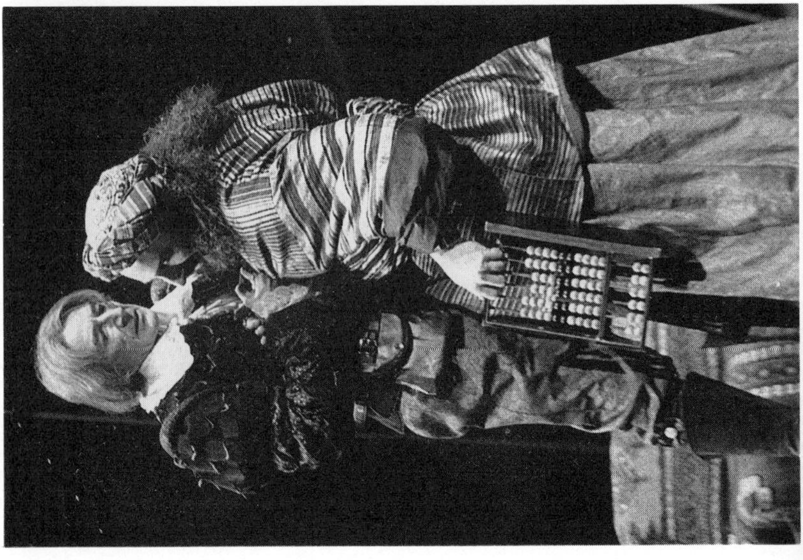

CHAPTER III

Wayward genius in the high temple of bardolatry: Theodore Komisarjevsky

> Frank Benson returned for the last time to Stratford at a Whit Monday matinée of *The Merchant of Venice* acted by the Old Bensonians in the old manner, the Venetian scenes in sequence followed by the Belmont scenes. Lilian Braithwaite travelled down to play Portia; Cedrick Hardwicke, Tubal; Robert Donat, Lorenzo; Nigel Playfair, Arragon. It was an afternoon of pardonable emotion, and the curtain fell when Benson's Shylock left the strict court of Venice; anything else would have been anti-climax. Presently, to the sustained roar of cheering, Bridges-Adams placed a laurel chaplet at Benson's feet.
> J. C. Trewin, *Shakespeare on the English Stage*, p. 137

Frank Benson's last performance at Stratford, on 16 May 1932, had symbolic as well as emotional significance. Benson had served his apprenticeship with Irving at the Lyceum; not surprisingly, then, as manager of the Shakespeare Festival until 1919, he perpetuated Victorian stage practices, and his *Merchant*, as Trewin's account indicates, clearly was cut from Irving's mould, reaching a tragic climax at Shylock's departure from the trial. Unknown to all but perhaps managing director W. Bridges-Adams, however, was that at this matinée, Victorian *Merchants* gasped their last; for Bridges-Adams, in a calculated move to catapult the Festival into the twentieth century, had invited Russian-born Theodore Komisarjevsky to stage *The Merchant* as the first guest director at the new Shakespeare Memorial Theatre. Komisarjevsky had begun his career at his sister's theatre in St Petersburg (she was the noted actress Vera Komisarjevskaya) as assistant to her *regisseur* – a word he preferred to director – Meyerhold. Later he became the director of first the Imperial Theatre and then the State Theatre in Moscow, where he gained fame as an interpreter of Chekhov; and two years after the Revolution he left for the Continent and England, where his involvement in expressionist and other avant-garde theatre movements, along with his erudite treatises on the evolution of theatrical styles and, particularly in England, his successful stagings of Chekhov, brought him to the attention of Bridges-Adams (Beauman, pp. 125-6; Mennen, pp. 386-7). For the hidebound Stratford Festival, he was a radical choice; and the play he chose to direct could not have been more deeply encrusted in stage tradition or, as the account of the Benson matinée suggests, riper for his revolutionary pluck. As Ivor Brown remarked in the *Week End Review* (30 July 1932) after seeing Komisarjevsky's *Merchant*, Stratford would no longer be 'just a repository for the dry bones of the Bensonian convention', for the Russian iconoclast had gone there 'with the clown's poker and the costumier's largesse, wherewith he has given the solemn tradition a ludicrous trouncing. What is both remarkable and admirable is that the governors of the theatre invited this wayward genius into the high temple of Bardolatry, and gave him full freedom to use his talented, capricious hand.'

Komisarjevsky deliberately set out to overturn the pictorial realism, the attention to historical detail, the naturalistic acting, and the moral sententiousness that had characterised *Merchant*s for more than fifty years. He used a complete text (all but fourteen lines), restoring scenes to their correct sequence and reinstating characters (Arragon, the Gobbos) often cut; he emphasised all the elements of farce and festive comedy that Irving and his disciples had so studiously suppressed; and above all, he eschewed the tragic conception of Shylock, which he identified with nineteenth-century actor-managers for whom, he believed, star turns and the profit motive were more important than artistic integrity. With a Marxist view of how theatre had evolved, he argued that economics were the decisive factor in the rise of the actor-manager system: 'those actors who were enterprising and dexterous enough to make money by their performances enforced their leadership upon theatrical companies. Their management served neither social ideas (a lot they cared about them!) nor theatrical art, but the interests of their own self-exhibitionism and their pockets.' The megalomania inherent in this system, he protested, gave actor-managers 'a monstrous idea of their own artistic worth' and promoted 'anarchistic-individualistic' ideas inimical to the 'basic elements of theatrical art – dramatic action expressed by the synthesis of an ensemble of players and of different arts' (*Civilisation*, pp. 10-11, 75-6). By championing such a synthesis, of course, Komisarjevsky appealed – with a political difference – for a return to the organisation of the Elizabethan theatre as a collective enterprise.

A star Shylock in a mercantile Venice became, for him, a metaphor for the greed of a bourgeois theatre he abhorred. Although Irving – 'an aristocrat of Merchants' as he was of actor-managers (p.102) – was not exempt from his lash, Komisarjevsky inveighed most heavily against a German Jewish actor named Bogumil Dawison, who, he complained,

> transformed Shakespeare's comedy ... into a tragedy and acted Shylock as a leading character, in the same manner as many English and Continental actors did after him. Dawison transformed the twisting, comic devil outplayed by Portia into a deceived, noble and emotional Jew, thereby upsetting the whole balance of the comedy and introducing a false social motive, quite alien to Shakespeare's gay, fairy-tale world, represented half mockingly, half lyrically, in *The Merchant of Venice* (p. 84).

The phrase 'false social motive' is the key to Komisarjevsky's dismissal of the Victorian conception of the play as a study in racial prejudice. In his eyes, the ennoblement of a 'twisting, comic devil' was clearly wrong: it pandered to a false sense of social morality and cheapened the play with sentiment. For all its engagement with issues of race and class, he argued, *The Merchant* remained fundamentally a fantastic comedy; and as such, it did not comfortably lend itself to the 'realism' of nineteenth-century bourgeois theatrical practices in which its spirit too often had been entombed. The English penchant for archaeological productions and naturalistic acting in particular, as 'practised by H. Beerbohm Tree and Henry Irving, [is] considered in this country, even to the present day, to belong to what is called the legitimate and sound Shakespearean tradition'. But Komisarjevsky objected that these practices had 'nothing to do with Shakespeare' and criticised the alacrity with which the reactionary English 'delighted in a repetition of those nineteenth-century liberties, which, obscuring the real sense of Shakespeare's plays, in no way serve their interpretation' (pp. 100-1).

In his production of *The Merchant*, therefore, which opened just two months after Benson's valedictory performance, Komisarjevsky set out to restore the 'real sense' – by which he meant the theatrical or ludic sense– of Shakespeare to English audiences. His agenda was strongly influenced by the writings of German anti-naturalist Georg Fuchs who, averse to the '"monkey-like" imitations of everyday life', championed the essential *irrationality* of the theatre and argued that sets, costumes and acting alike should imaginatively express the emotional and rhythmic movement of the play (*Civilisation*, pp. 130-3; also Mennen, pp. 388-9). Komisarjevsky thus drew on a pot-pourri of styles and periods, considering (like Fuchs) the ideas and emotions of a play to be a synthesis of a diverse history of human thought, not representative of one specific time or culture (*Costume*, p. 159). Meyerhold had experimented with similar expressionist techniques in his work for the Moscow Art Theatre, so it was perhaps not surprising that his protégé Komisarjevsky should evolve a production style for *The Merchant* that was playfully and wildly eclectic, its elements unified only by the 'creative work of [his] irrational self' (*Civilisation*, pp. 23-4).

His sets for Venice and Belmont reflected his training in Russia and on the Continent. In an essay called *Settings and Costumes in Europe*, he assessed the influence of cubism and expressionism on theatrical design and singled out for particular praise Picasso's set designs for Diaghilev and his own for productions in Moscow, which, he said, were inspired by the principles of Kokoschka (pp. 12-13; also *Costume*, pp. 160-2). In *The Merchant*, his set for Venice combined cubism with the colouration of the Fauves: a topsy-turvy array of brightly-coloured buildings and bridges at odd angles, staircases that defied perspective, dizzying towers, barber poles, and a Bridge of Sighs that split right in two before the eyes of the audience (see photograph 3); and it was all bathed alternately in a crimson or pea-green glow, colours such as 'one has never been so lucky to see ... on this earth' (*Birmingham Post*, 26 July 1932). The Venetian painted cloth, used for front scenes, was equally expressive, depicting a canal with sails, a cock-eyed column holding up a vaulted ceiling, crooked houses and bridges in the distance, and, atop it all, a crescent moon. Spectators at the opening night were astonished – a few were appalled – by Komisarjevsky's ingenuity. He has provided 'the Venice of popular dreams,' exclaimed the *Birmingham Gazette* (26 July 1932), 'a mass of broken Bridges of Sighs set at the eccentric angles a man might view them from late at night.' The *Daily Express* was more hostile:'The set was riotously out of perspective ... The pillar of St. Mark's leaned drunkenly against a nightmare Venetian tower surrounded by a confusion of flying bridges' (26 July 1932). Commenting on Komisarjevsky's fantastic use of stage machinery, the *Birmingham Post* observed that 'Venice split in two and the Lion of St. Mark went one way while the Bridge of Sighs went the other', and *The Times*, seeking a rational explanation for such nonsense, suggested that Komisarjevsky must have intended to 'set before us the histrionic Venice of the untravelled Elizabethan' (26 July 1932).

Most reviewers welcomed both his designs and his ingenious use of the machinery of the new stage as an invigorating slap in the face of tired tradition, but there were dissenters. The *Birmingham Mail*, only partially grasping Komisarjevsky's purpose, complained that the crooked architecture of Venice and 'generous elasticity as to period' contributed to 'the artificiality of the whole thing' and protested that his 'method of scene changing becomes ... wholly destructive of illusion' (26 July 1932). *The Times*, finding such artifice 'reckless and affected', asked whether or not there was 'something to be said ... for beginning with strict realism the telling of stories as incredible as the stories of the pound of flesh and the caskets' (26 July 1932). And the *Daily Express* displayed an almost humorously philistine contempt (if not incomprehension) of the production's anti-naturalist bias: 'In a sentence,' the reviewer concluded, 'Komisarjevsky tried to practise his flair for expressionism and burlesque on the finest drama of a Jew that has even been written – and failed in miserable confusion' (26 July 1932).

Such 'confusion' – or, less pejoratively, eclecticism – governed the design of costumes as well. Komisarjevsky was an authority on costume design, having written a history of *Costume of the Theatre* in 1931, just prior to his production of *The Merchant*. The expressive quality he had brought to the sets he also recommended for costumes, which, he thought, should reveal facets of character through symbolic or surreal association, not historical accuracy. He announced in advance that his costumes for *The Merchant* would 'represent a mixture of Veronese and English of the period of James I' (*Birmingham Mail*, 26 July 1932). Yet even this is misleading, for the costumes, though they had 'an air of Renaissance sumptuousness', in fact were fantasticated, drawing inspiration from various *theatrical* traditions rather than from one or two cultures or periods. As Ivor Brown wrote in the *Observer*, assuming the voice of Komisarjevsky, 'We do not ask your rational attention. But it is a gorgeous fairy-story and we shall fancy-dress it for your delight' (31 July 1932). And fancy-dress it he did. The Venetians were outlandishly flamboyant in huge ruffs, vividly coloured doublets and hose;

and Antonio was most flamboyant of all. This sad merchant, customarily attired in sombre colours to reflect his disposition, here sported a pair of flame-coloured tights that 'gave the lie immediately ... to the traditional view' of his character. In addition, he wore a grotesquely exaggerated ruff which, according to the *Birmingham Post*, made 'his face like the head of John the Baptist on a charger' (26 July 1932); and throughout the trial he 'preened himself in the little mirror that hung from a ribbon round his neck, emphasising the impression given in the first scene', during which he fondled a rose, that the reason for his melancholy was that he was indeed in love – with himself (*Stratford-upon-Avon Herald*, 29 July 1932). Komisarjevsky thus transformed Antonio, whose motivation is always something of a problem for directors, into a 'depraved exquisite' (*Daily Telegraph*, 26 July 1932), a near relation to Malvolio, 'a Venetian dilettante in a poetic languor' who, one feels, 'would not much mind the cutting off of his flesh so long as it did not disfigure his aesthetic magnificence' (*The Stage*, 28 July 1932).

Komisarjevsky's irreverent wit expressed itself in other costuming as well. Gratiano, with humorous topicality, was coiffured to look like Rudolph Valentino (*Evesham Journal*, 30 July 1932); and Portia's suitors, traditionally played for their exotic appeal, here appeared as buffoons. The Prince of Arragon, a foppish grotesque who bowed to Portia with swaggering affectation, was accompanied by a 'fat little attendant' (*Coventry Herald*, 30 July 1932) who reminded one reviewer of a creature out of *opéra bouffe* (*Sheffield Telegraph*, 1 August 1932). The Prince of Morocco was even more outlandish. Usually played as 'a dusky paladin with a good deal of sex appeal', he was reduced to 'an out-and-out blackamoor, so like Al Jolson that one expects him to drown his disappointment with a stave of "Sonny Boy"' (*Birmingham Mail*, 26 July 1932). In the words of another, he was 'made up as a nigger minstrel with a Mexican sombrero on his head' (*Birmingham Gazette*, 26 July 1932); and still another saw him as 'a black-faced embodiment of the Captain' who shows his 'derivation from the Commedia dell'Arte' (*Birmingham Post*, 26 July 1932).

Morocco's derivation from El Capitano suggests how indebted Komisarjevsky was to the *Commedia* tradition, a style whose extravagant use of colour and comic exaggeration he found wonderfully expressive. He had devoted a long section of his book on costume to the *Commedia*; his description of El Capitano therein as a braggart soldier in stripes with tight breeches, a wooden sword, and a small tabarro with long feathers clearly illustrates Morocco's lineage (*Costume*, p. 117). The *Commedia* style inspired costume designs for other characters as well. Portia, for example, was dressed as a Columbine, the sweet associations of pastoral simplicity made ironic by the worldliness with which Fabia Drake played the role. Even more explicitly, the Gobbos, father and son, were attired like a piebald Scapino and Pantalone – the young man in patches and ruffs, the old man in yellow slippers, red breeches and stockings, a tight jacket, red bonnet, and a half mask with a long nose. Such costumes suggest how far Komisarjevsky wished his *Merchant* to be regarded as play – as the product of an eclectic theatrical imagination – rather than as a representation of any recognisable society.

*

'Perhaps the Lancelot Gobbo of Bruno Barnabe comes nearer to his heart than any of the players,' speculated the *Birmingham Weekly Post* (30 July 1932), and the speculation was surely right. For Barnabe had trained in mime under Komisarjevsky at the Royal Academy of Dramatic Art and had researched clowns of the *Commedia*, so that his role as the production's presiding genius of comedy was inevitably informed by that tradition. Komisarjevsky set the play during carnival, a time of music and dance when Venice 'has no period but that of eternal masquerade' (*Observer*, 31 July 1932). To create that festive mood, the production opened with a masque of pierrots led by Barnabe, who assumed the role of Harlequin. Fantastically dressed in a striped suit and a yard-high hat, Harlequin strutted on to the stage and beckoned to his mummers. They, all dressed in black and white dominoes and wearing masks with long noses, appeared from every corner of the set, pirouetting over the bridges of Venice and dancing acrobatically to a version of Bach's Toccata and Fugue in D Minor played by a concealed orchestra (*Midland Daily Telegraph*, 26 July 1932). Then, on a cue from Harlequin, they scampered off to make way for the first actors in a comedy – *The Merchant of Venice* – that was to be performed, presumably, as a part of the carnival celebrations: Antonio and his friends suddenly appeared behind Harlequin, as if he had summoned them up. Two or three reviewers took the performance of *The Merchant* that followed to be a 'revels' play; but as Barnabe soon reappeared in the habit of Lancelot Gobbo– his double role readily apparent to the audience – one could, alternatively, interpret this opening sequence as Lancelot's dream, establishing a more profoundly irrational world in which the role-play and absurdities of carnival take on, for the dreamer, a reality of their own. In either case, the festive license of the opening scene made the fantastic premises of *TheMerchant* – the terms of Shylock's bond, the lottery by which Portia must be won, the cross-dressing of all the play's women: such things as prove problematic in realistic productions – explicable. 'One found the old and too familiar material joyously rewrought into a dazzling pattern of fantasy,' wrote one reviewer (*Sheffield Telegraph*, 1 August 1932). Komisarjevsky has created a world, concurred another, 'where everything ... becomes excusable, and nothing outrageous' (*Birmingham Mail*, 26 July 1932).

The Gobbos, in fact, set the tone for the revelry in the play-within-the-play. The lengths to which Komisarjevsky went to emphasise their clowning are revealed by elaborate stage directions in his prompt book. At their first meeting, for example, not only does Lancelot attempt to disorient his father by spinning him around, he also pushes Old Gobbo right into Bassanio on 'To him, father' (II.ii.97), pushes him again – so hard that the old man falls down – on 'as my father shall specify' (102), then picks him up and *carries* him to Bassanio. This horseplay continues throughout the scene. In subsequent scenes, furthermore, Old Gobbo toddles dutifully behind his son – even though the text does not specify his presence– so that the two of them can perform running gags together, like the *lazzi* of *Commedia* tradition (Mennen, p. 395). In II.iii, when Lancelot bids a tearful farewell to Jessica, Old Gobbo is there to wipe his son's eyes with a giant handkerchief. In II.v, he adds a funny double echo every time Lancelot echoes Shylock's 'Why, Jessica!' And when Shylock advances on them – 'Who bids thee call?' (7) – Lancelot falls backwards over his father, the two of them winding up in a heap on the floor. Lancelot himself is also introduced into scenes where Shakespeare did not intend him to be. In Belmont, he is on stage – and given comic business – throughout Bassanio's wooing of Portia in III.ii; he is there again in III.iv, when Portia puts Lorenzo in charge of her house; and his clowning with Jessica and Lorenzo dominates III.v, right up to his entrance at the end to announce, in mime, that dinner is ready.

The roles of Lancelot and Harlequin merge again in Act V. Lancelot's presence there, of course, is justified: he enters at l.39 with news of Bassanio's impending arrival, and there is no indication that he departs thereafter. But where other directors had usually found a way to usher him off as a figure too low to intrude on the play's romantic conclusion, Komisarjevsky wished to round out his fantasy with the clown. Barnabe at first sat unobtrusively by the proscenium to observe; but the director soon found comic business for him to do. Where the text indicates *A tucket sounds* (121), Lancelot mimicked the blowing of a horn, making a joke of Lorenzo's subsequent line to Portia, 'Your husband is at hand, I hear his trumpet' (122). The joking continued when, as Bassanio spoke his aside 'I were best to cut my left hand off/ And swear I lost the ring defending it' (177-8), Lancelot, happy to be of service, offered him a knife – a humorous allusion to the trial scene just past. And when all the couples had departed (even Antonio entered into the spirit of their festivity) Lancelot was left alone. He summoned the pierrots, just as he had once done as Harlequin: they entered as before, pirouetted around him, then bounded off as quickly as they had come, leaving him to yawn and stretch. This brought the revels full circle: clearly the audience was to think of the two hours' traffic as the fruit of a clown's imagination, if not his dream, no more substantial than the *The Taming of the Shrew* may become when it is preceded by the induction with Christopher Sly.

It is instructive to recall that Irving, too, had incorporated dancing pierrots in his production of *The Merchant*; but there, they were participants in the masques Shylock commanded Jessica to ignore, a momentary diversion – naturalistic enough, in context – from the sobriety of the bond plot and a frivolous contrast to the tragedy of the Jew. In Komisarjevsky's *Merchant*, the pierrots required no such justification. They represented the spirit of carnival and, like so much else in the production, defied naturalistic explanation. Even the entrances and exits of characters playfully violated the illusionistic 'world' defined by the proscenium arch. Aware that audiences were disappointed that performances continued to be confined by that arch in the new Shakespeare Memorial Theatre, Komisarjevsky took the liberty of breaking through it. Barnabe, as Lance, led the way by effecting his first entrance hand over hand down a rope hung from a gallery over the apron of the stage (*Daily Telegraph*, 26 July 1932); and later on he performed his scenes with Jessica on a tower located outside the proscenium. Venetians climbed on to the stage from the orchestra pit 'as if landing from gondolas' (*Sheffield Telegraph*, 1 August 1932); and Portia and her suitors arose as if from nowhere on an elevator which, as we shall see, occasionally took them to heights well above the stage. Perhaps the *Birmingham Gazette* described the situation best: 'Nobody came on the stage from the wings – they all came on as if conjured by magic from nowhere, either from behind masked figures, from out of the orchestra well, from beneath the stage by trap doors, or else they were let down from the flies above' (26 July 1932). Such effects were comically disorienting. By keeping the audience uncertain where characters had come from or where they were going, they enhanced the surreal quality of the production and made spectators themselves participants in the dream.

✻

New theatrical technology allowed for a fluidity of play unknown on the Victorian stage; and if Komisarjevsky used that technology to excess, at least he did so in order to thwart the expectations of representationalism to which audiences had grown accustomed. Set changes between Venice and Belmont flamboyantly called attention to their own theatricality: at the conclusion of the very first scene, when Bassanio spoke to Antonio of a lady in Belmont richly left, 'the audience was permitted a full view of the rolling stage in action. The Venetian street scene ... divided in the centre, half sliding off on each side'; and as the cyclorama changed from apple green to deep pink, 'a lift carrying Belmont rose to stage level with Portia and Nerissa poised like Dresden china figures – a theatrical reinforcement of Bassanio's description of Portia's virtues' (*Midland Daily Telegraph*, 26 July 1932). The Belmont set, more classically formal in style, contrasted with the riotous disproportions of Venice: it consisted of a cluster of steps, geometrically designed to look like sculpture, and a large, free-standing wall panel in the shape of a scroll on which were painted musical instruments in the style of Picasso. The overlapping of scenes achieved while the set change was in progress established both a rhythmic and a visual counterpoint between Venice and Belmont that, as Richard Mennen suggests, reinforced the stylistic differences between those two worlds inherent in the text (p. 390); and these differences became even more apparent when, in subsequent scenes, the Belmont set moved to even greater heights.

In contrast to the scenes in Venice, which opened with a flurry of activity, each of the wooing scenes began as a *tableau vivant*, with Portia and Nerissa statuesquely rising from the depths as the lift took them to a level eight feet above the stage, the suitors rising only to the level of the stage below, where they were to make their choices from caskets located beneath the platform – literal-minded critics persisted in calling it a 'roof garden' – on which Portia was standing. 'The purpose of this device,' wrote the critic of *The Times*, 'is to show us the shining, desirable Portia poised on high, while her unwelcome suitors blunderingly woo her on a lower level, and to let her descend later to Bassanio's level' (26 July 1932). But Komisarjevsky had more in mind, for this arrangement also commented wryly on the representational way in which the casket scenes had been staged in the past. Three decorated panels covered the 'pavilion' beneath the upper platform (*Birmingham Mail*, 26 July 1932), on the middle of which the three caskets were fancifully *painted* – an urn with a smiling face for gold, a purse for silver, and a plain bucket for lead. None of them was in any sense real. The reviewer for the *Daily Telegraph* protested that 'the casket scenes happened in a horrible little curtain grotto beneath Portia's garden' and thus failed to convey the romantic opulence he expected (26 July 1932); but the literalism of his response was countered by others who recognised that those caskets 'were painted ... very much after the manner of a Victorian pantomime' (*Birmingham Post*, 26 July 1932) and in their comic presentationalism served not only to satirise the absurdity of the lottery, but to burlesque the tradition of theatrical representationalism as well.

Komisarjevsky applied irreverent brush strokes not only to the design but to the direction of the wooing scenes. If the suitors' costumes were drawn from various comic traditions, so too was their behaviour. In one inspired moment noted by most reviewers, 'the Prince of Morocco, black-faced and with thick, red lips, [rose] out of the ground under a red umbrella' held by his black servant (*Birmingham Gazette*, 26 July 1932; also *Evesham Journal*, 30 July 1932). Portia viewed him from above with disdain, and indeed he seemed to deserve little else; for his manner was as theatrical as that of a black minstrel, and when he found the death's head inside the gold casket, he rolled his eyeballs and delivered 'Oh hell! What have we here?' (II.vii.62) not as a prince, but 'just as a motorist would who has burst a tyre' (*Stratford-upon-Avon Herald*, 29 July 1932). The swaggering Arragon, too, proved more fool than prince: he was constantly upstaged by his fat little attendant who nodded in agreement at comically inappropriate places, such as when Arragon, seeing the fool's head he had chosen, asked, 'Are my deserts no better?' (II.ix.59). Neither suitor could possibly have proved worthy of Portia, and so – as the set impishly implied – she kept her distance.

When Bassanio arrived, however, she 'descended' – as *The Times* put it – 'to his level.' She was not a traditionally romantic Portia: Komisarjevsky's conception of the play would not have allowed that. In fact, as Fabia Drake reported in a BBC broadcast in 1959, he had told her that she must play the scene with Bassanio 'not sentimental – physical' (Mennen, p. 393). Those three words, she said, liberated her from the stumbling block of tradition and charged her with what she called 'a new vibrancy' – and what reviewers called a youthful zest for love. She 'clearly sustains some human warmth beneath the porcelain poses,' reported the *Week End Review* (30 July 1932); and where once Ellen Terry was criticised for being too forward with Bassanio, Drake clung to him and at one point impulsively threw her arms around his neck without fear of censure. Sexual desire, apparently, would prompt her to do anything – even flout her father's will. When Bassanio asked to be left to his fortunes and the caskets, the lift rose to the upper level, but Portia remained below with him – 'leaning, languorously, against the edge of the proscenium' (Mennen, p. 393) – ready to be of assistance. And assistance he needed, for his values were no more pristine than hers: money, apparently, weighed as heavily as love in his desire to win the lottery. Not surprisingly, then, when it appeared that Bassanio was about to plump for the golden casket, Nerissa – obviously at Portia's prompting – put him 'on the right track' by 'shamelessly stress[ing] the syllables in the "Fancy" lyric which rhyme with "lead" – until he could not possibly go wrong' (*Birmingham Mail*, 26 July 1932).

Ellen Terry, writing in 1908, defended Portia's right as an independent woman to circumvent her father's will in this way, though she had never stooped to such subversion in performance. But 1932 was a more liberated age, and Fabia Drake's Portia was unabashedly determined to marry the man of her own choosing. Male reviewers, however, objected to her strategy for doing so. The *Daily Telegraph* called it 'an uncommonly dirty trick' which under-mined the idealism that should have made Bassanio the *inevitable* winner of the lottery. The *Christian World* concurred that Portia's trick undercut the play's romantic fictions with a baser reality, reducing the hero and heroine to mere poseurs so that 'Bassanio's lengthy discourse on the relative values of gold and silver and lead is turned into a piece of hypocritical attitudinising' (4 August 1932). But perhaps such criticism took the production too seriously; for in the world of carnival, the release of inhibition means everything and morality counts for naught – or, as the *Birmingham Gazette* put it, 'the arraignment of morality is incidental ... the comic interlude all important' (26 July 1932). This is not to suggest that the comedy was devoid of moral observation;indeed, Komisarjevsky used the license of carnival to make pointed social criticism about the values of the bourgeoisie. 'All those young men,' he announced in advance, 'Bassanio, Lorenzo, Gratiano, Salarino, and the rest – will be put in their place. They will be shown as the dissipated, fast, bright young people like the crowd we have in London today' (*Birmingham Mail*, 7 July 1932): Komisarjevsky alludes to the spoiled darlings of England's monied classes who seemed oblivious to the fact that the economic system which had kept them rich had also led to a terrible depression. In his production, then, comic romance gave way to topical satire, and moral sententiousness to a light-hearted indictment of contemporary social values.

That same topicality informed the trial scene, which Komisarjevsky staged as farce, overturning the tradition that had for so long made it the tragic capstone of the play. His satirical intentions were made clear in an interview: 'The court scene,' he said,

> will present some new aspects. If such a law could exist as that by which the Jew could take his pound of flesh, then most certainly it would be allowed to shed the victim's blood and the claimant could not be expected to cut the flesh to the exact pound. The thing would be absurd. That scene represents the crash of justice in the face of prejudice. (*Birmingham Mail*, 7 July 1932)

The key word here is *absurd*, for Komisarjevsky believed that the power of the fable lay in its illogic, in its irrational theatricality. 'Justice is brought to nought by a girl,' he continued, citing Portia's 'sweet unreasonableness' as the principle governing the scene.

Komisarjevsky thus designed the trial to bring to a climax the irrationality, and amorality, of a dream. Appropriately played on the Belmont set rather than in Venice – the levels had been rearranged, with the geometrical steps now forming a dais for the Duke – the scene reflected the surrealist style of Portia's world and the priority of her (questionable) values. The costuming, too, reflected Komisarjevsky's satirical intent. 'I shall try to bring out the power of that scene,' he said,

> by having all the senators of the Doge's Court sitting around in a uniform dress, their faces covered by uniform masks. Not a human face will be visible but Portia's, and in the background there will be painted a shadowy ensemble of the court crowd – the sort of people who gloat over sensations in our present-day courts. (*Birmingham Mail*, 7 July 1932)

In the event, the crowd painted on the scroll-shaped wall had the faces of sheep; the magnificoes, costumed in scarlet robes and ruffs, had faces made up in white rather than masked; and, during the proceedings, the entire court followed Portia and Shylock like spectators at a tennis match, looking mindlessly now this way, now that (Mennen, p. 395).

The action at the trial was rife with a comic invention that illustrated the patent injustices of the judicial process. The old Duke, who kept nodding off during the trial and waking up with a start 'like his prototype in "Alice"', could in no way dispense justice (*The Stage*, 28 July 1932): he even fell asleep while his doddering clerk read the letter from Bellario (Shakespeare assigns those lines to the Duke himself) – its opening line, 'Your grace shall understand, that at the receipt of your letter I am very sick' (IV.i.150-51), delivered so as to suggest that the Duke's letter had caused Bellario's illness (Mennen, pp. 395-6). The jury, according to one reviewer, 'brought to mind the Ku-Klux-Klan', an association Komisarjevsky would have welcomed (*Coventry Herald*, 30 July 1932); but as I have already noted, the defendant on whose life they were to pass judgement, Antonio, preened in the mirror that hung about his neck as if the only thing he feared about death was the disfigurement of his face. Was such a man – vain product of a comically decadent bourgeoisie – worth saving?

If such absurdities blunted the point of Komisarjevsky's satire, so too did Portia's appearance from the orchestra pit as a contemporary young barrister sporting 'a Henry Lyttonish wig and bicycle wheel spectacles' (*The Stage*, 28 July 1932) – a disguise reminiscent of that worn by Kitty Clive who, in Macklin's *Merchant*, aped the mannerisms of famous lawyers of *her* day. The wit of Fabia Drake's performance perfectly matched that of Komisarjevsky's conception: most reviewers found her Balthasar a refreshing departure from tradition, 'a credible ... young doctor of laws, and not merely a young woman who' – *pace* Ellen Terry – 'had previously played the part in a scarlet robe' (*Birmingham Post*, 26 July 1932). Drake took the scene more 'as a frisky adventure in male impersonation' (*Sheffield Telegraph*, 1 August 1932) than a serious attempt to instruct the court in Christian virtue; and when Komisarjevsky told her that the 'quality of mercy' speech should be delivered not as a declamation but simply as an answer to Shylock's question, 'On what compulsion must I?' (179), she was happy to oblige: 'Portia, leaning over her desk, snaps the poor old Jew's head off with the retort – the effect is electrical' (*Birmingham News*, 22 May 1933).

In the most blatant rejection of stage tradition, this trial scene tried to dramatise 'the crash of justice in the face of prejudice' *without* encouraging the audience to feel much pity for Shylock. True, stage directions in the prompt book indicate that Gratiano spat at Shylock and pushed him to his knees, but Komisarjevsky did not want such business to elicit sympathy for a man who, according to him, was little more than a caricature of malice. How, one wonders, can prejudice be regarded as ignominious if its object is so clearly deserving of it? 'The point of Shylock is revenge, and revenge can never be sympathetic,' he claimed. And although 'there is a hint of triumph about the Jew, even at that crucial point in the court when after everything has been taken away from him he admits that he is crushed with the plaint that he does not feel well' (*Birmingham Mail*, 7 July 1932), Komisarjevsky thought it wrong for that hint of triumph to be magnified into the tragic exit that had won Irving so much praise. *The Times*, discerning in this Shylock a 'vulpine and instinctive' nature at odds with the tragic dignity of Shylocks past, approved of the way in which Komisarjevsky handled his departure from the trial: 'Rightly, [Shylock] lets himself be dismissed from the Court without the least straining after heroic gesture, making an exit that well befits the crushed and sordid usurer who ... would now be only too content to take his three thousand ducats and let the Christian go' (26 July 1932). In this way, Komisarjevsky succeeded in offering an alternative to Irving's interpretation as no director had done for over half a century.

✳

It is symptomatic of Komisarjevsky's success that reviewers focused not so much on individual performances as on the overall aesthetic of his production – its style, its tone, its design. This, I think, was the real breakthrough of his *Merchant*: that it diverted attention from the nineteenth-century notion that the play was 'about' character and drew attention instead to the directorial *concept*. The star actor was thus supplanted by the director, or, to use Komisarjevsky's term, the *regisseur*, who, more than any actor-manager would have found possible, was expected to synthesise all the elements of a production into an artistic whole. 'The *regisseur* is a spiritual leader, a kind of magician, psychologist and technical master,' he wrote, who must be flexible rather than tyrannical and adapt his concept to 'an individual actor's mode of expression', because he 'respects the creative individualities of his actors and knows that no more can be achieved by the methods of the drill sergeant than by committee meetings' (*Civilisation*, pp. 18-19). The acid test of Komisarjevsky's willingness as a *regisseur* to adapt his concept to the 'creative individualities of his actors' came in his debate with Randle Ayrton over how Shylock should be played.

Regarding Shylock as a role that had been inflated out of all proportion by actor-managers bent on displaying their own egos, Komisarjevsky was determined to shrink the Jew down to a size befitting the villain of a comedy who appears, after all, in only five scenes. Komisarjevsky, one may recall, abhorred the way in which bourgeois theatre had sentimentalised Shylock – in England, that sentiment had led to the mawkishness of Frank Benson's farewell matinée– and he therefore strove to desentimentalise him. In Ayrton, he apparently found an actor suitable for the task. Noted for roles as diverse as Lear and Malvolio, Ayrton was described by fellow-actor Sebastian Shaw as

> a short squat man, with grey hair, a broad expansive face, a large nose. He was ugly ... but you were never conscious of that, just of his tremendous power. He had a curious, almost ugly voice too, slightly nasal in quality, but with the most extraordinary range: it could move in a moment from lightness and delicacy to rawness and passion. (Beauman, p. 88).

From this description, one may easily envisage Ayrton's Shylock as a malevolent stage Jew or even, in his more comic scenes, as a pantaloon from the *Commedia*. Instead of the traditional Jewish gaberdine he wore a brightly-coloured costume – the *Daily Mail* thought he looked like 'Mr. Willy Clarkson at an Albert Hall fancy dress ball' (26 July 1932) – and he played Shylock in a conversational tone 'with an amusing accent and a sense of humour which is quite unexpected' (*Birmingham Post*, 26 July 1932). Critics generally agreed that he revived a conception of the role too long dormant in the theatre. According to the *Observer*, Shylock was played as he might have been on Shakespeare's stage, as 'a wicked old scamp to be detested of the audience, a scamp with drollery inherent, but meriting all the punishment that comes his way' (31 July 1932). The reviewer clearly approved of Komisarjevsky's challenge to the sentimental tradition: 'Ayrton's performance is strong, clear, sardonic, and never sentimentalised or expanded with irrelevant goings on.' The critic of the *Daily Herald*, showing an anti-Semitic stripe to which the production obviously appealed, agreed that Komisarjevsky 'had the courage to show Shylock what I always thought him to be – a terrible old scoundrel. He made him as he was before Irving, in order to placate Jewish patrons of the theatre, pretended that a moneylender who wanted to cut a pound of flesh from a living man was really a noble-hearted gentleman' (29 July 1932).

Despite Komisarjevsky's claim that he intended the trial to expose racial prejudice, therefore, few critics interpreted it that way; and it is difficult to see how they could, given his attempt to turn Shylock into a grotesque suitable for the carnival entertainment his *Merchant* had become. But Komisarjevsky ultimately met an obstacle in Ayrton, who, as a veteran actor of the old school, would not – or could not – fully comply with his approach. Having played Shylock at Stratford before, Ayrton was well aware of the role's complexity and potential for tragic pathos; according to Fabia Drake, he was at first 'completely appalled by Komisarjevsky's interpretation' and apparently, for a time, resisted the invitation to see Shylock as in any way a caricature of revenge (Mennen, p. 394). The situation was a difficult one for the director: as Mennon reports, Bridges-Adams had chosen the company at the beginning of the season, as was Stratford's policy, and had allotted each production only five or six rehearsals. 'In other words, Komisarjevsky had not cast Ayrton, had no contractual leverage over him, and certainly had no time to cajole him into an interpretation he opposed and which may have been beyond his abilities' (p. 394). Yet lest we credit Ayrton with too much opposition, we should recall that the text itself resists the reduction of Shylock to comic villainy; and as an actor, Ayrton may simply have been responding more to the lines he was given to speak than to a director's concept. A few reviewers recognised in the power of Ayrton's performance something that transcended stereotype, and the terms in which they describe him are remarkably like those used to describe Macklin's performance two centuries earlier. Shylock 'is not quite all the monster that Mr. Komisarjevsky, reverting to the old tradition, would make him,' asserted the *Manchester Guardian* (26 July 1932); and the *Daily Express* remarked that his 'refreshing, cynical humour' in the first scene yielded later to 'a cold fury that was degrees above the tattered passions of more conventional Shylocks' (26 July 1932). Such fury reached its peak in III.i, when a storm of wind and thunder brewed during his confrontation with Solanio and Salarino – a loud clap punctuated 'She is damned for it' (26) – and gathered force as, Lear-like, he vented his passions with Tubal under an 'ominous coppery green' sky (*Western Sunday*

Independent, 31 July 1932). The effect of the scene may have been melodramatic, but in the opinion of one critic, it revealed the futility of trying 'to treat Shylock as a rascally and belaboured pantaloon' (*Sheffield Telegraph*, 1 August 1932).

The differences between Ayrton's and Komisarjevsky's conceptions of Shylock reflected the divergent potentials of the role as written. In his attempt to scale Shylock down to a size appropriate for a *Merchant* indebted to the traditions of mime, dance, *Commedia*, and farce, Komisarjevsky risked reducing him to a comic stage Jew; and to some degree Ayrton must have been willing to oblige, for a number of critics saw him as that – 'a nasty old card who gets uncommonly rough justice for behaving like an uncommon ruffian' (*Week End Review*, 30 July 1932). But the pressures of the text and Ayrton's own proclivity to play a more human role resisted that reduction, so that Shylock ultimately did not appear to most critics to be simply two-dimensional. The struggle between the comic type – which is a part of Shylock's heritage – and what *The Times* called Shakespeare's 'divination that the Jew is also a human being' may ironically have benefited the production by making it more accurately reflect the tensions within the text itself. The *Sheffield Telegraph* eloquently spoke of how those tensions were manifested in performance. Ayrton,

> the finest Shylock we have seen since Irving, played the game for his producer for all he was worth by stressing the grasping squalid side of the Jew's nature. But he was bound in honour to play the game for Shakespeare too, and from the glorious humanity [note here the vestige of Victorian assumptions about the play] ... of Shakespeare's treatment of Shylock there is no escape. Mr. Komisarjevsky has succeeded in making us forget Shylock when he is not there: but when he moves upon the stage, and until he quits it in pitiful disaster, the feast of fancy and artifice is ruled, in the old way, by the skeleton. (1August 1932)

The skeleton of which the reviewer speaks, of course, is that of Irving; and in strange ways, I would suggest, it dances in the shadows of Komisarjevsky's production as surely as it rattles through the prose of this review. Komisarjevsky went to great lengths to refute Irving's legacy: by dressing Ayrton in fantastical garb, giving him an exotic accent, and asking him to play the role for all its malicious humour, he tried to recapture the 'twisting, comic devil' that he thought the Elizabethan Shylock had been (*Civilisation*, p. 84) and thereby to put to rest the tragically heroic figure Shylock had become in the nineteenth century. Yet Victorian tradition permeated his thinking about the play so much that he was even prepared to borrow its most celebrated effect – the interpolated scene in which Shylock returns to an empty house – in a form altered to suit his more political purpose. Komisarjevsky's recollection of that effect in an interview for the *Birmingham Mail* suggests how deeply he felt the anxiety of influence.

> I have always felt that ... the traditional last scene is wrong. Shylock should not be allowed to knock at his own door to discover that Jessica has flown with a Christian. I shall arrange it so that after the lovers have gone off together, the young men of the fast dissipated Christian set will remain in the Venetian setting talking over the case. Shylock will cross the stage towards his house and find it seized, with two Venetian guards at the door. Then will be seen the reaction of those who convicted him unjustly. (7 July 1932)

Rejecting what he saw as the false pathos of Shylock's traditional return, Komisarjevsky nevertheless decided to appropriate that tradition to make a statement about social injustice. Without ever questioning whether the scene was in fact Shakespeare's, he vowed to use it to indict the strong-arm tactics of a 'dissipated' ruling class that had convicted the Jew 'unjustly': Shylock was to be barred from entering his own house. In the event, however, Komisarjevsky did not alter tradition even that much. Stage directions in his prompt book indicate that when the masquers have departed, 'Shylock enters ... sees money lying on floor and open door'; he 'calls Jessica three times', and then, hearing no response, 'closes door slowly'.

※

However fantastic his *Merchant* was, therefore, and no matter how he decried the 'false social motive' imposed on the play by previous directors (*Civilisation*, p. 84), Komisarjevsky was not oblivious to the moral, social, and political implications of its performance. True, he eschewed the psychological subtlety, the naturalistic style of acting, and the pictorial realism that had characterised productions of the preceding fifty years; but his production was not frivolous for all that. His new aesthetic was part of a revolutionary agenda, and he was abundantly aware of the social and political context in which it would be interpreted. Komisarjevsky himself averred that 'it is absurd to assert, as some do, that the art of the theatre is a purely aesthetic function and has nothing to do with "propaganda", either moral, religious, or political' (*Civilisation*, p. 2). In fact, I would argue that his production – even in its rejection of the past – covertly addressed the social divisions and political upheavals that were rocking Europe in the 1920s and early 1930s.

Komisarjevsky was an outspoken proponent of socialist dictatorships. In a book called *The Theatre and a Changing Civilisation*, which he published in 1934, just two years after his production of *The Merchant*, he lamented that Europe had languished for so long under effete democratic governments. The capitalist values of European society, he argued, had had a dire impact on the theatre, which held an unflattering mirror up to the bourgeoisie (pp. 1-14, *passim*). Under the direction of visionary *regisseurs* such as himself, however, the theatre could help to guide social reform; and in his eyes, such *regisseurs* found their political counterparts in the likes of Lenin, Stalin, Hitler, and Mussolini – dictators born out of the failure of imagination in European democracies. Where 'the old democracies pandered to the spirit of conservatism and to old people, and bred mediocrities, conflicting and mercenary passions and anarchy,' he wrote, the new leaders have 'genuine idealistic foundations' (p. x) – such idealism as should, in his view, bring about a revolution in the theatre as well. Of his own country, he believed that

> if the snobbish Russian aristocrats and the highbrow Russian intellectuals had possessed a power of vision and had collaborated with the Soviets upon their coming into power, and if the Jews and the Christians had not imagined that there were two separate Gods ... and if all of them together, including the cosmopolitan bankers ... had found a higher purpose in life than land and money-grubbing and organising the exploitation of man by man, then there would have been no revolutionary massacres in Russia nor any Jew-baiting in Germany'. (p. x)

Good sentences and well pronounced. From them, one might deduce that he saw reflected in *The Merchant* these very concerns about a capitalist culture – here, Renaissance Venice – so perniciously rich, so full of money-grubbing and exploitation, that it bred the sort of persecution Shylock suffers. Considered in light of his political ideology, Komisarjevsky's *Merchant* may be seen to have had a socialist dimension; and while it may not have sentimentalised the play's morality as earlier productions had done, it satirically observed how bourgeois decadence could lead to racial prejudice. That, at least, was Komisarjevsky's avowed intention: he conceived of the Venetians as 'dissipated' young idlers and Shylock as a man who, however malevolent, suffers injustice at their hands. The kangaroo court in sheep's clothing makes just this point.

But this interpretation of the production may be too charitable.

It is called into question by Komisarjevsky's argument, in the same text, that the purges of the Communist revolution in Russia, during which so many citizens were, 'as the expression goes, disposed of', and the herding of Jews to concentration camps during the 'Nazi upheaval' were, however regrettable, an understandable and even necessary consequence of 'any mass progressive movement'; for, he claimed, there has never been progress 'without bloodshed and injustice being inflicted on certain groups of people, and, however sentimental we may be, our feelings must not be allowed to blind us to the positive and progressive sides of the Fascist, Communist and Nazi movements' (pp. ix-x). For Komisarjevsky to claim, in an interview prior to his production, that Shylock was victimised by 'the crash of justice in the face of prejudice,' then to speak as an apologist for the herding of Jews to concentration camps in the name of progress smacks of hypocrisy, and suggests that his *Merchant* may have been informed by more extreme political views than he was willing to admit. We may recall how strenuously he objected to those actor-managers who sentimentalised Shylock as a bourgeois tragic hero; here, he objects to a 'sentimental' humanism – in other words, an abhorrence of atrocities– that would blind us to the achievements of socialist dictatorships. The objectivity with which he claimed to squelch such sentiment allowed him, in the name of art, to fashion Shylock as a figure most audiences could jeer at and dismiss as justly punished. The critic of *The Times*, covering his own response in the cloak of historical distance, spoke for many when he speculated that if an Elizabethan 'retained his taste for a little Jew-baiting he might have laughed uproariously at the despairing rage of the crafty alien usurer hoist with his own petard. Moral sensibility does not lend itself to such laughter, but we may confess that the hardening process so skilfully applied by the actors to our hearts is good for the play' (26 July 1932).

One could argue, of course, that treating any play as an exercise in style will result in a reductive view of humanity and lead, inevitably, to totalitarian theatre: the moral contradictions of Komisarjevsky's *Merchant* may thus appear to have sprung from the tyranny of style rather than from a consideration of politics. Nevertheless, Komisarjevsky achieved more than an aesthetic revolution in his production. He overturned as well a tradition of playing Shylock that for more than half a century had embodied the moral enlightenment of Western culture and dramatised the tragic consequences of racial prejudice. By dispensing with the traditions of bourgeois theatre, he dispensed as well with a sentimental Shylock – the one was a product of the other; and in his place he offered audiences (so far as Ayrton would allow) a 'twisting, comic devil' more appropriate, he thought, for the naïve 'fairy tale' world of *The Merchant* (*Civilisation*, p. 84). But there was nothing naïve about Komisarjevsky's conception of that world: as his remarks indicate, he knew that one cannot, by artistic fiat, divorce a play from cultural values and moral questions that have accrued over centuries of production. In fact, his Shylock was nearly indistinguishable from the anti-Semitic stereotype promoted by Komisarjevsky's favourite dictator who, at that very time, was turning Jews into scapegoats for the ills of the capitalist system in Germany and was even using *The Merchant of Venice* and *The Jew of Malta* as comic propaganda to advance his racist agenda in the theatre. And did Komisarjevsky, by analogy, do any less? By dehumanising Shylock as a 'crafty alien usurer', didn't he, as *The Times* attests, encourage audiences to harden their hearts against him and to laugh at his punishment and expulsion? From the perspective of sixty years, is it possible *not* to hear an ominous warning in the reviewer's claim that this 'hardening process' was 'good for the play'? Komisarjevsky, I would submit, staged *The Merchant* as a carnival of denial and found a receptive audience for it: indeed, the production proved so popular it was revived the following year. It must have tapped into the anxieties of a people who, in the throes of economic crisis, sought escapist entertainment and found it in the fantasy of a fortunate heiress; a people who, in their readiness to hiss the wealthy Jew, averted their gaze from anti-Semitic activities abroad that would, in years to come, make the tragedy of Shylock dwindle into insignificance.

CHAPTER IV

Aesthetes in a rugger club: Jonathan Miller and Laurence Olivier

The spectre of Henry Irving hovered uncannily over the National Theatre's 1970 production of *The Merchant of Venice*. Even the circumstances of production resembled those at Irving's Lyceum: Laurence Olivier, who, as director of the National, was the modern equivalent of an actor–manager, had not had a major new role, nor his company a successful production of Shakespeare, in several years, when Kenneth Tynan persuaded him that *The Merchant* might offer such an opportunity; and what was good for Olivier would, of course, be good for the National (Cottrell, pp. 360-1). Like Irving, Olivier was best known for his tragic roles – Hamlet, Richard III, Othello. When he assayed Shylock, therefore, it was clear that his *Merchant* would serve as a vehicle for a famous tragedian. Yet there were other similarities as well: just as Irving's Lyceum came to be regarded as a shrine to what was noblest and best in Victorian culture, so Olivier believed that the National Theatre had a duty to nurture his country's most civilised traditions and values. For him, therefore, as for Irving, *The Merchant* should not pander to popular prejudices with comic stereotypes, but promote 'a feeling of dignity and austerity'; it should eschew romantic artifice in order to 'search for reality'. To achieve a 'reality' his audience would recognise, Olivier decided to update the play to 1880, 'that period when the Victorians had found their maturity' (*On Acting*, p. 119) and, incidentally, the very time when Irving was revolutionising the way audiences viewed *The Merchant*.

What did Olivier mean by maturity? Most probably, that by the late nineteenth century, those economic and social relations determined by capitalist expansion had become so firmly fixed that they were ossified. England was no longer, as in Shakespeare's day, riven by the residual values of feudalism, but was a sophisticated market economy, its ruling classes dedicated to the expansion and control of global supply and demand. It was a world, as Olivier said, of 'tall hats and frock coats', of 'clean and polished fingernails' (*On Acting*, p. 119); a world in which merchants did business in City offices or on the stock exchange, not on quays; a world in which antagonisms between the landed gentry and the new monied classes had grown more subtle, since those with money had for centuries been acquiring land and titles and thus, to the common eye, were all but indistinguishable from the old aristocracy. It was a world where usurers were now called bankers or financiers; a world where Jews such as Rothschild and Disraeli seemed (but only seemed) at last to have overcome the obstacles that for so long had denied them the rights of citizenship. By updating the play to 1880, therefore, Olivier appropriated Shakespeare's text to explore a society in which the economic and social tensions emergent in Elizabethan England had become more intricate and codified.

Indeed, every age has appropriated *The Merchant* for its own purposes. By the ingenious cutting and repositioning of scenes, Irving had transformed the play into a tragedy of social alienation. His strategy was to appeal to the pride Victorians took in their enlightened racial tolerance; that fact that, to do so, he had to fashion his sixteenth-century Shylock as very much an English gentleman did not strike audiences as at all unusual. Shakespeare too, they surmised, was an eminent Victorian who had the misfortune to be born three hundred years before his time, and only they, having achieved the apogee of civilisation, could rightly discern the true message of *The Merchant*. In young Jonathan Miller, Olivier found a director who was willing to appropriate both Shakespeare's text *and* Irving's conception of it to demonstrate how the presumably enlightened Victorians to whom Irving appealed were themselves philistines, their prejudices all the more insidious for being cloaked in shows of courtesy and good will. Miller, a theatrical iconoclast with an interest in social history far keener than Olivier's, located the roots of modern prejudice not in theology, but in economic theory and power relations. 'Modern anti-Semitism,' he argues, 'as Hannah Arendt (*The Origins of Totalitarianism*) has shown, has something to do with nineteenth-century capitalism and politics rather than with biblical theories about the death of Christ.' Jewish financiers often provided the capital with which industrialists made their fortunes, but such provision did not guarantee them access to power or social privilege. In fact, Jews came to be blamed for exploitation, unemployment, market fluctuations, and other economic woes for which capitalists had no ready solutions. Miller used Shakespeare's text to develop such themes: he set Shylock 'within the context of the Rothschilds Banking House, which found that great wealth and prestige never meant exemption from the hatred and anti-Semitism of European society – whose rapid economic and political expansion the Rothschilds were helping to finance' (Miller, *Plays and Players*, p. 53).

What particularly interested Miller was not overt differences between Christians and Jews, but the ways in which ethnic groups '*look* for appearances which will substantiate their prejudices'. He therefore envisaged a Shylock not exotically different from the gentiles, but socially and culturally assimilated.

> Allowing Shylock to appear as one among many businessmen, scarcely distinguishable from them ... made sense of his claim that, apart from his customs, a Jew is like everyone else ... I felt that there was no need in a nineteenth-century setting to distinguish him except by the customs and rituals that he follows discreetly in his home. This highlights and emphasises the absurdity of the racial prejudice.
> (Miller, *Subsequent Performances*, pp. 155-6)

Updating the play thus served Miller's agenda as readily as an anthropologically 'correct' production served Irving's; both directors sought thereby to discover the origins of their own culture's attitudes towards Jews, and both suppressed the play's comic potential in order to present the 'real' – that is, the tragically verisimilar – Shylock as a representative of his whole persecuted race.

Where Irving strove for verisimilitude by reconstructing a Venice inspired by the paintings of Bordone, Giorgione and Veronese, Miller's Venice was inspired by photographs taken by the Count de Primoli at the end of the last century, photographs which depicted young men frequenting waterside cafés, the bustle of richly detailed piazzas, the faded splendour of *fin de siècle* society. Julia Trevelyan Oman attempted to capture the Venice of de Primoli's photographs behind the proscenium arch of the Old Vic, itself a nineteenth-century picture frame. Her set was a 'golden-ochre piazzetta' of colonnades and graceful arches, flanked by flats of a church and a borsa (*Drama*, Summer 1970). Upstage were two Palladian loggias, mirror images of one another, which swung open to reveal the interiors of, respectively, Shylock's house – tastefully sober in its deep-grained woods, bookcases and busts – and Portia's house, all golden draperies, overstuffed furniture, and Victorian bric-à-brac. By creating a richly pictorial set reminiscent of those on the Victorian stage, Oman confined the action to a novelistic world in which Miller's reading of the play would make sense. Such a set, however, as Peter Ansorge observed, did not 'easily absorb the violent, quick-changing rhythms of the Elizabethan drama – which were designed to portray human experience in an open context, as opposed to the closed, private world of the nineteenth-century novel' (*Plays and Players*, June 1970). At a time when the National's great rival, the Royal Shakespeare Company, was developing a self-consciously theatrical style modelled in part on the Berliner Ensemble – a presentational style which acknowledged the virtues of breaking through the proscenium arch to play directly to the audience – Miller's production was deliberately reactionary and illusionistic, evocative of 'the rather dull, Adriatic mercantile life that Italo Svevo re-creates in his novels' (*Subsequent*, p. 107).

The first stage directions in the prompt book indicate how realistically Miller intended his Venetians to go about their business: 'Extras coming from church ... Extras in background carrying parcels with sacks over heads ...'. And amidst this mundane activity, the play opens on the interior of the elegant Café Florian: 'twelve café chairs, three round tables, two oblong tables; white table cloths, brass coffee pot, cups, saucers, liqueur glasses, bottle of Strega, silver tray.' The props define a world of privilege and help to convey Miller's view that the play is driven by class divisions and social injustice.

Here Antonio sits, reading a newspaper on a banquette, sipping coffee. A distinguished grey-haired man in a morning suit, looking like an 'elder Forsyte, with rolled umbrella and spats' (*Daily Telegraph*, 29 April 1970), he speaks with two younger men who clearly are concerned more with his business ventures – and their own coffee – than with his sadness. Their attire and umbrellas identify them as City men, lesser merchants than Antonio; and when Bassanio enters, Miller makes us very aware of their antagonism toward the leisured class. 'We leave you now with better company,' Solanio sneers (I.i.59); and his sarcasm is echoed by Salerio when he speaks of the 'worthier friends' (61) whose company Antonio will prefer to theirs: these merchants thus betray disapproval, perhaps envy, of those who have inherited wealth and never had to work for it. Such disapproval may be warranted, too, for Bassanio and his companions are played as aristocratic idlers who pointedly snub their social inferiors – Bassanio's acknowledgment of Salerio and Solanio, 'Good signors both, when shall we laugh?' (66) is patently insincere – and exploit the generosity of their friend: Gratiano intercepts the waiter to drink a glass of strega intended for Antonio.

Predicated on class consciousness, the friendship of Antonio and Bassanio elicits a complex response. Jeremy Brett's Bassanio is no youth: a fortyish gigolo in a dashing check jacket who greets his patron 'with a gently teasing kiss on the upstage cheek' (*Punch*, 6 May 1970), he is worshipped by the dignified and understated merchant, a man who is just a bit too old to qualify as a friend and too intimate to be a father. With characteristic hyperbole, Miller suggests that 'the relationship between Bassanio and Antonio made me think of the relationship of Oscar Wilde and Bosie where a sad old queen regrets the opportunistic heterosexual love of a person whom he adored' (*Subsequent*, p. 107). However strained the analogy, Brett's Bassanio is clearly a cunning opportunist: sitting next to Antonio, he feigns ingenuousness as he discusses his debts, acts hesitant to say the word 'money', looks uncomfortable as Antonio presses him to get to the point; then, turning away and rising from his seat at the table, he describes Portia – 'In Belmont is a lady richly left' – to the accompaniment of a violin which strikes up on the word *richly*. The cloyingly romantic music (one critic called it 'Café Chopin') underscores the insincerity of the speech: Bassanio's delivery is arch, affected, calculating. Money motivates his quest for Portia as surely as it underlies his friendship with Antonio. Miller thus identifies Bassanio as a leech who will suck his friend dry: their parasitic relationship is quite at home in the Café Florian, where material success and moral impoverishment go hand in hand – where Bassanio, cheered to have prevailed so easily, slaps his gloves instead of a tip into the waiter's outstretched hand and saunters off, leaving Antonio to pay the bill.

It is to this world that Shylock would like to belong. Olivier seized the opportunity to give Shylock as much psychological depth as a tragic hero, paying careful attention to the subtle ways in which aliens learn to cope in a hostile environment, just as Irving had done a hundred years earlier. Yet unlike Irving, whose model was a Levantine patriarch, Olivier conceived of Shylock as a *Victorian* Jew, a banker striving for assimilation but not yet in command of the manners or *noblesse oblige* of a Rothschild. Driven by a first-generation desire for social respectability, he would paradoxically emulate those very gentiles he abhors. He dresses like them, only better: wearing a black frock coat over black striped trousers, carrying a silver-topped walking stick and a newspaper from which he reads current market prices through a golden pince-nez – 'then let me see, the rate' (I.iii.96) – he is every inch the financier. Only the yarmulka hidden by his top hat identifies him as an outsider.

In creating so compellingly believable a Shylock, Olivier eschewed the stage tradition that had so often caricatured the Jew: 'Shylock owed more to Benjamin Disraeli than to Fagin, physically and mentally,' Olivier avers. 'There was to be no stropping of knives on the soles of shoes, no fingering the sharpness of the blade, no splitting hairs with the curved edge, no spitting oaths on to the courtroom floor, no rolling eyes to the deaf gods. I was determined to maintain dignity and not stoop physically and mentally to Victorian villainy' (*On Acting*, p. 119). His reference to Disraeli is not merely fortuitous, for he admits in *Confessions of an Actor* 'to having been so impressed by the interpretation of Disraeli by Mr. George Arliss in an exceptionally good talkie made in 1929 that, to be honest, I lifted it (pinched is such a common word) for my playing of Shylock'. Even here, Olivier communicates the bourgeois sense of decorum – 'pinched is such a common word'– with which he invested his Shylock. From Arliss he borrowed the Disraeli curl on his forehead and the Disraeli mouth: he had a special front row of teeth made, with its companion extra lower gum, and took particular pride in the authenticity they lent to his appearance. 'These two little friends,' he admits, 'made my mouth area from just underneath my nose to the top of my chin protrude enough (one feature is sufficient) to lend a semitic look to my whole countenance without further sculptural addition' (p. 236).

This set of false teeth and gums helped him to affect an accent that spoke volumes about his social aspirations. As J. C. Trewin observes, Olivier's Shylock 'knows that he is an alien in Venice, but he seeks to ingratiate himself with the Christians, to imitate the affectations of their speech, to clip words like "meanin'" and "speakin'" ... [yet is] probably aware that his carefully nurtured accent can slip into plebeian vowel sounds, and that the game he plays is fruitless' (*Illustrated London News*, 9 May 1970). Irving Wardle, too, astutely concludes that although in appearance Shylock is virtually indistinguishable from Antonio, within ... he has been incurably maimed by the process of assimilation. His delivery is a ghastly compound of speech tricks picked up from the Christian rich: posh vowels and the slipshod terminations of the hunting counties. 'I am debatin' of my present state,' he spits out, fingering a silver-topped cane; and then spoils the gesture by dissolving into paroxysms of silent, slack-jawed laughter. (*The Times*, 29 April 1970)

Shylock is thus at once a creation and a victim of his society. He apes the dress, the manners, and the speech of his social 'betters', and even surpasses them in word-play. His delight in puns, for example, is never more outrageous than when, dressed to dine with the Christians in a cream-coloured stole over black tails, he delivers lines rich in social resonance – 'Well, thou shalt see, thy eyes shall be thy judge,/ The difference of old Shylock and Bassanio' (II.v.1-2) – pronouncing the middle syllables of 'Base-aini-o' in such a way as to make a plural anus of his host (*Punch*, 6 May 1970). At times such as this, he seems supremely confident of his place in the community of gentiles, superior to them in wit and style. Yet in so far as he exaggerates their affectations or does not quite get the accent right, he verges on the grotesque; and the hint of grotesqueness, of course, only reinforces the prejudices of those who all along have known that he was not one of them. Benedict Nightingale summarises the problematic social position of Olivier's Jew: 'He is a foreigner in a public school, an aesthete in a rugger club, a gargoyle in a gallery of classical faces, a profoundly emotional being in a world where emotions embarrass people, and one can readily imagine the history of snubs and mortification behind him' (*New Statesman*, 8 May 1970). Like many a nineteenth-century critic, Nightingale imagines a social and psychological history for Shylock. Olivier's performance invites him to do so.

In order to refashion the play as a realistic portrait of late Victorian society – a society in which Jews were nominally assimilated and prejudices more covert than they had been in Elizabethan England – Miller had to adjust Shakespeare's text. Such adjustments are evident as early as I.iii. When Antonio enters to enquire about the loan, Shylock tips his hat to him, and the courtesy is returned. These men will be civil to each other, for civility is the badge of all their tribe; only by dodging and circling one another do they betray their deeper antagonism. Miller cuts the entire aside (33-44) in which Shylock confides,

> I hate him for he is a Christian;
> But more, for that in low simplicity

> He lends out money gratis, and brings down
> The rate of usance here with us in Venice ...

– thereby effacing both the economic and the religious motives for Shylock's wanting to catch Antonio 'upon the hip'. Such sentiments clearly belong to an earlier age, just as the aside itself does (an Elizabethan device that has no place in illusionist theatre); and when we are denied the privilege of overhearing Shylock's thoughts, his motives for agreeing to the bond remain necessarily opaque (Sullivan, pp. 33-4). Like the Venetians, we must try to fathom his motives by closely observing his behaviour, and his behaviour gives us much to think about. It has great humour and mimetic vigour: his gentle greeting to Antonio, 'Your worship was the last man in our mouths' (52), is accompanied by masticatory jaw movements; and when he tells how Jacob 'peeled me certain wands' (76), he inserts his walking stick through his outstretched hand with corkscrew movements, which suggests not only the peeling process, but animal copulation as well (Billington, p. 84).

Yet Shylock drops his mask of bonhomie when Antonio insists on an answer. With controlled fury he turns on his old rival: 'Signor Antonio, many a time and oft/ In the Rialto you have rated me/ About my monies ...' (98-100), unearthing a buried pun in *rated*, the word he has just emphasised while checking his paper for the current rate of usance (96). He lispingly ridicules Antonio's aristocratic accent on 'you come to me, and you say,/ "Shylock, we would have monies"' (107-8), pointing his stick accusingly on '*you* say so,/ *You* ... ' (108-9), the explosive force of each *you* laying bare the humiliation to which the Christian community has subjected him. But he regains his composure to propose the 'merry' bond; and in this context, it is precisely that – a bond made in jest, a loan of three thousand ducats gratis, an uncharactistic show of generosity from a Jew known for sharp business practices. Olivier delivers his lines with ingratiating humour: 'let the forfeit/ Be nominated for ...' – and here he pauses, searches for an idea; and when it comes, he tosses it off with wry wit while touching Antonio's lapel – 'an equal pound/ Of your fair flesh' (141-3). In the world of Victorian business, a bond which specified the forfeiture of a pound of flesh would have been simply incredible. Here, Shylock appears to use it as a throw-away, in self-mockery – proof, perhaps, of how mistaken the Christians have been in him. Pleased with Antonio's consent, he removes his glove to offer his hand; but Bassanio's objection to the condition leaves him again humiliated, his 'kind' offer spurned, his hand unshaken. Contemp-

[82]

tuously, Olivier slings his stick over his shoulder and does a marvellous false exit – 'If he will take it, so; if not, adieu' (162) – spinning on his heels the moment Antonio relents. Having exposed the distrust with which Christians and Jews regard each other, the scene returns to feigned civility, doffed hats, and smiles.

※

Miller thus encourages his audience to discover in Shakespeare's Venice a precursor of modern society. The play was ripe for his revision. For a century, certainly since Irving, it had been widely recognised as a play whose comic form did not comfortably resolve the issues of racism and social class it broached, and the horrors of the Holocaust only served to sharpen our focus on them. By updating the play to the late nineteenth century, Miller forced audiences to confront those issues without the reassurance provided by the historical 'difference' of an Elizabethan staging. The society he created more closely resembled their own, the codes of conduct were familiar, the subtleties of prejudice readily recognisable. His interpretation often challenged what generations of playgoers had taken the play to mean, but in doing so it seldom worked against the text. Three instances stand out. First, Miller fashioned wooing scenes which subverted the romantic values traditionally ascribed to them. Second, he reshaped the drama of Shylock's revenge to make it more humanly credible. And third, he made discordant the ostensible harmonies of Act V. In these ways, he demystified a text encrusted with stage tradition and thereby inspired a generation of directors to review the play in light of contemporary cultural biases.

Where Irving's insistence on Shylock's essential humanity and Venice's realism clashed with Ellen Terry's romantic conception of Belmont, Miller's production was all of a piece, stylistically consistent throughout. In 'Miller's thoughtful deformation of Shakespeare,' writes J. W. Lambert, assuming a standard reading of the play, Belmont is not 'the neoplatonic fancy of an ideal world of love, music and moonlight' (*Drama*, Summer 1970), but the fantasy world of the *nouveaux riches*, a tasteless tribute to consumerism. *This* is what men seek, the lucre for which they hazard all they have; and as such, it becomes the focus of the play's capitalist values, not an alternative to them. Belmont – just as it might have done in an Elizabethan production – serves as the feminine mirror into which Venetians look to see their own greed prettily reflected.

Portia's first scene with Nerissa alerts us to the equation of

Belmont with Venice. The loggia opens to reveal Portia in her boudoir, every inch the chatelaine of Belmont: elegantly dressed in corset, bustles and petticoats, she moves comfortably amid her Victorian stuff – shawls and cushions, oriental carpets and lace curtains, chairs and settee, vases filled with lillies, ferns, and peacock feathers – the queen of all she surveys. As Nerissa opens letters from would-be suitors and reads off their names, Portia squints at slides of them through an antique viewer: the device quickly establishes both the period – the dawn of the technological age – and Portia's fondness for toys. Furthermore, it distances her from her suitors: they become mere excuses for her to display her wit. And this Portia has wit aplenty. Joan Plowright plays her with the command of a woman of years. Searching for a Jamesian source, Miller compares her with Isabel Archer (*Plays and Players*, March 1970); Nightingale less charitably calls her a bossy suffragette with little moral conviction (*New Statesman*, 8 May 1970); and Peter Ansorge, 'a new rich snobby spinster [with] a determination to buy a husband' (*Plays and Players*, June 1970). No young maiden who will submit to the will of her father, this Portia knows what she is about, and it is *not* her father's business.

Audiences were either amused or outraged by the way in which Portia – and Miller – sent up her suitors. By 1970, it had become customary to play the suitors for laughs: Komisarjevsky's satirical treatment of them had proved so popular that subsequent directors readily followed suit. The farce of Morocco's wooing scene is very much in the vein of Komisarjevsky: in a conflation of II.i and II.vii (by now, a convention), Morocco is caricatured as 'a diplomatic Al Jolson minstrel just back from the colonies' (*Plays and Players*, June 1970). Not the 'tawny Moor all in white' with three or four followers indicated by the stage direction, he enters alone, dressed in Victorian military regalia like a colonial officer in whom the ideal of cultural assimilation is turned to folly. His blue uniform, complete with epaulettes on the shoulders and a banner around the chest, suggests that he is a proud product of British imperialism, someone with a public school education who may do very well when he returns to his own country but should not expect to mix races with Portia. In fact, Portia and Nerissa shriek when they see him, shocked that someone of his leer might actually *win* the lottery. But the scene gives him short shrift: in the tradition of Irving, much of his eloquent speech in praise of Portia is cut (including lines 38-59), thus sharpening his focus on the caskets alone, which he inspects formally, arm bent at the waist, white-gloved hand gesturing, and his speech comically arhythmic with the kind of foreign pronunciations ('deserb' for 'deserve') that will forever make him the butt of jokes among the ruling class. Pausing at the silver casket to ask, 'What if I strayed no farther, but chose here?' (35), he breaches all decorum by sliding an arm around Portia's waist; she recoils from his touch. Once he has chosen, however, the scene hastens to its conclusion. The naked disappointment of his 'O, hell! What have we here?' (62), like that of Komisarjevsky's Morocco, underscores the pomposity of his proud boasts, and all that remains of his scroll reading is four lines – 65-6, 69, and 73 – which quickly deflate his social presumption and lend more point to Portia's tart dismissal of him and all of his complexion.

Miller's ingenuity shows to even better advantage in the scene of Arragon's wooing. Usually played as an effete young nobleman, Arragon here is reduced to a palsied *senex amans*, the last gasp of the titled aristocracy who, 'tottering into the contest as if from a ducal old folks' home, has entirely lost control of his motor faculties' (*The Times*, 29 April 1970). The staging makes a mockery of his suitability as a contestant for Portia's hand. 'Armed with spectacles rather than a scimitar ... clad in tails and white tie, white hair wildly erect ... Arragon walks blindly past the caskets, submitting to the two women's pushes in finding his way' (Schlueter, p. 171). Portia exasperatedly interrupts him as he rehearses the injunctions of his oath, cutting all but the first line of his speech; and taking the article of agreement out of his hand, she offers him a cup of tea instead, into which he keeps putting sugar cubes until, with a comic arbitrariness, he returns the eighth cube to the bowl and absentmindedly drops the silver tongs into his coat pocket. Massive textual cuts bring him quickly to his choice, but only a deft manoeuvre by Nerissa prevents him from putting the key into the wrong – the lead – casket. The prize he wins, the 'portrait of a blinking idiot', elicits a senile cackle; and as he departs, he kisses Nerissa's hand (though Portia has extended hers) and gives Portia the portrait to keep, promising never to marry.

Such comedy makes mischief of the casket plot; for if Portia's suitors are patently unsuitable – if their merits are exploded by absurd pomposity or grotesque senility – and if, furthermore, their hazarding for her entails no element of risk, then one cannot take the romantic premises of the lottery seriously. As June Schlueter argues, 'in agreeing to the conditions of the test, [Arragon] has hazarded nothing, for the prospect of continuing his royal line through a legitimate – or any – heir is as laughable as it is unlikely'. The imposition of hard conditions seems intended to limit choosers to those who might be worthy of Portia – 'a strategy that has worked with the suitors from foreign lands who have earlier taken their leave'. That Morocco and Arragon accept those conditions would seem to argue in them a merit lacking in the others. 'But the reduction of Arragon to dotage' – and, I might add, the reduction of Morocco to a figure of imperial fun – 'makes a mockery of this purpose' and raises the possibility that Portia, the prize, 'may be bestowed unearned' (p. 171).

Her father's inspiration for protecting her from the undeserving may not, after all, be foolproof. Yet Miller offers something in compensation, for by rigging the casket plot, he justifies Portia's taking matters into her own hands. If she does not teach Bassanio how to choose right, she may be condemned to a miserable marriage. In order to spare herself from the likes of Morocco and Arragon, therefore, she must feel no compunction about flouting her father's will; she must (with a relish that would have seemed even more timely in 1970 than today) liberate herself from male tyranny and assert her right to self-determination. A woman of forty, after all, should know her own mind about finding a husband, and it is only Plowright's expertly comic playing that keeps us from wondering why she hasn't married earlier, or what in God's name her father was up to by keeping his grown daughter closeted for so many years.

Portia meets her perfect match in Bassanio, whose designs on her money are as calculating as her strategy to catch him. With a gambler's instinct for winning, he follows the rules of romantic courtship to the letter, performing the casket ritual with mock sincerity and counting on Portia's ingenuity to help him out. Olivier admits that he had waggishly suggested Bassanio should be Portia's *only* suitor, coming disguised first as Morocco, then as Arragon, one way or the other guaranteeing a victory. Though the suggestion mercifully was not taken up – it would too radically have debased the moral and mimetic credibility of Belmont – it nevertheless demonstrates that for this production, Bassanio all along was conceived to be a self-serving poseur, and the outcome of the lottery a foregone conclusion.

Miller's staging provides ample opportunity for such role-play. The lovers enter III.ii in riding habits (Belmont apparently is hunt country), wielding their crops suggestively and discussing the lottery without much emotional conviction. Portia adopts a teasing tone when she tells Bassanio, 'I could teach you/ How to choose right,' then adds unconvincingly, 'but then I am forsworn./ So will I never be' (10-12); and she delivers her behest, 'If you do love me, you *will* find me out' (41, her emphasis) in such a way as to alert him to some chicanery to come. After such calculation, the mythic hyperbole of her paean to Bassanio rings false; indeed, much of it (53-60) is cut, denying him the status of young Alcides and her the unlikely role of virgin tribute. But enough remains so that her injunction 'Go, Hercules' prompts the audience to cynical laughter: there is simply too great a gap between the demigod she envisages and the charlatan we see to make the analogy credible.

We do not wait long to discover what her ploy is: she will use the song, 'Tell me where is fancy bred', to cue him which casket to choose. The possible subliminal message of the song, both in its focus on fancy's deceptions and in its implicit rhyme with 'lead', have long been noted; even Ellen Terry had entertained but dismissed the notion that Portia intends to subvert her father's will by such means. Miller, however, found the subversion irresistible. Bassanio is just about to address the caskets when two middle-aged sopranos, referred to in the prompt book as 'the Gemini', dressed in lead-coloured satin gowns with their hair pulled back into buns, bustle in and distract him. As they begin their *bel canto* duet, they advance on Bassanio, crowding the ornate pedestal on which the caskets rest and fixing their gaze unashamedly on the lead casket when they sing 'In the cradle where it lies' (69). When it is over, the performance of these leaden belles is rewarded with applause– ours and Bassanio's.

The ingenuity with which the Gemini give away Portia's secret is enormously amusing, but equally amusing is Gratiano's dimwitted response. Thinking he has got the clue, he points decisively to the silver casket. Bassanio, however, is more astute than his friend: having exchanged a knowing smile with Nerissa, he is prepared to play the part required of him. Brushing Gratiano aside, he addresses the caskets in the same declamatory style with which he described Portia to Antonio in the opening scene; and although the speech is drastically cut, he nonetheless says what he *needs* to say to appear a lover who will not be deceived with ornament. Pausing at the lead casket, 'here choose I' (107), he steals a glance at Portia, who puts her hands to her face in premeditated amazement. And when he unlocks it to discover – with all the surprise he can muster – her portrait, he launches into the most artificially Petrarchan of all his speeches, 'What demi-god/ Hath come so near creation?' (115-16), gesturing extravagantly as he praises each feature of her painted face, checking over his shoulder to see the effect of his hyperbole, and, confident of success, reaching a breathless climax on 'But her eyes!' (123) as she, like an ageing *ingénue*, bats her lashes and wipes away a tear.

The two lovers thus get what they want with their eyes open, feigning compliance with the rituals of courtship demanded by her father and by society. Their charade is splendidly ironic. In one sense, the lyric speeches which fall so trippingly from their tongues preserve the romantic ethos of Belmont. But those speeches are not for a moment believable; they are *acted*. Miller's cynical depiction of Belmont, therefore, provides no ethical alternative to the world of Venice as more conventional interpretations argue it should: all passion here is unfelt; all talk of love, mere pretence. When Portia wishes herself 'A thousand times more fair, ten thousand times/ More rich ... only to stand high in [his] account' (154-5), her sentiments do not redeem Bassanio's vocabulary of mercantile value, as they commonly are said to do, but instead reaffirm the very values that have brought him to her. Worth, in Belmont as in Venice, remains a commodity: 'the full sum of me/ Is sum of something' (157-8), Portia puns, as Bassanio surveys the riches he may now take title to. Thus, through the ambiguous language of value, Miller's Belmont codifies the risks and rewards of venture capitalism and perpetuates the romantic fictions – love, honour, obedience – by which a mercantile society disguises its fundamental greed. In Miller's hands, however, that disguise is joyously penetrable.

*

The joy Miller takes in demystifying Belmont has inevitable consequences for the bond plot, for against such chicanery as the Christians practise, Shylock's passion stands out as something finer, nobler, and more sincere. To ensure that we recognise the distinction, Miller reshapes the text to Shylock's advantage, cutting such obviously prejudicial lines as 'I did dream of moneybags tonight" (II.v.18) or, more significantly, the entirety of II.viii and Shylock's aside against Antonio. The Victorian gentility for which Miller strove makes these adjustments not only permissible, but necessary: Shylock in this period would not admit to hating Antonio because he is Christian, or because he lends out money gratis, any more than

Antonio would spit on Shylock in public or kick him over his threshold. The bond, as we have seen, becomes not a ruse to mask a deeper malice as it was for Irving, but a means by which Shylock strives to win the acceptance of the gentiles by playing according to *their* rules. And Miller revises Shakespeare's text most startlingly when he suggests that Shylock's revenge is motivated not by an implacable hatred of Christians, but by the loss of Jessica, and by this alone.

Miller seeks to explain Shylock's revenge as the anguish of a bereaved father. He had informed Olivier that the marriage of a daughter to a Christian is 'the very most appalling disaster that can happen in an orthodox Jewish family', who 'in such circumstances hold a funeral service for the errant girl, whose name is struck from the family records, and from then on she is dead to them. When it happens to Shylock as a Christian "joke", he is stirred to the boiling point of fury and proceeds to his vengeance as is not only natural but in fact his expected duty' (*Confessions*, p. 235). To excuse Shylock's lust for a pound of Christian flesh as a 'natural' and 'expected' behaviour may seem to strain the text, yet Olivier found a brilliant strategy for communicating to the audience just that in III.i. As the scene begins, he lurks on the balcony above his loggia, observing Salerio and Solanio as they gossip about Antonio. When he descends to them, in his shirtsleeves, obviously distraught, his accusation has a deadly force: 'You knew, none so well, none so well as you, of my daughter's flight' (III.i.20-1). Their mockery goads him to further fury, as does their mentioning the losses of Antonio, who obviously now will not be able to repay his debt to Shylock. Their intention is spiteful, but it backfires; for by mentioning Antonio's losses, they prompt Shylock to think about the merchant as a scapegoat for his own loss of Jessica. He screams uncontrolled, 'There I have another bad match: a bankrupt, a prodigal, who dare scarce show his head on the Rialto' (35-6), and then proceeds to the downstage railing where he rests for support, his back to the audience, as if gazing into a canal. As a bell tolls, apparently a death knell, he suddenly turns around, raises his hand to his lower lip with a look of malicious inspiration, and mutters, 'Let him look to his bond' (37). Here it occurs to him *for the first time* that the bond may serve as a vehicle for retribution: an Antonio for a Jessica. Miller thus invites us to feel that Shylock's 'depth of love for Jessica has become twisted into bottomless hate for Antonio by a kind of psychological *lex talionis*: his beloved daughter, his heart, has been taken from him by a Christian, so his revenge will be to remove the

[89]

heart of a Christian' (Perret, p. 147).

So inspired, Olivier speaks the rest of the speech rapid fire, the speed and tension of his delivery indicating that he at last has found an outlet for all the years of humiliation he has suffered. He bears down threateningly on Salerio and Solanio, who are mere reeds in the wind of his passion; their 'thou wilt not take his flesh' (40), spoken through nervous laughter, sounds as fearful as it is in-effectual. His series of rhetorical questions beginning with 'Hath not a Jew eyes?' (47) thus becomes not a plea for pity but a clarion call to revenge, 'senses, affections, passions' building to the kind of rolling-eyed emotion that characterised Olivier's Othello years earlier. He cuts the next four lines in order to arrive more quickly at the word 'revenge' (52), a word he insistently emphasises by slapping his right hand into the palm of his left and shooting the thumb of his left hand outwards like 'a butcher slapping a piece of meat on to a weighing machine' (Billington, p. 86). The speech reaches a climax when, as he arrives at the last question – 'what should his sufferance be by Christian example?' (55) – we await the expected answer, 'Why, revenge', but it doesn't come. He slaps his right hand into his left, extends his thumb, then, overcome with grief, pauses on 'Why' and, panting heavily, cannot utter the final two syllables. The effect is breathtaking: 'revenge' never echoes more clearly in our ears than here.

Shylock's emotional intensity contrasts sharply with the coolly detached playing of the Christians, and the contrast is sharpest when Shylock enters his house, leaving Salerio and Solanio, unmoved by his grief, to observe Tubal's approach with smug disdain: 'Here comes another of the tribe' (61). There is, to borrow Shylock's phrase, more difference between their blood and the Jews' than between red wine and Rhenish: where, typically, productions suggest some conspiracy between the Jews, with Tubal serving as Shylock's collection agent, Miller advances the idea that Tubal, another top-hatted banker all in black, has come to offer condolences to a grieving friend. A sense of mourning haunts the scene: Olivier enters with a dress draped over his arms – the very dress Jessica has shed onstage to take on a male disguise at the end of II.v – stroking it, as if it were his daughter's hair, and sighing 'Why, there, there, there, there' (66). The image resonates with Shakespearian associations of fathers lamenting the loss of children, just as the line itself anticipates Lear's cry that Cordelia will come again 'never, never, never, never'. Miller points out:

In *King Lear*, as in *Merchant*, a daughter who betrays her father seems, in his eyes, to die when she denies him her love. Holding the empty dress, Olivier appeared to be carrying the corpse of the departed daughter, as Shylock wishes when he says 'I would my daughter were dead at my foot, and the jewels in her ear! Would she were hearsed at my foot, and the ducats in her coffin!' (*Subsequent*, p. 108).

With a debt to Freudian psychology, Shylock here sublimates his grief by fixating on the loss of his ducats; he is one of those people who, as Benedict Nightingale observes, 'under stress become obsessed with details, minutiae, rather than face trouble squarely' (*New Statesman*, 8 May 1970). Therefore, when he hurls the dress to the floor and, stooping over it with his arms extended backwards in an Othello-like paroxysm of grief, wishes his daughter dead at his foot, we understand his words to express his deeper wish to have her back.

Shylock's exchange with Tubal is sometimes played for laughs. The information Tubal metes out, alternating news of Jessica's expenditures and Antonio's losses, moves Shylock to such extremes of agony and ecstasy that his behaviour may seem ludicrous. In this production, however, Shylock's mood swings are psychologically credible, poignant rather than comic, and Tubal parcels out information sparingly to protect Shylock's feelings, not to toy with them. Reduced almost to incoherence as he babbles 'no ill luck stirring but what lights o' my shoulders' (74-5), Shylock pricks up his ears at the news of Antonio's ill luck. 'I thank God, I thank God!' (81) he cries in falsetto, beating Tubal on the breast with his fists and then, on 'Is it true, is it true?', breaking into a gleeful dance around the dress that calls his sanity into question. Much noted by critics, this skip-like dance was inspired by the little jig of triumph done by Adolf Hitler in a railway carriage at Compiègne when he heard that France had surrendered. Olivier, who remembered the newsreel, 'was delighted with the unpredictable peculiarity of this gesture' (*Subsequent*, p. 108). But joy quickly yields to sorrow. Returning to his senses and to Tubal, he asks (adding his own words to the text), 'Didst thou hear naught else in Genoa, hm?' (84); and learning that Jessica has sold the turquoise he had of Leah, he sinks to his haunches to protest that he would not have given it for a wilderness of monkeys. The prolonged wail that escapes his lips on the first syllable of *wilderness* leads to a fit of sobbing – and blowing his nose into a large handkerchief – during which Tubal's consolation goes unheeded (Foulkes, 'Shylock', p. 32). Then, regaining his composure, he draws himself up, walks to the table, removes a tallis from the drawer, folds it, touches it to his lips, and drapes it over his head as he bids Tubal to meet him at the synagogue. This image has a profound significance: for the first time in the production, Miller reveals the importance of Jewish heritage to a man who has striven to deny it but who now, at a time of emotional dislocation, turns to it for solace. Going to the synagogue affirms, for Shylock, a world of values he has all but forsaken; it is a place to reclaim his birthright. Shylock's passion recalls him to his roots. And when he vows to have the heart of Antonio, his intention is less economically motivated than Shakespeare ever intended: the rest of his line, 'for were he out of Venice I can make what merchandise I will' (101-2), is tellingly omitted.

With the help of textual adjustments, therefore, Miller enables Shylock to become a tragic figure maimed by his struggle for assimilation. The authenticity of feeling in this scene surpasses anything of which the gentiles are capable. Yet to communicate such feeling, Olivier resorts to a heroic acting style seemingly at odds with the naturalism towards which the production has striven. In III.i, Olivier forsakes restraint for the grand gestures he had once used in *Othello*, his pinched nasal tone giving way before the thundering crescendos of heroic passion. By breaking out of the restrained acting style in which he aped his Christian 'betters', Olivier draws a powerful dramatic contrast between himself and the 'civilised' society which has failed to assimilate him. He was attacked for this: one critic wrote that 'once Olivier crumbles the business man is forgotten ... and we watch another version of Othello falling back into dark, tribal blood rites. The Venetian setting dwindles into a cardboard background for an "heroic" performance ... Olivier's Shylock isn't a Jew, but an actor with a Jewish director up his sleeve' (*Plays and Players*, June 1970). Yet for all its wit, this criticism betrays a cultural bias, an expectation of stereotypical Jewish behaviour that at once belittles Miller's achievement and ignores the dramatic *function* of Olivier's shift in acting style. As Michael Billington observes, 'the terrifying and exhilarating spectacle of a full-scale piece of heroic acting' is strikingly incongruous 'in an orderly, mercantile late-nineteenth-century setting' and makes tragically significant 'the tension between period and style' (p. 83). The heroic style in which Olivier displays his grief effectively isolates him, both morally and aesthetically, from the society of his fellow actors.

✻

This scene, not the trial, is the climax of the production; it is a bravura demonstration of how one who is ostracised from a genteel but closed community must break under the pressure of failed expectations. At the trial, Shylock tries to compose himself once again in the only way he can, by aping *their* manners and playing by *their* rules. Determined not to reveal the nature of his injury to those who have injured him, he refuses to give a reason for seeking Antonio's life other than the 'lodged hate' he bears him, allowing mildly offensive analogies (some men 'cannot contain their urine' [IV.i.50] when they hear a bagpipe) to work as defences against a world that has proven itself his enemy. The one thing he *can* rely on, he thinks, is the law, whose ostensible impartiality underpins the economic system and helps to maintain Venice's credibility as an arena for international trade. Shylock knows he is appealing to the self-interest of the ruling class when he warns, 'If you deny [the bond], let the danger light/ Upon your charter and your city's freedom!' (38-9). He is aware that he has them in a bind: if they honour the spirit of the law and maintain its proper indifference to individuals, then Antonio will be murdered; if they violate it to save one of their own, then they will risk discrediting the legal foundation on which Venetian enterprise depends (Eagleton, pp. 35-8).

Miller's staging of the trial is appropriately muted, restrained, and bloodless. Such restraint was not to everyone's liking: Harold Hobson complained that 'in the long history of *The Merchant of Venice* the trial scene can never have generated so little excitement; it is as flat as a puncture' (*Sunday Times*, 3 May 1970). The exciting public spectacle Hobson might have preferred, however, would have been singularly out of place in a society whose members gather in small chambers to make gentlemen's agreements and to assert their corporate privilege (from the Latin for 'private law'). Miller's Victorian power-brokers set great store by form: soberly dressed in business suits, they shake hands upon entering and sit in red leather chairs around a large table. Shylock, briefcase in hand, makes up one of them, tapping his fingers impatiently as they try to strike a bargain, smugly reminding them that the law protects his rights as well as theirs. Like them, he preserves the veneer of civility. This court is no place for him to carry scales or sharpen a knife against the sole of his shoe – a servant sharpens the knife behind him, and he intimates that the scales are ready off stage – nor is it a place for Antonio, sitting opposite him, to betray his anxiety, trained as he is in the art of the stiff upper lip. All that distinguishes Shylock from

Antonio, in fact, is the yarmulka he wears, and that is little enough to lend plausibility to Portia's question, 'Which is the merchant here and which the Jew?' (170; see photograph 4).

Portia herself, however, is implausible. Her disguise strains belief in the most fanciful of productions, and it becomes an absurd incongruity in Miller's, where the leap of faith required to accept her as a man seriously compromises the naturalism he seeks to impose on Shakespeare's text. Such incongruity is the inevitable result of an attempt to suppress the allegorical and folkloric origins of the play in favour of its more topical, realistic potential: the cross-dressed heroine appears to have strayed in from another play far more naïve than this. Joan Plowright is clearly not comfortable playing Balthasar. Yet her costume (black juridical robe, black hat, white cravat), her resonant voice, and her assertive, businesslike demeanour make her convincingly masculine, if not convincingly male, and suggest that she might (if only women were allowed) survive as well as men in the corporate world of Venice. No young fairy-tale princess with a penchant for performing miracles, she, like Shylock, strives to establish her legitimacy through a knowledge of Venetian law.

The scales of justice, of course, are tipped against Shylock. The pretence to impartiality, the insistence on the disinterestedness of the law, only makes Portia's quibble seem the more underhand and Shylock's defeat the more prearranged. Miller conceives of the quibble much as Terry Eagleton does, as an absurd adherence to the *letter* of the law at the expense of its *spirit*, a reading of the law which, 'aberrant because too faithful,' skates 'perilously close to promoting "private law"', or class privilege. As a strategy, it is perfectly in keeping with Portia's manipulation of the lottery in Belmont: it bespeaks a morality far more 'interested' than she would admit to. Such a strategy, of course, 'threatens to bring the law into disrepute', just as Shylock warned it would. The 'ruthless precision' with which Portia interprets the text 'parallels Shylock's relentless insistence on having his bond'; and by forcing the Christians to outdo his own legalism, Shylock is, in a sense, vindicated (Eagleton, p. 37). Such vindication brings small comfort, however, when the Christians use the law not only to deny Shylock his pound of flesh, but to dispose of his life and living as well. Shylock's case may blow the sanctimonious cover of Venetian law and expose it as the handmaiden – or whore – of those in power, but this production does not allow us to forget that Shylock suffers nonetheless.

In defeat, Olivier returns one last time to the heroic tradition of Irving. When he hears the penalties against an alien, he turns around to utter a cry that will not come; then 'his quivering hand reaches out for the rail to steady himself'. When Antonio demands that he presently turn Christian, Shylock crumples over the rail, just as Irving had done, where two Jews in attendance help him to his feet; and as he mutters 'I am content' (390), his back rigid and eyeballs bulging, he is apparently suffering a seizure or stroke. This prepares us for the most celebrated moment in the production, when, a few seconds after his long Irvingesque exit, he emits an otherworldly keening, 'sharp and intense at first and then barbarically extended– that reminds one of a wolf impaled on a spike and dying a slow death' (Billington, pp. 88-9). If Olivier 'wanted something to remain ringing in the ears long after [he] was in the dressing room, something that would stay with the audience through the sweetness and light of the final romantic comic scene' (*On Acting*, p. 130), he certainly succeeded. His wailing left the Christians momentarily speechless in the knowledge of what they had done: Bassanio in particular seemed troubled, raising a hand in protest, then turning his back to the others (Perret, p. 153). On the Victorian stage, such an effect might have required the omission of Act V as irrelevant to the tragedy that has just occurred.

✳

Shylock's grand exit casts a pall over Act V, just as Olivier wished. The return to Belmont has little sweetness and light; and despite the lovely Victorian conservatory in which the lovers meet, their games do not affirm marital harmony so much as anticipate discord. Miller rejects the romantic resolution towards which the play's comic form would seem to point and insists instead on the text's resistance to closure (Howard, pp. 122-6). This resistance is immediately apparent in Lorenzo and Jessica's mythic celebration of the night. In most productions, their nocturne takes the form of playful banter: references to such doomed lovers as Troilus and Cressida, Dido and Aeneas, Pyramus and Thisbe are but comic provocations to a declaration of love. In Miller's version, however, these references portend disharmony in Belmont, for Lorenzo and Jessica speak at cross purposes, he attempting to humour her, and she, sadly disillusioned, accusing him of false promise: 'In such a night/ Did young Lorenzo swear he loved her well,/ Stealing her soul with many vows of faith,/ And ne'er a true one' (V.i.17-20). On each line, Jessica moves further downstage away from Lorenzo, while he, oblivious to what she feels, follows her, intent only on teaching her all he knows about music. Looking priggish in his white summer suit, Lorenzo is 'a dogged, middle-class didactic Hampstead mini-intellectual' who punctuates his observations with stabs of his pipe and spreads out a handkerchief before sitting down to give Jessica 'a much-needed education, during which ... she falls asleep, like Miranda bored rigid by Prospero, but without the latter's textual sanction'(*Drama*, Summer 1970).

If Miller finds no textual sanction for this, neither does he expressly contradict the text: Jessica's interaction with the Christians is something Shakespeare sketched so lightly that a director of Miller's imagination could virtually invent her character. With a sensibility born of his own study of social anthropology, Miller asks questions of Jessica most directors would not think to ask: How does she adjust to having betrayed her father? Does she regret having given up her home and her religion to marry a Christian – and, in particular, *this* Christian? How does she feel when, introduced at Belmont, her first task is to condemn her father before a group of people largely unknown to her? Does such disloyalty win her acceptance? How is she, a Jew, treated at Belmont? The answers Miller provides are far from reassuring. They transform Jessica's brief scenes into a tragedy to parallel – and extend – her father's.

Throughout the production, she has acted melancholy, not at all the giddy, venturesome girl one might expect. Wearing attire as subdued as Shylock's, she has led a life of puritanical sobriety; even her elopement is undertaken not in the spirit of carnival, but with apprehension. Her relationship with her father is formal. She gives him a kiss upon entering (II.v) and hands him his gloves, hat, and walking stick as he departs to dine with the Christians; and when he entrusts the keys of the house to her, he lays his hand gently on her head – a relatively demonstrative sign of affection in the repressed Victorian society Miller creates. This father and daughter share a strong familial bond, a bond based on love, duty, and obedience to patriarchal values. And when these values, however confining, are so sincerely expressed, one can only wonder why Jessica would wish to exchange them for those of the hypocritical Christians – unless she is motivated by the same hunger for assimilation her father is.

In Belmont, Jessica pays for her mistake. The Christians there are as patronising to her as members of an exclusive club might be to a Jew brought one evening as a guest. Portia manages to forget her name on two occasions, addressing Lorenzo as 'you and ... ah ... ah ... [with a prompt] Jessica!' (III.iv), and treats her with condescension both as a woman and a Jew. Coming from Shylock's sober household, Jessica cannot but be struck by the crass materialism and emotional chill of the group she has married into: she can no more be assimilated into their society than could her father. Her reluctance to embrace the Christians' values is strongly implied when she admits, 'I am never merry when I hear sweet music' (69); but Lorenzo, ever out of tune with her, provides an academic explanation for her melancholy full of analogies that only 'intellectualise her emotions' (*Queen*, June 1970) and reveal how little he understands her. The potential for such discord resides in the text, but it took Miller's sensitive ear to mark the music.

Even when the principals enter from their victory in Venice, Miller holds romantic harmony at bay. He uses the episode of the rings to bring all values into question. Traditionally, this episode has been seen to recapitulate within a comic frame the theme of hazarding all one has and ultimately to reaffirm the lovers' faith to one another. We know that Portia's and Nerissa's test of their husbands has been all in fun and that they themselves, even after lying with the doctor and his clerk, are as pure as driven snow. Yet the comic banter about infidelity sounds curiously tainted when spoken by characters we have been taught not to trust: with their cavalier disregard of the spirit of oath and law still fresh in our minds, we hesitate to credit the faith they swear to one another now. Miller explains,

> We are led to the conclusion ... that there are no unarguable moral axioms, and that the weight one gives to any principle can be redistributed from one occasion to the next. And that is really what the whole play reflects, as it raises questions about those to whom you owe debts of gratitude, of loyalty, whether filial, cultural, social, or that of friendship, and shows the contradictory tensions that arise from the different pulling threads. (*Subsequent*, p. 157)

By keeping those contradictions before us, Miller refuses us the comfortable closure that a traditional performance of Act V would bring. Even the manna Portia drops in the way of starving people to ensure a happy ending tastes bitter and leaves the starving unsatisfied. Manna comes in the form of two pieces of paper: one a letter that tells Antonio his argosies have suddenly come to harbour, the other a deed in which Shylock bequeaths his estate to Jessica and Lorenzo. In a less socially conscious production, these pieces of paper might bring great joy to the recipients by guaranteeing them a livelihood. Here, however, they remind us of the various ways in which the monied classes throughout the play have secured their fortunes by manipulating others with letters, bonds, deeds, wills – documents that unfailingly serve the interests of those who interpret them. Antonio's letter may be added to this list. Portia delivers it with a wry detachment that winks at the 'strange accident' (278) by which she chanced on it and thereby pokes fun at the romantic ethos that would have us credit such accidents. In real life, things like this do not happen. Lost argosies do not miraculously come to harbour any more than cross-dressed women save men's lives in court. Such fictions disguise the more ruthless means by which the rich stay rich.

Miller uses Shylock's deed of gift, however, to focus our attention on the cost to others of keeping the Antonios of this world rich. In the text, Jessica does not respond to the deed or speak at all; Shakespeare leaves her with a silence to be interpreted as the director wishes. Usually she plays the happy convert, apparently satisfied with the outcome of the trial and eager to take part in the nuptial festivities. Miller, however, fills her silence with unspoken remorse. Jessica does not regard the deed as any kind of gift: as she pores over it, she walks slowly away from the group, conscious of betraying both her father and her heritage, guilt and doubt darkening her face. As the lovers exit laughing, Lorenzo, puzzled by her sadness, leaves her to her thoughts and joins the others. Only Antonio remains with Jessica, each of them holding a piece of paper – he the letter, she the deed. But when he catches her eye and, instinct with sympathy, extends a hand to her, she turns away. Realising his own complicity in causing her grief, he crumples up the letter and reluctantly exits. As our focus narrows to Jessica alone, we hear an offstage voice plaintively intoning the Kaddish, 'the eternal wail and lamentation of Orthodox Jewish prayer' (*Daily Express*, 29 April 1970). It is a dirge for the father who is now dead to her; it is a dirge for the daughter who would retreat from a world to which she, like Shylock before her, has tragically committed herself. The moment is inspired: it unsettles rather than affirms, it counters comic reconciliation with tragic isolation, and it crystallises the process of alienation that Miller has used the play to explore.

I say 'used' the play because, in the eyes of most who saw the production, Miller appropriated Shakespeare's text to foreground themes that preoccupied western societies in 1970 but may not have preoccupied Shakespeare in quite the same way: the moral bankruptcy of the bourgeoisie, the hypocrisy with which those in power stay in power, the subtle ways in which society marginalises its minorities, and, in particular, the insidious effects of prejudice on those minorities who strive to be assimilated. These concerns are implicit in the text; in the production, they are made explicit by Miller's understanding of social relations. He inscribes contemporary cultural concerns in an Elizabethan text and, according to Ronald Bryden,

> virtually rewrites the original to do so. Out goes much of the comedy, out Belmont's fairy-tale romance. Instead, there's the assumption that the central, unavoidable experience of the play is that explosion of frank, murdering tribal hatred at the core of it; that the task of any revival is not to skirt around this, but to create afresh a believable world from which it can spring. (*Observer*, 3 May 1970)

Perhaps, in 1970, it was inevitable that such hatred was seen as the core of the play: society was divided over the same questions about wars of imperialism and global hegemony that had divided Victorians a hundred years earlier, and that made Miller's decision to set the play in 1880 particularly apropos. To many in 1970, the world seemed to be run by a conservative élite. The American military was seeking to determine the future of South East Asia, famine and revolution were sweeping Africa, students were protesting throughout Europe and America, and blacks were demonstrating for civil rights. Establishment had become a dirty word, and those who opposed it grew increasingly incensed with the ways in which those in power imposed their values on other cultures and kept minorities oppressed.

This context may help to explain the impact Miller's *Merchant* had on its audiences. 'An angry black or an embattled student will very likely hear the voice of his own defiance in Olivier's Shylock, and should certainly recognise his quintessential enemies, complete with top hats, canes, Waspish accents and polite contempt,' wrote Benedict Nightingale (*New Statesman*, 8 May 1970). 'In a period like this, increasingly conscious of its insistent minorities, wary of its silent majorities, and nervous of bloody conflict between the two, it looks like the play Shakespeare ought to have written.' The *ought* raises the most fundamental question of all, for by accommodating the play to a social and political context in many ways different from Shakespeare's, Miller essentially fashioned a play of his own. He appropriated Shakespeare's text, and with it his cultural authority, to advance an ideological agenda peculiar to his own time. Was Miller's *Merchant* Shakespeare's?

This question, of course, can only be answered with another: whose Shakespeare? Miller did what any director of Shakespeare does: he tailored the play to suit his cast, his venue, and his audience. Invariably, in the process of staging a Shakespeare play, a director will adapt and revise the text in light of current cultural assumptions and values: such revision is sometimes conscious, sometimes not. Irving revised *The Merchant* as radically for his age as Miller did for his; and like Irving's, Miller's production, especially after it was televised worldwide in 1973/4, in effect *became* the play for a generation of audiences. By calling into question what the play traditionally was thought to be about, Miller discovered a new way of looking at *The Merchant* that made Shakespeare – at least for the moment – our contemporary.

CHAPTER V

The BBC *Merchant*: diminishing returns

Ten years after his production for the National Theatre, Jonathan Miller had the opportunity to produce *The Merchant of Venice* again, this time for the BBC as part of its ambitious plan to record all of Shakespeare's plays. In the interim, he had radically altered his view of the play, which he now saw as 'totally symmetrical in its prejudices', with Shylock as culpable as the Christians (PBS Interview, 23 February 1981). 'We did not want to make him into a pantomime devil or merely a noble, all-suffering victim,' Miller declared, modifying his approach of a decade earlier; nor, he said, should the play be made to redress the wrongs of recent history, for 'if the only point of view you have is the point of view of your own time, the past becomes foreshortened and very flat' (*New York Times*, 22 February 1982). In his attempt to honour the past by reflecting *its* ideological biases – not our own – in his new production of the play, Miller strove to be truer to what he understood Shakespeare's original intentions to have been than he was in his 'Victorian' *Merchant*.

Miller's new-found respect for tradition may in part have been a response to the BBC's brief that productions for the series be 'orthodox', by which was meant no tampering with the text and no updating of the period. This requirement apparently was dictated by American corporate sponsors who, fearful of directorial intervention, wanted school children to see their Shakespeare dressed in doublets and hose in the best Old Vic tradition. Such traditions are themselves, of course, the historically naïve products of nineteenth-century theatrical practice; but Miller, undaunted, made a virtue of necessity. 'The requirement that I stick to something which is recognisably period happens to coincide with an interest of mine, which has been growing in the last year or two, in trying to return to the sixteenth century because it is interesting in its own right' (*Quarto*, pp. 9-12). Miller therefore redefined orthodoxy as an academic challenge. Citing the work of recent social historians, he set out to reconstruct the fundamental 'Elizabethanism' of the plays, creating for each one a sort of period verisimilitude that would demonstrate how Shakespeare engaged the social and political attitudes of his audience (Bulman, pp. 571-81).

It may seem odd that I credit Miller with responsibility for the BBC *Merchant* when in fact the production was directed not by him, but by Jack Gold. My reason for doing so is that Miller, as executive producer of the series during 1980-1, habitually exerted a strong influence over his directors. When not directing himself (which he often did: six productions in two years), he hired directors who had little or no experience with Shakespeare and who therefore might prove susceptible to the power of his suggestion (Wells, pp. 48-9). Gold, known primarily as a film director, was an apt pupil, and Henry Fenwick's account of the production makes clear that Miller was omni-present during the taping and helped to shape Gold's interpretation of the play (pp. 17-25). I do not mean to imply that Gold was merely a puppet: his comments suggest that he brought considerable intelligence to the text and exercised decisive control over the televisual strategies of the production. Nevertheless, as a newcomer to Shakespeare, he proved remarkably receptive to Miller's concept of Elizabethan 'tradition', so much so that hereafter, when I speak of Gold, the reader should bear in mind that it is often impossible to distinguish his work on *The Merchant* from that of Miller.

The likeness of their vision is apparent in their rationale for having Warren Mitchell play Shylock as an ethnic Jew. In an interview with Fenwick they claimed that Shylock's 'Jewishness' was authentic because a triumvirate of Jews – Miller, Gold, and Mitchell – made it so. 'Watching non-Jews trying to be Jews is just awful,' declared Gold, with an oblique reference to Olivier and other Shylocks of the English school. 'I've seen two versions and it's like watching Englishmen trying to be American ... it's always phoney.' Mitchell's Shylock, on the other hand, was resolutely unassimilated, antagonistic to the proprieties of bourgeois Venetian behaviour: 'there was no way he could act that wasn't Jewish' (Fenwick, p. 23). His looks were emphatically Semitic: he was short, square, and balding, his curly grey hair wildly unkempt, his beard thick, his attire a black gaberdine and yarmulka. His gestures were of a piece with his looks: his nodding head and quick hands, far more expressive than those of the gentiles, marked him as typically 'Jewish', and he spoke with a thick Middle European accent that most critics identified as Yiddish – an anachronism which immediately stamped him for modern audiences as the alien he would have been in sixteenth-century Venice (*Shakespeare on Film Newsletter* 5 [May 1981] 2). This squat, domestic, garrulous little man, this comic figure with a plaintive face, was the Shylock whom Gold and Miller called authentically Jewish.

Yet their claim for Mitchell's authenticity may be questioned, for in fact his portrayal bordered on caricature. His Shylock was laden with 'an incessant series of bromidic Jewish mannerisms' that seemed at times to reduce him to a stock figure from old comedies (*Christian Science Monitor*, 20 February 1981): always ready with a laugh or a genial shrug, he rolled his eyeballs on 'Yes, to smell pork' (I.iii.27) and frequently invaded the space of others, crowding them like a salesman too insistently pushing his wares. For one critic, he resembled 'a seedy pawnbroker' (*New York Times*, 23 February 1981); for another, 'a poor Jewish pedlar in some place like Pinsk' (*The Listener*, 18-25 December 1980). Such responses reveal how strongly Mitchell harked back not to the Elizabethan stage Jew – a tradition to which Miller might have appealed – but to the more recent stage 'Yid' of music-hall revues and vaudeville skits. This heritage made it hard to take Shylock's villainy seriously (Shapiro, *Shofar*, p. 7); and indeed, Mitchell shamelessly exploited the traditions of music-hall performance. Appropriating the comedian's direct address to his audience, he spoke his asides straight to the camera, breaking the illusion of naturalism with a theatrical device to ingratiate himself with the viewer. He used it first on 'How like a fawning publican he looks' (I.iii.33), a speech Miller excised from his earlier production so that Olivier could preserve his decorum as a Victorian gentleman. Mitchell delivered the speech *sotto voce*, winning the viewer's confidence with his easy familiarity and direct eye contact. He used the device even where the text did not warrant it, as when, leaving to dine with the Christians, he addressed 'But wherefore should I go?/ I am not bid for love ... ' (II.v.12-15) not to Jessica, but to the camera – acknowledging the audience as blatantly as stage comedians do.

Laughter throughout characterises Shylock's relationship with the Christians: more than a mark of his garrulous disposition, it works in subtle ways to weave a complex web of deception and intimidation. At the outset, it seems primarily to be the means by which Shylock disguises his malicious intent with false *bonhomie*, most obvious when he laughs at the absurdity of the 'merry bond' and gets Antonio to laugh along with him. Yet later on it serves to disguise his pain, and the suggestion of its darker purpose complicates our response to Shylock. Uncomfortable laughter rings throughout the scene in which he is taunted by Solanio and Salerio. It begins when they engage him in a game of verbal wit. As Marion Perret observes (p. 156), Shylock's anger over his daughter's 'flight' (21) prompts them to refer to her as a bird, and his pun in response to Solanio's use of 'dam' (25) – 'She is damned for it' (26) – encourages them further to belittle his pain in word play. But their game is also physical: when Shylock complains, 'My own flesh and blood to rebel!' (28), Solanio – taking the complaint as a comic reference to sexual desire – lunges for his genitals: 'Rebels it at these years?' (29). And in the exchange that follows, Salerio, played by a burly Welsh actor who towers over the diminutive Mitchell, locks his arm around the Jew's neck from behind, laughing genially as if to pass off the stranglehold as good humour. At this point Shylock in self-defense laughs too, trying to act as though he is enjoying their game; but his laughter as he catalogues Antonio's abuses – 'thwarted my bargains, cooled my friends, heated mine enemies' (45) – grows increasingly forced and creates a disquieting sense of his helplessness. Even his explanation for Antonio's behaviour – 'and what's his reason? I am a Jew' (46) – a line that introduces a speech customarily accorded the reverence of holy writ, here simply feeds the hilarity of his tor-mentors. 'Ah!' they exclaim in mock surprise, with comic gestures that mirror those of Didi and Gogo in *Waiting for Godot*; and to each of the rhetorical questions that follow they respond with mimicry until, inspired by 'If you tickle us, do we not laugh?' (51), they tickle Shylock mercilessly and reduce him to tears. The kinship between laughter and tears so feelingly dramatised here provokes Shylock's climactic question, 'And if you wrong us, shall we not revenge?' (52). The moment he utters the word revenge, all laughter stops: Shylock has put a stop to this physical abuse in the only way he could, by threatening to take measure for measure. The Christians have not taken him seriously up to this point; nor perhaps has the audience, who may have been lulled into a sense that he is no more than a stage Jew. Here, quietly swearing revenge, all passion spent, he gains a more human dimension.

Shylock warns his audience elsewhere, too, against too easy an acceptance of the anti-Semitic stereotype. The chief means by which he does so is to nod knowingly or look at the camera each time one of the Christians launches into a diatribe against Jews or usury, as if to say, with Ronald Reagan, 'There you go again'. When, for instance, Antonio asks Bassanio to mark how 'the devil can cite Scripture for his purpose' (I.iii.90), Shylock is seen standing behind them nodding his head, obviously having heard it all before. He makes us more conscious of the anti-Semitism that permeates his culture, and we are therefore inclined to nod with him when, later on, Antonio vents even more racial spleen in a speech that curses his 'Jewish heart' (IV.i.80). Gold uses this strategy most tellingly at the trial, when Shylock is shown smiling with feigned interest at Gratiano's furious invective – 'O be thou damned, inexecrable dog... Thy currish spirit/ Governed a wolf ... ' (IV.i.128-38) – while he whets his knife on his shoe and tests its sharpness on a hair pulled from his head. The camera's relentless focus on Shylock's murderous intent as we simultaneously hear the sort of anti-Semitic vituperation that has led him to seek revenge teases us to link the two as cause and effect, and perhaps, by so doing, to accept such abuse as sufficient provocation for murder. Gold's strategy at once preserves and subverts the stereotype of the villain Jew.

This tension between caricature and credible humanity also informs the two scenes in which Shylock comes closest to winning our compassion. In the first, during his exchange with the dignified, Hasidic Tubal, Gold alienates us from Shylock by demonstrating the selfishness of his cause. When Shylock laments, 'The curse never fell upon our nation till now' (III.i.67-8), Tubal opens his arms as if to query whether, in his private grief, Shylock has forgotten sixteen hundred years of Jewish history; as Michael Shapiro notes, the emphasis in Shylock's reply, '*I* never felt it till now', bespeaks an isolation from other Jews and an obliviousness to their suffering that likens him to Marlowe's Barabas (*Shofar*, p. 8). Tubal further under-scores Shylock's inhumanity by stopping his mouth in horror when he wishes his daughter dead at his foot. Such apparent lack of paternal feeling, however, is contradicted by the anguish Shylock expresses when he hears that Leah's ring has been pawned for a monkey. A doleful cello accompanies the look of pain that crosses his face as he recalls his beloved wife; and the camera continues to play over his face when, bidding Tubal to meet him at the synagogue, he rends his cloak in a ritual gesture of mourning.

At the trial, too, Gold goes to some lengths to alienate us from Shylock. Little humanises him: implacable in his hate, he gloats over his bond, waves his knife in the faces of his adversaries and, in close-up, uses the point of that knife to find just the right spot on Antonio's bare chest to make his incision. This inhuman behaviour, however, is balanced by the brutality with which the Christians dispense mercy to him in the form of conversion. Forced to his knees, Shylock suffers a cross to be hung around his neck and, in close-up, is made to kiss it. The camera here again, as at the conclusion of III.i, lingers over his expression of agony. Such moments permit us to pity the man who has endured the loss of his ducats, daughter, wife, and religion. They are effective precisely because they contrast with the prevailing theatricality of Mitchell's interpretation, investing with humanity a character who elsewhere flirts with caricature.

Gold and Miller further adjust our perspective on Shylock by making attractive those characters who have most cause to hate him, Lancelot Gobbo and Jessica. Such emphasis bears witness to how fundamentally Miller's view of the play had changed since 1970, when the comedy of Lancelot's servitude and Jessica's elopement intruded awkwardly on the social realism of Venice – or since 1973, when those scenes were cut altogether from the televised version of that production. In Miller's 1980 *Merchant*, the scenes are played in full. Lancelot's stage ancestry is as readily identifiable as Shylock's: appearing from beneath a bridge to deliver his monologue straight to the camera, he resembles Scapino from the *Commedia*, an appealing scamp whose ingenuity at getting a new livery we admire and whose casual cruelty to his father seems comically justified. His appeal is of a piece with Jessica's, for she too betrays her origins in Italian comedy of intrigue – the resourceful daughter who outwits her father in order to join her lover. Where in 1970 Miller disguised those origins by refashioning her as a melancholy Jew in whom her father's tragedy would be re-enacted, in 1980 he used her as an exuberant gauge of Shylock's unnaturalness. She is passionate, outspoken, and disdainful of his inhibitions; and in so far as we approve of her affair with Lorenzo, we censure the father who would obstruct it. Leslee Udwin's dark, deep-voiced Jessica knows how to assert herself in a man's world. Like Lancelot and Shylock, she addresses the camera directly to win our confidence: 'Alack, what heinous sin is it in me/ To be ashamed to be my father's child!' (II.iii.15-16) she asks, and we do not doubt the sincerity of her question. She mocks Shylock behind his back, mouthing 'Fast bind, fast find:/ A proverb never stale in thrifty mind' (II.v.52-3) even as he speaks it – a proverb she no doubt has heard too often. And the same mockery informs her determination to leave him by donning a male disguise: she spits 'I have a father, you a daughter, lost' (55) directly into the camera, confiding her plan to us while clutching the ring Lorenzo has sent her.

Sexual passion is the key to her relationship with Lorenzo. Although Gratiano insinuates that money must motivate his desire for her – 'Now, by my hood, a gentle and no Jew!' reveals only how impressed he is by the weight of the ducats she has thrown down (II.vi.52) – Lorenzo clearly is as much in love with her as she with him. In fact, they cannot keep their hands off each other. Their banter at the opening of Act V is sexually charged: Jessica, clad in a white nightgown that all but exposes her ample breasts, delivers 'In such a night as this ... ' repeatedly in the most seductive tones, wrapping her arms around Lorenzo's neck, with her lips nearly touching his as the camera moves in for a close-up. When a messenger interrupts them with news that Portia will return before dawn, an embarrassed Lorenzo stops her from apparently reaching inside his shirt (her hand has moved below the range of the camera); but their love play continues when, reclining on a moonlit bank, he puts his hand inside her gown while ironically disparaging 'this muddy vesture of decay', the body (64). Such sexual subtext makes their romantic charges and countercharges sound suspiciously like foreplay, and that is exactly what Gold had in mind. Insisting on a naturalism ingrained in the medium, Gold argued that their scene together, while full of exquisitely romantic verse, is nevertheless '*not a poetry contest*. They happen to be two realistic characters, so I turned it into a sexual contest ... [They] have probably been making love to each other non-stop ever since [their arrival at Belmont] and can't wait to get each other back into bed' (Fenwick, p. 18). Such a conception liberates Jessica from her father as absolutely as guilt kept her bound to him in Miller's previous *Merchant*. In both productions a realistic subtext is allowed to transform the artifice of the verse, but the latter production at least keeps Petrarchanism in the service of love, not betrayal.

※

It should not surprise us to hear Gold or Miller speak of how to make Shakespeare seem more real or natural, because television has long been regarded as an intrinsically naturalistic medium. The main problem in adapting Shakespeare for television, according to Sheldon Zitner, is how to translate 'plays written for a highly stylised stage to a medium whose typical visual imagery is more realistic in detail and effect, and whose visual and emotional frames are much more restricted' (p. 35). Television's framed image, as Raymond Williams suggests, has a 'direct cultural continuity' with the room in which we sit to watch (p. 9): it creates little sense of depth, works best in medium distance and close-up, and tends to diminish large theatrical effects. The televised version of Miller's 1970 production played to these strengths. In its attempt to recreate the Venice of a hundred years ago, the stage production already had a strongly naturalistic bias: one may recall that Julia Trevelyan Oman's set was inspired by *photographs* taken by the Count de Primoli. The medium of television simply realised that bias more fully. The Venetian scenes occurred in richly detailed interiors where characters were framed in their 'natural' space: the ornate Café Florian, the understated ducal chamber, and Shylock's house which, decorated with classical busts, oriental rugs, and walnut bookcases, looked as elegant as any in Mayfair. Furthermore, the theatrical origins of the production were suppressed: all the frankly non-illusionist asides, the slapstick comedy of the Gobbos, and Jessica's stealing away in the habit of a boy were, as I have mentioned, omitted, and direct address to the camera would have been out of the question. Other striking stage moments were reconceived for television. Shylock, for instance, no longer entered carrying Jessica's dress in III.i, but instead was discovered holding her picture to his breast, stroking it as he might stroke her hair, to create a smaller, more intimate effect. Although the outdoor scenes in Venice (what few there were) betrayed their studio origins, those at Belmont were absolutely 'real': filmed on location at an English country house, they showed sweeping lawns, vast terraces, and Portia and Bassanio leading their horses back to the stables after a morning's ride. Television thus helped Miller to fulfil his ambition of fashioning *The Merchant* as a naturalistic nineteenth-century drama suitable for Masterpiece Theatre.

By 1980 he had come to understand the conventions of television differently. Where before he had avoided theatrical artifice by radically reshaping the text, now he was willing to exploit the theatricality of the television medium itself: Shakespearean realism, he acknowledged, was not necessarily the same thing as naturalism. Conscious that earlier productions in the BBC series had faltered in their attempts at naturalism – shooting *As You Like It* on location had only made its comic artifices look absurd: one cannot translate pastoral to a real countryside and expect it to be credible – he sought visual analogues for the television screen in Renaissance painting, choosing to allow the conventions of one medium to inform our perception of another. Where previous directors had looked to television itself for inspiration, Miller looked to the gallery – to Titian, Tintoretto, Veronese. As John Wilders, the series' literary consultant, commented, 'the television screen resembles the stage in that it depicts characters who move and speak, but its two-dimensional surface, rectangular shape and surrounding frame, also make it look like a picture'. Visual quotation from paintings of the period, therefore, 'calls attention to the artifice of the plays and does justice to those tableaux which are as much a part of Shakespeare's dramatic language as is his dialogue' (*Times Higher Education Supplement*, 10 July 1981, p. 13).

Miller's use of such visual quotation in the productions he directed, beginning with *Antony and Cleopatra*, proved so controversial that it renewed critical interest in the series; not surprisingly, then, all the directors and designers who worked for him followed his lead. Oliver Bayldon, for instance, spoke almost as glibly as Miller of the artists who had inspired his design for the two 360-degree backcloths used in *The Merchant* – Venice's a mottled blend of ochre and sienna, Belmont's of blue and grey. On his list one finds Canaletto, Turner, 'some shades of Piper ... Monet crept in too, of course' (Fenwick, pp. 18-19). The costumes likewise were patterned on those in Renaissance paintings. According to their designer, Raymond Hughes, the palette used for costuming the Venetians was Titian's: blacks and oranges, burnt umbers and dull greens to capture 'the moody, gloomy sections of the play' (Fenwick, p. 20). These ornate costumes bespoke great wealth – furs, plumed hats, doublets and capes trimmed with gold – and did not distinguish social rank. All the gentiles looked noble, and the Jews were costumed no less richly, though they wore more sombre colours, Jessica in a dress of brown, Shylock and Tubal in black. The costumes for Belmont were altogether more ethereal and softer in focus, their blues and greens drawn from Canaletto and (though Hughes does not acknowledge the source) Botticelli. Portia moved through her garden like a queen of pastoral in an olive green dress, her golden tresses adorned with a coronet of laurel: the allusion to

Botticelli's *Primavera* signifies the mythic dimension that this Portia was allowed to achieve.

Gold, however, was not so determined as Miller to replicate the details of a particular artist's vision; rather, he intended only to create the *impression* of a Renaissance canvas. Where Miller and his disciple Elijah Moshinsky (whose *All's Well* and *A Midsummer Night's Dream* alluded to works by Rembrandt and Vermeer) laboured to create static tableaux, Gold believed that the essence of television lay in movement. He did not want to be bound by the sets; thus he required them to be minimal and abstract in order to allow the camera to move. 'I used the sets with an enormous amount of freedom and usually on single cameras,' he recounted. 'I could do long tracking shots right across the studio if I wanted to; it really was like being on location in Venice, though there was no pretence that we were in a real place' (Fenwick, p. 20). The qualification – that there was no pretence of 'real place' – is instructive: it reveals that Gold, like Miller, understood that the reality of Shakespearian drama is inherently different from that of most television drama. He explained his concept of reality in spatial terms. 'If you imagine different planes, the thing closest to the camera was the reality of the actor in a real costume ... then beyond the actor is a semi-artificial column or piece of wall, and in the distance is the backcloth, which is impressionistic.'

The sets for *The Merchant*, therefore, do not disguise their studio origins, but capitalise on them. Venice is composed of three freestanding Doric columns, an archway (in which Shylock is first seen in a striking silhouette), walls of peeling plaster, and a small bridge in which one sees reflected water (obviously a lighting effect) from the canal below. It is a set with many angles – characters appear from around corners, or through arches, or from under bridges – and one delights in discovering the ingenuity that allows these structural units, most of them on casters for easy mobility, to keep reappearing in apparently different places. The Belmont set, on the other hand, has a greater feeling of space and does not attempt to trick us into believing that we are in different places. All the action occurs within one arena – a kind of formal garden with a studio floor – in which artifice is palpable. The isolated structural units forbid any sense of architectural illusion: a grand, free-standing staircase leads into the garden; beyond it stands a fanciful pavilion or gazebo modelled on an Edwardian folly, 'a curlicued Temple of Atalanta' with a filigree dome that allows light and shadow to play in it

(Fenwick, p. 19). Flanking the gazebo are abstract, pyramid-shaped shrubs and, next to them, free-standing pillars resembling those in Venice only more delicate. Even the caskets are located in this space, directly across from the gazebo. A gauze curtain is swept aside to reveal the three pedestals, standing starkly against the mottled-blue backcloth as if themselves a part of the garden. In fact, indoors and outdoors are not differentiated here: by framing nearly all the elements in a single shot – pedestals with caskets, pillars, pyramidal shrubs, gazebo (see photograph 5) – the camera makes us keenly aware that Belmont is a studio and that the actors occupy an artificial space. Only their acting can convince us of the play's reality.

※

The television camera functions much as the director of a stage production, only its power is more absolute. It serves as the eyes of the audience, directing attention to one part of the studio and away from another, denying the spectator any choice of where to look. Furthermore, the camera not only restricts but also diminishes what the audience sees. Unlike Shakespeare's public theatre, it affords little sense of depth, and long shots tend to trivialise ceremonial scenes and reduce crowds of actors to so many ants. The medium, in short, is incapable of presenting the complex group dynamics on which Elizabethan drama so heavily depends. It handles best a group of two or three figures, commonly focused in close-up, whose 'talking heads' more easily fit a small frame. Using the techniques available – montage, cutting, camera movement and angle – the television director must therefore try to arrive at some compromise between the theatrical demands of the text and the requirements of his more intimate medium.

Gold sought such a compromise by occasionally breaking conventional televisual strategies – the kind of camera work that has become, in Graham Holderness's phrase, 'the familiar discourse of television' (p. 69) – with more overtly theatrical techniques. Such devices as characters' delivering their asides to the camera, for example, make us acutely aware of our role as spectators: they break the illusion on which television customarily depends and acknowledge the artifice of the medium. Gold used his camera most theatrically for the wooing scenes in Belmont. We view them from a distance as through a proscenium arch, the camera placed where an audience might sit. Blocking of the scenes is frontal, with Portia and the attendants grouped formally behind the suitors as though on a stage; and the camera remains for the most part stationary while each of the three suitors makes his choice. All of them address their speeches directly to the camera, dropping the more naturalistic device of thinking aloud (the cinematic solution for dramatic monologue) in favour of playing to the audience. The trouble is, the audience is absent; and without its immediate response, actors on television cannot successfully replicate the dynamics of live theatre. The result, as one critic complained, is that the wooing scenes have seldom been less funny or convincing (*Cahiers Elisabéthains*, 19 April 1981, p. 128).

Gold, however, was determined to convince us of the love Portia and Bassanio feel for one another, and so for their scene together he resorted to more traditional televisual techniques. Portia speaks her hyperbolic praise of Bassanio (III.ii.40-62) in close-up but not *to* the camera; we simply hear her reverie (she is thinking aloud) and see in her face a radiant sincerity. And once Bassanio has made his choice and turns to claim her with a loving kiss, the camera moves in to capture them at close range, peering over their shoulders as they speak to one another, catching them in profile as they embrace, *showing* us how heartfelt their love is. The camera, as it scrutinises their faces, speaks more than words. Gold's camera work is unobtrusive; it offers what television has conditioned us to regard as natural ways of seeing. Through it, he allows us to credit Bassanio and Portia as the hero and heroine of romance: he a noble knight and pure, seemingly unaffected by the mercantilism that might have motivated his quest for her golden fleece; she a dewy-eyed damsel who, in a telling slip, reverses the priorities of her wish to be, for his sake, 'A thousand times more fair, ten thousand times/ More rich' (154-5). This Portia would be a thousand times more rich but ten thousand times more fair. Money, as John Kerrigan observes, seems to play little part in this affair of the heart: Gold systematically suppressed the play's cash nexus in favour of romantic sentiment (*Times Literary Supplement*, 19 December 1980). The problem for some critics was that he used the intimacy of the medium to engage us with that sentiment uncritically, so that instead of viewing romantic tradition through the lens of social history as a manifestation of aristocratic privilege, he may unwittingly have recreated the sort of fancy-dress, ideologically naïve Shakespeare popular with audiences forty years ago.

Gold's success in reducing Shakespeare's most expansively theatrical scenes to the intimate dimensions of television can perhaps be better judged by his treatment of the trial scene. Seven years earlier Miller, in adapting his National Theatre production for television, had chosen to minimise the trial's theatricality by dramatising it as a private hearing, confined to the Duke's chambers where the opposing parties could sit around a table and air their grievances with gentlemanly decorum. Miller had elected to sacrifice the public dimension of Shakespeare's traditionally climactic scene in order to achieve the naturalism he thought television required. Critics complained that the scene had never been less exciting; moreover, its naturalism made the disguises of Portia and Nerissa look jarringly out of place and the premises of the bond plot seem absurd. The theatrical fictions of the play worked against Miller's use of the medium.

Gold found a way to preserve the scene's theatricality while making the action acceptably 'real' in televisual terms. His strategy was to create a number of discrete smaller scenes within the larger scene Shakespeare wrote, juxtaposing a sequence of private moments with the public occasion of the trial. His use of the camera was so adroit that it never called attention to the artifice of his technique. He introduced the scene with a tracking shot, following the fur-trimmed Duke from above and behind as he strode into a hall crowded with bystanders and proceeded to his canopied dais. This shot clearly established the trial as a public spectacle in the grand tradition of the nineteenth-century stage: Irving would have been at home in it. But as soon as the Duke turned to speak with Antonio, the camera narrowed its focus to the two men, who thus were allowed to address one another with a familiarity that belied the formal context. In effect, Gold used the camera to establish private relationships within the public ceremony of the court proceedings. He returned to this strategy again and again: the Duke, commanding that room be made for Shylock (whose entrance had been picked up in a long shot), called him forward to reason with him quietly as the frame tightened to exclude all onlookers; but Shylock, unwilling to submit his grievance to private arbitration, turned back to the court on the line, 'If you deny it, let the danger light/ Upon your charter and your city's freedom!' (IV.i.38-9), raising his voice as the camera widened its focus to include those onlookers whom the Duke had excluded. The reverse of this occurred when Shylock, called upon to justify his un-willingness to take money instead of flesh, chose to address the Duke alone, suggesting in conversational tones that there was a Venetian precedent for his bond: 'You have among you many a purchased slave ...' (90). For television audiences, their exchange had greater impact because the camera reduced it to a private confrontation.

Gold's strategy benefited most those moments that tend to lose force when they are played too histrionically. This was especially true for Antonio's farewell to Bassanio, which the medium allowed to culminate in a passionately whispered 'Say how I loved you' (271), and Bassanio's equally impassioned confession that he did not esteem his wife above Antonio's life. As the camera closed in on their embrace, this became the most intimate of scenes. The lines were not spoken for others in the court to hear, so they had to be *over*heard; as a result, those who responded to them could do so only in reaction shots, their responses revealing private pique rather than public wit. Portia spoke 'Your wife would give you little thanks for that' (284) as an aside to Nerissa, and Shylock delivered 'These be the Christian husbands!' (291) – a line often played for laughs – in *sotto voce* to the camera, as a prelude to his sad reflection on the fate of his daughter.

The dynamic interplay of public and private moments also offered a solution to the problem of how to make Portia's playing 'Balthasar' credible. The most theatrically naïve of the play's conven-tions, the male disguises worn by Portia and Nerissa are particularly troublesome for television, whose insistent focus on faces makes their identity immediately clear to viewers and thus strains the credibility of the trial. Such disguises, as Miller's earlier production would attest, subvert all attempts at naturalism. Gold, however, used the camera to preserve a balance between the self-conscious theatrical artifice of their assumed roles and a televisual realism sufficient to compel belief. Portia's entry in a jurist's robe of vermilion and black is tactfully captured in a distance shot: it creates a sense of her role as public defender and spares us the embarrass-ment of wondering why those gathered at court do not spot her at once as a woman. Having established her public role, she proceeds to alternate formal address to the court with private appeals to Shylock, modulating her voice from the stentorian (male) to the more conversational (female). In a medium shot, she quotes the terms of the bond to the men assembled around her, proclaiming in grave tones that the pound of flesh must be 'cut off/ Nearest the merchant's heart' (228-9; see photograph 6). Suddenly, the camera moves in to a close-up as she urges Shylock in more intimate tones to 'Be merciful:/ Take thrice thy money; bid me tear the bond' (229-30). Shylock replies to her in kind, offering an explanation for her ears only, until Antonio interrupts their *tête-à-tête* by calling for judgement. Portia then resumes her masculine voice – 'Why then, thus it is' (240) – and the camera once again backs away to make us aware of the public occasion.

Portia thus uses the intimacy of the medium to deliver as personal appeals lines which are usually spoken as public address, moving in and out of her roles as 'Portia' and 'Balthasar' with more frequency and greater nuance than is possible on the stage. This has the ultimate effect of making her male disguise more credible, because we can more easily see the woman struggling within it. Clearly, she offers Shylock every opportunity to save himself: knowing the hold the law has on him as an alien, she repeatedly pleads with him to show mercy, to understand her message aright. The subtleties of her facial expressions and modulations of voice suggest that she is as concerned to save Shylock as she is to save Antonio: television allows us a privileged glimpse into her motives that theatre audiences are denied. Only when Shylock proves intransigent, his knife poised over Antonio's flesh, does Portia submerge her identity fully within that of 'Balthasar' and proceed to judgement. The camera, in a long shot, frames the whole court as Portia, now acting as prosecutor, reads from a book of Venetian statutes what 'justice' may be offered Shylock. His humiliation is public; and in a high-angle shot, as from the dais on which the Duke sits, the camera shows Gratiano and Salerio pushing Shylock to his knees to beg for mercy.

Such techniques ensure that the play will not be received as Shylock's tragedy. In terms of both ethos and art, Portia has controlled the trial: the intricacies of her role-playing have made her, for once, more interesting than Shylock and have assured us of her benevolent purpose. With Miller whispering in his ear, however, Gold could not allow the problematic morality of the play to remain unexplored. The trial concludes, as Marion Perret observes (p. 160), not on a celebratory note, but on two close-ups that poignantly mirror one another: Shylock kissing the cross that Salerio presses to his lips, and Bassanio kissing Portia's ring before relinquishing it under pressure from Antonio. Both kisses signify a breaking of oaths – Shylock's to his faith, Bassanio's to his wife – that has the potential to muddy the waters of reconciliation with which Belmont would baptise all comers. Miller, as we have seen, allowed such unresolved problems to disrupt the comic closure of his production for the National Theatre. But Gold does not go so far: his Shylock has been too stereotypical for his defeat to dampen the festivities of Act V, his Bassanio too noble for the question of loyalty to Portia to be taken seriously. True, Gold pointedly alludes to Miller's earlier production by having Jessica pore over her father's deed of gift (accompanied by the cello that once underscored his grief). But as this hint that she may feel compunction for having treated her father badly is unsubstantiated by anything that has gone before, her last-minute remorse seems gratuitous; and in the event, she takes Lorenzo's hand and happily exits to join the others. Likewise, the concluding tableau of Antonio sitting alone and unpartnered, gazing in the direction of the happy couples, is insufficient to disturb our sense of comic closure. The implication that his abiding melancholy springs from unrequited love for Bassanio has by now become a theatrical commonplace and cannot by itself resist the play's romantic affirmations. In effect, Gold used such moments as *gestures*, as if he wished to acknowledge the play's potential for raising subtextual problems but was ultimately unwilling to sacrifice to them the comic resolution he had so carefully prepared for.

Critical response to the production was mixed. Some reviewers approved of Gold's restraint, praising his direction as 'simple and direct' (*Shakespeare on Film Newsletter* 5 [May 1981] 2) and carefully balanced so as not to offend, indebted to many traditions but slave to none. Others found Gold's lack of intervention objectionable, protesting his reluctance to foreground such issues as greed, racism, disloyalty and sexual ambiguity as a wilful denial of the play's performance history. In fact, Gold may not have known that history. By his own admission inexperienced as a director of Shakespeare, he may have been more concerned with simply *telling* the story than with the cultural implications of that story. And where critics such as John Kerrigan might have wished for a more radical manipulation of the medium to heighten our awareness of the play's artificiality – 'to expose the artifice of the screened spectacle and reveal subtleties within it which a theatre audience, restricted to a single point of view, would miss' (*Times Literary Supplement*, 19 December 1980) - Gold's impulse was to fall back on the conventional techniques with which he was familiar, reducing stage artifices to the dimensions of the small screen to create a convincing 'reality' in televisual terms. His success in doing so may be measured by the number of critics who found his *Merchant* balanced, simple, direct and inoffensive. In the theatre, these are not necessarily terms of praise. In television, they usually are.

CHAPTER VI

Cultural stereotyping and audience response: Bill Alexander and Antony Sher

Bill Alexander's production of *The Merchant* for the Royal Shakespeare Company in 1987, revived the following year in London, grappled with the play's offensive subject matter more daringly than any production in recent memory. Refusing either to rehabilitate Shylock as the play's moral standard-bearer (as Miller had done in 1970) or to treat him from a safe historical distance as a comic 'Elizabethan' Jew (as Miller had done in 1980), Alexander courted controversy, seeming almost to invite accusations of racism. The controversy sprang in part from his refusal to honour the distinctions between romance and realism, comedy and tragedy, sympathy for and aversion to Shylock, from which stage interpreters have traditionally felt they had to choose. By intensifying the problematic nature of the text, Alexander modulated the dynamics of audience response: he goaded audiences with stereotypes only to probe the nature of their own prejudices; he confronted them with alienation in different guises in order to reveal the motives for scapegoatism. His Shylock was grotesque – at once comic, repulsive, and vengeful. Yet he was made so in part by those Venetians who needed someone on whom to project their own alienation; Venetians who, in their anxiety over sexual, religious, and mercantile values, were crucial to the transaction Alexander worked out between Shakespeare's text and contemporary racial tensions.

Take, for example, Alexander's innovative staging of the trial scene, the acid test of a production's credibility. At a key moment, when Portia conceded that Shylock was entitled to his pound of flesh, the preparations for surgery were chillingly unconventional. The Duke, habited like a Catholic Monsignor with a large silver cross around his neck, fell to his knees to intone a *Salve Regina*; Bassanio, dissolved in tears, threw himself prostrate before the disguised Portia; Antonio was taken forcibly upstage and bound to a pole as to a cross; and Shylock, who had been on his knees to sue for justice, suddenly rose in triumph, raised his clenched fists to heaven to demand 'A sentence!' (IV.i.300), and moved downstage to begin a ritual that played on age-old fears of Jewish bloodlust.

Such rituals, of course, have nothing to do with Judaism, though, as Derek Cohen argues, Shakespeare may have thought they did when he had Shylock immediately follow his vow to 'have the heart of [Antonio] if he forfeit' (III.i.100-1) with a request that Tubal meet him at the synagogue, as if a synagogue were 'a mysterious place where strange and terrible rituals were enacted' (p. 109). Alexander's production, however, forced that association on us. Shylock performed his ritual while chanting in Hebrew: in the absence of any appropriate prayer in Jewish liturgy, Rabbi Dr Allen Podet, adviser to the production, supplied a Seder night prayer which calls upon a vengeful God to 'Pour out Thy wrath upon the nations that know Thee not and upon the kingdoms that call not upon Thy name' (*London Theatre Record*, 23 April–6 May 1987). The cacophony created by these rival incantations – Shylock's Seder prayer and the Duke's *Salve* – signified a clash of ideologies which, as I shall argue later, had more to do with the dynamics of power than with religion; but Shylock's compulsive behaviour was fascinating to observe because it *appeared* to spring from some deep religious conviction, or 'messianic madness' (*Daily Mail*, 30 April 1987), or Abraham-like determination 'to visit the wrath of Jehovah upon the Gentiles' (*Independent*, 1 May 1987). As he chanted, he doffed his black gaberdine and donned a tallis, sprinkled a few drops of blood from a horn case with his hand on to a white cloth, then poured out the rest, lifted the cloth to heaven, and swept upstage to place it at Antonio's feet as if in preparation for a ritual slaughter. As the chants grew more cacophonous, Shylock made a wide arc, swinging his arms in rhythm; then, with startling violence, he ran at Antonio to tear his shirt off. Like one possessed, he circled behind Antonio, cupped one hand around his victim's neck, and in the other raised a dagger above his head. The crowd screamed.

Suddenly, as if by miracle, Portia cried 'Tarry a little!' (IV.i.301). Her voice full of anxiety, she had to shout to be heard; but as she explained the law, the crowd fell silent. Her quibble about 'no jot of blood' may have been a desperate remedy, but it stopped Shylock dead. In an interview for *Drama* Antony Sher, who played Shylock, noted with dismay that audiences spontaneously applauded this moment. 'The problem with this production, which seeks to point out racism, is that we may appeal in exactly the wrong way to any racists in the audience ... Often, in the trial scene, when the tables are turned on me, there's a roar of delighted applause. I feel hurt by that. It's like being at a Nazi rally' (p. 29). Sher may have found such a response disconcerting, but it clearly demonstrated the power of the production to persuade audiences to buy the absurd premise of the folklore plot – to believe that the Jew would actually *take* his pound of flesh. Alexander's staging stripped bare Shylock's motives, revealed the origins of the scene in primitive rituals of human sacrifice, and, in the name of humanity, begged audiences to condemn it. Jeremy Kingston's review for *The Times* (27 April 1988) made just this point: 'I do not know the nature of the earnest rituals that Sher performs with shawl and prayer before advancing on his victim, but it is the sort of scenic colour that in other epochs would have the mob baying for Jew blood.' Audiences were thus *invited* to cheer Portia's victory over Shylock. That cheer did not necessarily signify that they condoned anti-Semitism (though some perhaps did), nor that the production was morally unambiguous. It did signify, however, that emotionally, at that moment, they sided with the Christians against the Jew.

Sher deliberately made Shylock offensive – so offensive, in fact, that the production itself was attacked for promoting an anti-Semitic stereotype. Although such attacks unduly simplified the moral complexity of the production, Alexander nevertheless encouraged audiences on a visceral level to loathe Shylock and, consequently, to suspect that they were being coaxed into the very racial intolerance which, according to Sher, the production took pains to expose. In outward appearance, Sher's Shylock was exotically unassimilated – 'a lip-smacking, liquid-eyed Levantine bargain hunter', according to the *Jewish Chronicle* (8 May 1987). His 'bright robes and flashing eye' reminded one critic of 'Holman Hunt's biblical canvases at their most dreamingly hallucinatory' (*Financial Times*, 27 April 1988), and another of drawings by David Roberts (*London Daily News*, 30 April 1987). Squat, bear-like and barefoot, dressed in bulky gaberdine with unkempt hair and a straggly beard, Shylock was played with the coarse physicality for which Sher is noted: he gestured 'with not just his hands but his entire body' (*The Listener*, 14 May 1987), and his gait was 'a sort of seafaring waddle interrupted with sudden ferocious descents to a crouching position' (*Financial Times*, 30 April 1987). Grimly determined, he moved through Venice with 'the thrusting quality of someone used to pushing his way ... through stone-throwing, catcalling mobs' (*Guardian*, 1 May 1987). This portrayal, then, in its dangerous unpredictability, recalled unassimilated Shylocks of earlier times, from Macklin to Kean.

Sher took this approach for good reason. In the interview for *Drama*, making a veiled allusion to Olivier's celebrated performance nearly two decades earlier, he stressed that he wanted to break with recent stage tradition and to portray Shylock as 'someone obviously apart. The modern trick is to put *The Merchant* into the eighteenth or nineteenth century and present Shylock as an assimilated, sophisticated Jew. We didn't want that' (p. 28). In defiant rejection of the patrician, westernised Shylock who had held the stage for so long, Sher – a South African and a Jew by birth – portrayed an Eastern Jew closer to his own Semitic roots. Just as he had in his celebrated portrayal of Richard III, for which Olivier's performance had proved a similar obstacle, Sher sought to overturn the tradition of 'English' characterisation and to play Shylock afresh. He conceived of characters – English king and Levantine Jew alike – from an alien perspective, in light of cultural models different from those traditionally offered to British actors. Thus, where Olivier's Shylock was elderly, dignified, and patriarchal – a Rothschild or a Disraeli – Sher's was younger, earthier, and crass – a rug dealer at a bazaar. What Hugh Richmond writes of Sher's Richard was true of his Shylock as well: 'it needed only a hint that Olivier had used a bit of business for Sher to reject it outright, as if the truly Shakespearian idea of art as an accumulation of insights from successful precedents were intolerable' (p. 109).

In particular, Sher explicitly rejected the narrow focus on anti-Semitism common to post-Holocaust productions:

> We didn't want our production to be about anti-semitism only but about racism more generally. Curiously, although I was born Jewish, *The Merchant of Venice* has always said more to me as a South African. There's something about the way in which Shylock is moved to exact extreme penalties by the extent of the barbarism he endures which seemed to me to have applications to South Africa and the Middle East today. (p. 28)

Sher, therefore, drew his image of Shylock not from Jews who today, in Israel as elsewhere, are largely westernised, but from other Semitic peoples far more threatening to the middle-class audiences who flock to Shakespeare in London and Stratford: Arabs, Palestinians, Iranians, peoples who are associated in the western mind with frightening and unpredictable extremes of behaviour, with Islamic fundamentalism, death threats, and acts of political terrorism. Sher's Shylock invoked the image of such alien and often misunderstood peoples, ignorance of whose traditions and values all too readily has led to racial prejudice. His behaviour at the trial played on audiences' fears of religious fanaticism, the blood ritual recalling not Judaism, but the vengeful outbursts of an ayatollah bent on destroying the Great Satan – and settling for the heart of Salman Rushdie.

Sher calculated his performance to play on bourgeois audiences' intolerance of racial difference. When we first see him in I.iii, he is squatting cross-legged on a cushion under a black canopy, as if in a souk, an abacus and scales beside him, beads in hand – 'a gypsy Jew in a canopied lair' (*Financial Times*, 30 April 1987). He is wearing a striped kaftan over baggy trousers and a turban on his head, his gestures broad and Semitic, and his pinched, nasal delivery punctuated by a nervous, high-pitched laugh which irritates when it would most ingratiate. Sher uses his vocal limitations intelligently: to compensate for his thin and reedy tenor, he affects an accent full of awkwardly self-conscious pronunciations, such as 'Wenice' for Venice and 'suffeesent' for sufficient. By mispronouncing words in this way, he teasingly appeals to his listeners' linguistic snobbery – both the Venetians' and the audience's – and invites the ethnic ridicule that Third World pronunciations typically provoke. Worse, he laughs at his own jokes (the pun on 'pie-rats' evokes an uncouth snort), pretends at first not to see Antonio, then confides to the audience in an intimate sing-song, 'I hate him for he is a *Kleestiun*.'

Sher taunts the audience with his Middle Eastern stereotype. He plays on the insecurity of the privileged classes, on their fear of minorities who, having learned to be overtly solicitous, sneer behind their backs and try to wrest power from them. When Bassanio comes to beg money of Shylock, as Miriam Gilbert astutely observes in her production notes, he asserts his power simply by remaining on his cushion. Bassanio, standing uneasily in front of him, shifts from foot to foot; and when Shylock asks, 'May I speak with Antonio?' (I.iii.25), Bassanio does not spy the trap: pausing to consider, he awkwardly offers what he thinks is the dinner invitation

Shylock is fishing for, only to have that invitation turned viciously against him: 'Yes, to smell pork ... ' (27). Shylock's strategy changes when a more powerful antagonist, Antonio, appears on the scene. Turning with mock surprise to greet him, he grovels and fawns as the merchant steps forward – 'Your worship was the last man in our mouths' (52)– the rug dealer in spite of himself, eager to make a sale. Yet, in a gesture that smacks of cultural defiance, Shylock goads Antonio with vulgarity. When explaining to him how 'Yakov' got his ewes and rams to do the deed of kind, he vigorously slaps his fist against his open palm to imitate coital sounds – at one point doing so right in Antonio's face. Here is the alien rubbing his obscenity in the nose of Christian decorum. Even more crudely, to seal the bond Shylock spits in his hand before offering it to Antonio. Such behaviour is provocatively offensive. We do not blame Antonio for reviling Shylock. We would do the same. Sher dares us not to.

*

Audience response to Sher's Shylock is complicated, however, by his mistreatment at the hands of the Christians. Antonio, the chief offender, is played as a virulent anti-Semite, self-righteous enough to feel that he need not treat Shylock any better than a dog. Physical violence characterises even their first encounter. When he grows irritated by Shylock's rehearsal of the terms of the bond, Antonio grabs the abacus out of Shylock's hand, hurls it across the stage, then turns to him and asks, 'Well, Shylock, shall we be beholding to you?' (I.iii.97). An odd way to gain one's attention, such violence clearly asserts Antonio's cultural privilege: he knows he need fear no reprisal, and he flaunts that knowledge. As Shylock shrinks before him, Antonio continues to bully, brusquely raising him up with both hands on 'lend it not/ As to thy friends' (124-5; see photograph 7) then, on 'lend it rather to thine enemy' (127), shoving him centre stage, where Shylock crumples into a ball and offers, in turn, 'kindness'.

Physical intimidation is present in other scenes too, where Shylock is mercilessly ridiculed, jostled, and beaten. In II.viii, for example, Salerio observes that all the boys in Venice follow Shylock to mock him, 'Crying his stones, his daughter, and his ducats' (24): a group of street urchins actually materialises in Alexander's production, and they are worse than Salerio reports. They hound Shylock in early scenes, making noises before his door and drowning out his lines with cat-calls; later, when he enters lamenting the loss of his daughter, they mimic him with 'My ducats! My daughter!' and pelt him with stones. Blood streams down his forehead. Yet such violence, however malicious, is mere child's play compared with that of Salerio and Solanio. When Shylock accuses them of knowing of Jessica's flight, they taunt him both verbally and physically, gloating over his losses and tossing him between them like a beanbag. When he cries, 'She is damned for it' (III.i.26), they push him to the floor and prod him with sticks, as one would a steer, beating him as he rolls downstage towards the precipice. When he reaches it, they threaten with their sticks to push him off the edge and into the canal. This threat lends a mordant irony to the line with which Shylock stops their intimidation: when asked what Antonio's flesh would be good for, he replies, casting a glance at the water beneath, 'To bait fish withal' (42).

That line introduces Shylock's famous self-defence, and in it he turns the tables on his oppressors. On 'if you wrong us, shall we not revenge?' (52), he suddenly grabs the stick with which Salerio has beaten him and threatens them with it. Shylock now holds the position of power. Alexander thus underscores the production's governing idea: 'The villainy you teach me I will execute, and it shall go hard but I will better the instruction' (56-7). The point is made visually: Shylock has seized the weapon from his assailants and may, by their example, use it. Their violent abuse has driven him to seek a like revenge on Antonio – a point pounded home each time he beats his breast on the word 'revenge'. Shylock has become their monster, their Frankenstein, offering them a grotesque image of their own Christianity. Sher explains the idea with a contemporary analogy: 'the more violent is the segregation and racism, the more bloody will be the revenge so that brutality breeds brutality and you end up with people putting car tyres round their enemies' necks and igniting them' (p. 29).

Alexander makes this idea clearest in the motif of spitting – a motif so powerful that Peter Hall borrowed it (as he borrowed so much else from Alexander) for his production of *The Merchant* with Dustin Hoffman in 1989. Like the presence of the street urchins who pelt Shylock with stones, spitting is inspired by the text: Shylock complains in I.iii. that Antonio has voided his rheum upon his beard, and Antonio threatens to do so again. That very scene bears witness to Shylock's complaint. As he exits, Antonio spits forcefully in his direction, making spiteful a line – 'Hie thee, gentle Jew' (I.iii.170) – that might have been delivered more genteelly. Indeed, spitting punctuates most of the key moments of victimisation in the play. It begins at the outset when, silent and silhouetted upstage, Tubal stands alone. Salerio and Solanio enter across the bridge and, unprovoked, spit on him as they pass. That one simple action sets the tone for the whole play. They spit on him again when he enters to Shylock in III.i, this time baiting him as well with a chorus of 'Jew, Jew, Jew!' Their authority in this scene, as we have observed, has been challenged by Shylock, who vows to 'better the instruction'; thus their hatred is displaced on to the less threatening Tubal. Shylock, bemoaning the theft of his ducats but having successfully fended off his Christian aggressors, gently wipes the spit off Tubal's beard in one of the production's rare moments of tenderness.

It is fitting, then, that when Shylock has gained the upper hand and leads Antonio off to jail, he abuses him in kind. Shylock will have none of Solanio's pleas for mercy: 'I'll not be made a soft and dull-eyed fool,/ ... To Christian intercessors' (III.iii.14-16); and as a full stop, he spits. Before leaving, he spits again at the manacled Antonio: the Christians have taught him such behaviour. The gaoler and Solanio draw swords, but Shylock, confident of the law's protection, exits laughing. The scene concludes with Solanio spitting in the direction of Shylock's exit, just as Antonio has done in I.iii.

By such means, Alexander dramatises both the reciprocity and the violence of prejudice. Shylock imitates what he has learned from the Christians; thus he should be no more culpable than they are. The production challenges us, however, by pitting our ethical abhorrence of racism against our visceral response to those who are alien to us – by setting our rational tolerance at odds with those fears that feed racism. This unsettling disjunction is strikingly demonstrated at the trial, when Shylock, now with the authority of the law behind him, instructs the entire court on the nature of prejudice. Called upon to justify his insistence on the bond, he replies that prejudice needs no rationale: 'So can I give no reason, nor I will not,/ More than a lodged hate and a certain loathing/ I bear Antonio' (IV.i.59-61). The law is amoral: it legitimates prejudice by denying the need for rational cause and protecting what is emotionally based. If the law sanctions it, one can hate with impunity. To illustrate the point, Shylock seizes from the ranks of onlookers a black attendant and holds the young man directly before him, face out, for the whole court – and audience – to see. Pointing him first to one side, then the other, he poses an embarrassing question:

> You have among you many a purchased slave,
> Which, like your asses and your dogs and mules,
> You use in abject and in slavish parts,
> Because you bought them. Shall I say to you,
> 'Let them be free! Marry them to you heirs!' (90-4)

Shylock's logic is disturbingly clear. If Venetians need no cultural sanction for denying slaves a place in their daughters' beds, so, it would follow, Shylock needs no sanction for claiming his pound of Christian flesh. So too, it would ironically follow, Venetians need no sanction for anti-Semitism: it is simply an accepted clause in the social contract, beyond the need for moral justification. Shylock thus explains to the court the rules of a closed society which have victimised him, and which he now intends to turn against his oppressors.

Alexander's staging invests the text with remarkable topicality, creating 'that special sense of discomfort and uneasy excitement which you experience when an apparently remote argument unexpectedly cuts close to the bone' (*Sunday Times*, 3 May 1987). Cutting through all pretence of social morality, it illustrates the universality of racial intolerance and exposes the mechanisms by which prejudice is made legitimate. In effect, Alexander magnifies anti-Semitism by having us view it through the lens of discrimination against blacks, a form of racism that strikes contemporary audiences with a force that anti-Semitism has largely lost. Drawing on his experience as a South African, Sher makes us face the question of moral culpability squarely: for as he holds the slave in front of him, we see Shylock and the slave as one. Visually, the two victims of racism merge, and we project on to Shylock the anti-black prejudices that have become so insidious and commonplace in western culture – prejudices that Alexander's overwhelmingly white middle-class audience, without realising it, may share. The potency of the stage image depends on our identification with the oppressors; we are placed in a position of complicity with a group of Venetians whose moral hypocrisy we might otherwise judge from a safe distance.

※

Alexander tested our complicity in other ways as well. Our attitudes towards the Venetians themselves, for example, may have been coloured by more subtle prejudices that he skilfully drew out and manipulated, for the Venetians were characterised by a homosexuality which many in the audience found objectionable and which inevitably complicated their responses to the Venetians' Jew-baiting. Ironically, in a production that presumed to expose the nature of racial prejudice, Alexander encouraged his audience to indulge prejudices of a different but equally insidious sort. Homosexuality, of course, is latent in the text, and recent productions have used it increasingly to explain Antonio's otherwise unaccountable melancholy. In no production, however, has it been so pervasive or served so overtly as a metaphor for social alienation: comments by no fewer than fifteen reviewers attest to its importance.

Alexander dramatises a homosexual relationship in the very first meeting of Antonio and Bassanio, where Antonio reveals the love of a world-weary man for a disingenuous youth. Elegantly attired in a satin doublet of Caroline style, he asks with distaste what 'lady' it is to whom Bassanio has sworn a secret pilgrimage, turning his back on the handsome young man as he does so. Reviewers had no doubt about his sexual orientation: he is 'a solidly middle-aged homosexual' according to Frank Rich (*New York Times*, 16 June 1987), 'a man hopelessly in love with Bassanio' (*Sunday Telegraph*, 3 May 1987), 'a repressed homosexual' (*Time Out*, 6 May 1987), and a 'tormented closet gay' (*Guardian*, 1 May 1987) whose 'homosexual passion' for Bassanio is 'touchingly signalled' in the opening scene (*Daily Telegraph*, 29 April 1988).

Bassanio, for playing on the older man's love, was condemned as a 'bisexual opportunist' (*The Listener*, 14 May 1987) who 'appears to exist on the instincts of a successful rent boy' (*Daily Mail*, 30 April 1987). The accusations are not unfounded. When he speaks of coming freshly off from his debts, confiding 'To you, Antonio,/ I owe the most in money and in love' (I.i.129-30), he lays one hand casually on Antonio's shoulder, the other on his chest, fingering his ruffled collar. In response, Antonio places both hands on Bassanio's shoulders, leaving them there just a moment too long to signify mere friendship, and John Carlisle's rich, ironic bass teases an unwonted sexual innuendo out of 'My purse, my person, my extremest means/ Lie all unlocked to your occasions' (137-8). When Bassanio begins to sing Portia's praises, Antonio moves away from him to sit on a mooring post downstage, but Bassanio knows the art of manipulation. On 'O my Antonio, had I but the means' (172), he approaches his benefactor from behind, goes down on one knee and places a hand on his shoulder; when Antonio, jealously unmoved, says he cannot raise the present sum, Bassanio moves his right arm around

Antonio's waist. That does the trick. 'Therefore go forth,/ Try what my credit can in Venice do' (178-9), Antonio says as he rises; but he is not pleased. The words 'fair Portia' (181) are spit out of his mouth like tart wine. The men embrace, but before they release each other, Antonio plants a kiss, full and frank, on Bassanio's lips. Bassanio steps back, surprised but not offended, as indeed he should not be: his behaviour has provoked that kiss.

Critical responses to this scene reveal as much about the critics – and their gender – as about the scene itself. Noting 'the passion of Antonio's kiss', Martin Hoyle in the *Financial Times* commented that the overtly homosexual bias of the production brought to mind 'Germaine Greer's recent remarks on the basic homosexuality of the English' (27 April 1988). If Hoyle's response was self-consciously and even defensively male (note how he takes these men as his countrymen, not even pretending to see them as Venetian), Mary Harron approached the scene with a woman's concerns in mind. Remarking that Bassanio was 'presented more blatantly than usual as Antonio's former lover', she wrote in the *Observer* that 'there is much sexual tension and pathos in the opening scene between these two, creating a thread of suspense every time Portia sees them together, as we wonder – how much does she know?' (3 May 1987). Attempting critical objectivity, Paul Taylor of the *Independent* protested that homosexuality precluded a 'straight' reading of the text; for, he asked, how can Christian magnanimity be taken seriously 'if Antonio's generous funding of Bassanio's wife-hunting is overplayed as the selfish stratagem by which a depressed homosexual manages to keep an emotional hold over – and wrest a few impassioned kisses from – the friend he is bound to lose?' (28 April 1988). How, indeed? The discomfort apparent in such responses was felt by many in the audience as well. One had only to listen to comments during the interval to recognise that Alexander's ploy had worked: viewers were at once fascinated and repelled by the strategies with which Antonio and Bassanio advanced their selfish ends.

By mirroring this unrequited love of an older man for a youth, the relationship between Salerio and Solanio suggested that homosexuality makes the whole world kin. It is significant that reviewers bothered to mention these minor characters at all: the *London Daily News* found them 'a wimpish lot, tending to bisexuality' (30 April 1987); the *London Evening Standard*, 'decadent, cruel ... and rather mixed up about their homosexual longings' (30 April 1987). Salerio, a middle-aged courtier more fashionably dressed than Antonio, hungers for Solanio, his effete young protégé who sports a plumed hat and is rather heavily made-up. Together, they embody the values of a jaded Venetian culture. Their grilling of Antonio in I.i, for example, seems aimed at getting Antonio to confess not why he is so sad, but who his new lover may be: 'Why then, you are in love' (1.1.46) is spoken with particular relish. Later, when Salerio describes Antonio's leave-taking from Bassanio, his intentions towards the younger man undermine the pathos of his account. Kneeling beside Solanio, who is lying provocatively centre stage, Salerio grows passionate as he recounts how Antonio, 'his eye being big with tears,/ Turning his face ... put his hand behind him,/ And with affection wondrous sensible/ ... wrung Bassanio's hand' (II.viii.47-50). As if in sympathy, Salerio reaches for Solanio's hand and reclines next to him, apparently ready to make a sexual advance; but his young paramour abruptly rises and, in effect, spurns him. Such sexual game-playing continues in III.i , when they lament Antonio's ill luck. Solanio has been weeping, presumably in grief for his friend. When Salerio leans down to kiss away the tears, Solanio wipes the kiss off his cheek, once again rejecting the older man's attentions. Steve Grant in *Time Out* thought it a 'positive idea ... to have Salerio lust unsuccessfully after a somewhat petulant Solanio' (4 May 1988), for their interaction reinforces the sexual tension running through Antonio's scenes with Bassanio. In Salerio and Solanio, however, homosexuality is reduced to type, and their behaviour courts the disfavour of an unsympathetic viewer.

In the homophobic view of many in a bourgeois Stratford or London audience, Alexander's Venetians would seem particularly repugnant because the 'business' they have with each other, the mercantile self-interest commonly ascribed to them in the play, is dramatised through the dynamics of homosexual gamesmanship. Sexual commerce among these men employs the logic of capitalism, and audiences inured to exploitative business practices – audiences hesitant to call Bassanio morally bankrupt simply because he exploits a friend to win an heiress – may nonetheless disapprove of those practices when they serve homosexual ends. Such disapproval is implicit in some of the reviews quoted above. Alexander panders to popular prejudices: he makes us queasy about siding with the Venetians against Shylock not only because they are so calculatedly dishonest with one another, but because their dishonesty is bound up in stereotypes of homosexual behaviour that culturally 'enlightened' audiences have been taught to disavow. As in the trial scene, the production plays our ethical tolerance against our irrational responses to otherness, and by so doing makes those responses an issue we must confront. We may resent Alexander for soliciting our disapproval of these men, just as we may resent his daring us to dislike Shylock; for by identifying homosexuality as one source of that disapproval, he puts us in a position of complicity with the very closed-mindedness that the production ostensibly would have us repudiate. The critic who protested that 'Antonio's crush on Bassanio is amplified so that effeteness becomes a cheap token of the gentiles' malignity' proves my point (*The Listener*, 14 May 1987).

Antonio, in fact, is the only member of this Venetian community who commanded much critical respect. Tall, thin, patrician and gravelly voiced, John Carlisle portrays him with tragic longing as Portia's unsuccessful rival for Bassanio's affections. The staging highlights that rivalry. At the conclusion of I.i, for example, after Bassanio has departed, Antonio stands alone midstage, with his back to the audience, while the stage is cleared and reset for Belmont; Portia sweeps on and stands beside him, facing out to greet all comers. The tableau is brief, but telling. A similar tableau, with Antonio and Portia standing on stage together, occurs at the intersection of II.vi and II.vii; but here, the ambiguity of Antonio's sexual identity makes the suggestion of their rivalry more intriguing. In II.vi, after the revellers have gone, a solitary figure in a long black cloak enters downstage right; the figure is hooded and holds the mask of a young woman to its face. The text indicates that this is Antonio, come in search of Gratiano to tell him that the ship is about to sail for Belmont. In this production, however, we do not know the identity – or the gender – of the silent masked figure: it is simply a reveller come too late. When the figure lowers the mask, however, and Gratiano asks in surprise, 'Signor Antonio?' (II.vi.62), the audience may share his surprise, for Alexander uses transvestism unexpectedly – and powerfully – as a metaphor for self-alienation. Critics saw Antonio as a man 'out of love with himself' (*Sunday Telegraph*, 3 May 1987), 'whose melancholy amounts almost to a yearning for death' (*Daily Telegraph*, 29 April 1988); as 'a sad-to-be-gay merchant' (*Guardian*, 28 April 1988) who 'would actually prefer death to restricted life' (*Guardian*, 1 May 1987).

As someone who knows the pain of alienation, Antonio may understand the cause and intensity of Shylock's lust for his pound of flesh: a culturally conditioned self-hatred that causes the outsider to lash out at one more vulnerable than himself. Their mutual understanding is conveyed at the trial in a bit of business following Antonio's exhortation to 'Let me have judgement, and the Jew his will' (IV.i.83). The two antagonists circle one another at centre stage, the victim and his prey eyeing each other suspiciously. When, in desperation, Bassanio offers six thousand ducats for three, Antonio and Shylock stop to share a laugh at his naïveté. They know what motivates an alien to act as he does, and it is not money. This idea of self-hatred, of course, risks feeding a bourgeois audience's notion of homosexual neurosis. Indeed, Alexander may have had some such thing in mind; for clearly, at the trial, Antonio sees martyrdom as a way to bind Bassanio to him emotionally for ever. When Bassanio says, 'What, man, courage yet!' (111), Antonio pushes him to the floor with unanticipated fury and, standing over him, spits out his confession, 'I am a tainted wether of the flock,/ Meetest for death' (114-15). Then, in a sudden reversal, he tenderly raises Bassanio and completes the speech: 'You cannot better be employed, Bassanio,/ Than to live still and write mine epitaph' (117-18). In effect, he compels the young man's consent in this as he has not been able to in an affair of the heart. His subsequent speech to Bassanio, 'bid [Portia] be judge/ Whether Bassanio had not once a love' (272-3), is accompanied by an embrace more passionate than any other in the play, Bassanio burying his head in his lover's shoulder, and Antonio stroking the hair and neck of his young friend.

Such intimacy prompts Shylock's dismissive – and knowing – aside, 'These be the Christian husbands!' (291). The Jew, till now himself the powerless object of so much derision, turns his scorn on men whose scarcely concealed sexual orientation could make them as scorned as he. Bassanio certainly takes the line as an accusation: breaking from Antonio, he spits viciously in Shylock's beard. His motive for doing so is obviously defensive. Furthermore, it suggests that those who spat on Shylock earlier may also have done so defensively, projecting their own alienation on to one who is a likely victim because more obviously alien than they. Their anti-Semitism thus would seem to derive in part from their homosexuality, as a form of transference. David Nathan, writing in the *Jewish Chronicle*, makes this connection: the 'self-hatred' Antonio feels for being 'homosexually drawn to Bassanio', he suggests, 'adds to the depth of his anti-Semitism' (8 May 1987). Anthony Deneslow asserts more judgementally that 'we can have little sympathy' for those Venetians who, because they are 'homosexually-touched' (curious phrase), 'hiss and spit at their victim' (BBC Radio London, 30 April 1988). In

Alexander's production, therefore, alienation is not limited to the Jews. It infects the whole society – a society whose notions of class, whose rules of conduct in sex as in business, even whose religion, alienates men from one another and, worse, from themselves.

The violence with which these men use Shylock as a scapegoat is most brutal at the trial. Their ringleader Gratiano distils all the brute bullying of which we know his society to be capable. When, for instance, Shylock announces, 'I stand here for law' (IV.i.142), Gratiano rushes at him and spits directly in his face: no-one objects. Later, when Shylock praises Portia as 'A Daniel come to judgment' (219), Gratiano leads Bassanio and Solanio in a chorus of 'Jew, Jew, Jew!', bearing down on him like dogs baying for *his* flesh until Portia calls them off (*Spectator*, 9 May 1987). Once Shylock has lost his case, however, their aggression is unleashed. When Portia instructs Shylock to get 'down, therefore, and beg mercy of the Duke' (359), Bassanio and Gratiano wrestle him to the floor, Bassanio pinning his arms while Gratiano stands with his foot planted firmly on Shylock's back. From this position, the Duke's mercy must surely sound strained to Shylock. Even more strained is that of Antonio who, now unbound, strides centre stage to pick up the knife Shylock has dropped and, volunteering to return half of his goods provided Shylock presently turn Christian, hurls it into the floor – on the word 'Christian' – at the very spot where Shylock performed his blood ritual. In essence, he strikes at Shylock's heart: he may speak of mercy, but he achieves revenge. In victory, these Christians are as merciless and barbaric as Shylock was in demanding the bond.

With disturbing accuracy, then, Alexander dramatises how alienation born of ideological difference leads inexorably to violence. In doing so, he makes credible and immediate a folkloric plot which often, on the stage, strains credibility. What conditions, after all, could lead a man to cut out the heart of another? Confronting us with modern cultural analogues for the racism Shakespeare knew, assaulting us with stereotypes of religious fanaticism, black servitude, and homosexuality, he adroitly manipulates our moral perspectives: he appeals to popular prejudices here, upsets them there, and by so doing would make us aware of how deeply we are implicated in perpetuating social conditions that cause minorities to feel alienated. There is, of course, no guarantee that encouraging an audience to indulge its prejudices will lead to the self-awareness Alexander intends: one cannot control audience response. To attempt to sensitise people to their own prejudices by causing them to *feel* those prejudices entails risk. Anthony Sher attests to this risk when he complains that audiences applauded his defeat at the trial and thereby illustrated the very racism that the production sought to overcome: 'The problem ... is that we may appeal in exactly the wrong way to any racists in the audience.' In ways perhaps deeper than Alexander had anticipated, therefore, his *Merchant* functioned as a contemporary parable of culturally sanctioned hatred.

*

Kit Surrey's expressive set sharpens the production's focus on ideological kinship and conflict. The playing space is uncluttered, almost bare: a platform of dark wooden planks suggests a Venetian quay or landing stage, with gondola poles resting against the proscenium arch on each side of it; dank mist rises around it as from a canal, and at each corner is a mooring post on which actors may sit. Upstage centre, a narrow bridge leads off the platform; most entrances and exits are made across it. And looming high overhead, spanning the stage, is a wooden bridge evocative of the Bridge of Sighs – a bridge 'that creates an immediate sense of intrigue, of conversations overheard', a bridge that captures the brooding menace of a Venice 'all gloomy shadows and smoky golden light' (*Observer*, 3 May 1987). In this virtually empty space all the Venetian scenes are played; and though Surrey was criticised for not having sufficiently distinguished the ducal court from the Rialto – one literal-minded critic complained that the trial was 'set, unsatisfactorily, out of doors' (*Sunday Telegraph*, 3 May 1987) – this lack of distinct locations makes a metaphoric point: the proceedings at court are only 'the floating continuation of sectarian strife in the streets' (*Financial Times*, 30 April 1987).

If the open space itself is neutral, the backdrop is not. Surrey stripped the stage of the Royal Shakespeare Theatre right back to its brick wall (a wall recreated for the London revival). The plaster on it is cracking – this is clearly meant to suggest an old edifice – and it is adorned with two opposing images: slightly to the right of centre, a Byzantine icon depicting the Madonna in gold leaf; slightly to the left, scrawled in yellow chalk, a Star of David. This opposition potently expresses the play's ideological conflict. The Madonna indicates that the wall belongs to a church – the Church of Rome, locus of ecclesiastical power and hegemony; on its wall, Judaism is reduced to an obscene graffito which hints at institutionalised prejudice. The identification of the wall with the Church is confirmed when, as the play begins, bells toll and a *Kyrie* is intoned. Clearly, this production will take Roman Catholicism seriously as the culturally and politically dominant force it was: the ecclesiastical attire and silver crucifix worn by the Duke at the trial are not fortuitous.

This visual representation of ideological conflict is picked up in the attire of other characters. Most of the Venetians wear large crucifixes around their necks. The largest and most ostentatious are sported by Salerio and Solanio, who also cross themselves frequently when speaking of Antonio's misfortune. We needn't regard such behaviour as hypocritical; it is habitual. In so far as they typify the attitudes of their church, they may indeed be 'good Christians' in the tradition of those Roman Catholics (even the Pope himself) who tolerated the anti-Semitic policies of Adolf Hitler. Memories of Hitler's purges inform our response to the Jews' costuming too. Tubal, in the play's opening tableau, stands with his back to the audience; on his coat is emblazoned a yellow Star of David, the badge of all his tribe. Similarly, in II.v, before leaving to dine with the Christians, Shylock dons a black coat which, when he turns to go, reveals a Star of David just like Tubal's. As Victoria Radin reminds us, Jews who lived in the Venetian Ghetto during the Renaissance were forced to wear such insignias (*New Statesman*, 13 May 1988); the costuming is thus as historically authentic as it is evocative of the Holocaust. Either way, these Jews are 'marked' men.

Alexander employs religious symbols to define Jessica's plight as well. Behind Shylock's back, Lancelot Gobbo hands her a golden crucifix on a chain, a gift from Lorenzo. Lorenzo has given it to Lancelot in II.iv when he says 'Hold here, take this' (19). The line is usually interpreted as a reference to money; but as so often in this production, religion takes the place of currency. The ideology of the market-place is transferred to the Church. Jessica hides the crucifix from her father but kneels to kiss it once he has gone: it becomes the crucial symbol of her desire – and failure – to be assimilated into the Christian community.

A crucifix dangling from a chain is the final taunt Shylock suffers before being thrust out of the court after the trial: it is the mocking gesture of a closed society for whom Christianity signifies power and exclusion, not mercy and acceptance. The gesture has been anticipated when Antonio, in III.iii, dangles the chain by which he is being taken to prison in front of the gaoler, who instinctively crosses himself. Antonio himself is on the end of the chain, as one who suffers martyrdom, a role he plays nearly to death at the trial; like the Jews in the play, he knows the pain of unfulfilled desire. When Jessica arrives at Belmont, therefore, the crucifix and chain have accumulated considerable meaning. She carries them with her, along with a book of prayer from which she reads, as tokens of her cultural assimilation. But in fact, she is not accepted at all. Pointedly isolated by hosts who do not make her feel welcome – Nerissa ignores the request to 'cheer yond stranger, bid her welcome' (III.ii.236) by skirting around her – and baited by a Lancelot Gobbo who actually makes her fear damnation as Shylock's daughter (III.v), she is divided from the Christians by an accent similar to her father's, by her hair (long dark curls, like his), and by her Semitic looks and coloration. Even her costume betrays a difference: although the green Turkish harem suit she wore in Venice has been replaced by a white dress that would seem to signify her assimilation in Belmont, beneath it she still wears the red skirt she wore as an overskirt in Venice. It marks her as the Jew's daughter yet. Visually, she retains vestiges of her Judaism despite those tokens of Christianity she embraces; for the insiders at Belmont, therefore, she remains an outsider – 'Lorenzo and his infidel' (III.ii.217).

Act 5 reveals the influence of Jonathan Miller's emphasis on disharmony, particularly in Jessica's relationship to the Christians. Here, as they all enter the house to celebrate their nuptials, Jessica runs after Lorenzo, eager to take part and thereby to deny her obvious difference from them. On her way, however, she accidentally drops the crucifix she has been carrying. She breaks from Lorenzo to fetch it; but Antonio, who has spied it first, snatches it up in one fell swoop (a visual echo of what he has done with Shylock's knife at the trial) and, seeing her kneel down to get it, dangles it before her, just out of reach. The lights fade on the disquieting tableau of Jessica extending a hand to receive what can never be hers. In Miller's production, Antonio empathised with Jessica as one who, like her, knew what is was to feel isolated. In Alexander's, however, Antonio 'works off his own frustrated resentment by trying to exacerbate hers' (*Independent*, 28 April 1988). By taunting her with the crucifix – just as Solanio has done to Shylock at the trial – he reiterates the bitter lesson that no Jew may ever be permitted entry into the smug club of Christians for whom religion has more to do with power than faith.

※

When a production is so centrally concerned with issues of racial prejudice, male bonding and institutionalised power, one might expect the female world of Belmont to be overshadowed. In fact, Alexander's Belmont is ideologically of a piece with his Venice; its inhabitants subscribe to the same patriarchal assumptions and prejudices that the Venetians do. Belmont is a place where women honour tradition, where a dead father's will counts for more than a living daughter's wish, where the goal of every woman is to give herself and all her goods to the man she loves, and where Christian duty may be honoured more in the breach than the observance.

Some critics complained that this Belmont lacked magic, that it was too spare, too much like Venice: they wanted a green world to pose alternatives to the mercantile values of Venice. But that was not Alexander's aim. Ethically, his Belmont occupies the same space as Venice, and Kit Surrey's bare set helps to enforce the idea (much as an Elizabethan stage would have) that the worlds are reflections of one another – 'Belmont, it would seem, is just across the lagoon from the watery Republic' (*London Daily News*, 30 April 1987). Belmont basks in a warmer light than Venice, and the stage is softened by a beige oriental rug that is rolled out to cover much of the platform. A Bible on an ornate stand, upstage right, on which each suitor must swear his oath, symbolises the divine inspiration ascribed to Portia's father; and on the back wall, the Madonna is now lighted with votary candles, the Star of David visible only in shadow. Such minimal changes in the set ensured fluid scene changes and encouraged audiences to draw comparisons between the two worlds and their inhabitants.

If the men of Venice sported their Catholicism cavalierly, the women of Belmont take religion more dutifully. Dressed like 'Dresden shepherdesses' (*Independent*, 1 May 1987), their gowns adorned with large bejewelled crucifixes, they clearly have been educated at a convent school. They believe unblinkingly in male prerogatives: they cross themselves every time God is mentioned, and Portia never questions the will of her father. For her, God and the father are one and the same, a power to be honoured and obeyed. This faith in patriarchal authority allows Portia to endure the casket lottery obediently – but not without protest. She ridicules anyone whose manners differ from her own, be he English, French, German or Neapolitan. Male critics were quick to point out in Deborah Findlay's portrayal an 'unusual disdain' for her suitors uncharacteristic of most Portias (*London Daily News*, 30 April 1987). She is 'as nasty as she ought to be but so rarely is', wrote the critic of the *Financial Times* (30 April 1987); and others concurred, calling her 'tart' and 'astringent' (*Guardian*, 1 May 1987; 28 April 1988), 'icy and fastidious' (*Daily Mail*, 30 April 1987), 'hard-sharp' and 'unsentimental' (*London Evening Standard*, 30 April 1987), and 'sharp, impatient ... bossy, dully energetic [and] determined' (*Sunday Times*, 3 May 1987).

Pórtia is especially disdainful of the Prince of Morocco, but Alexander complicates the audience's response by making him a stereotype worthy of her disdain. Morocco woos Portia with all the arrogance of a man who regards women as chattels. Entering with a flourish, all in white save a turquoise sash, he grandly removes his cape and hands it to her to hold: as a woman, she of course would be his servant. He then puts on a bravura display of male potency, brandishing his scimitar so as to intimidate her: 'The best-regarded virgins of our clime/ Have loved it' (II.i.10-11) carries more than a hint of sexual ravishment and draws a knowing giggle from the audience. Then, as he begins to sing Portia's praises in the tradition of a sonneteer – 'From the four corners of the earth they come/ To kiss this shrine, this mortal breathing saint' (II.vii.39-40) – he seizes her hand to kiss and, in the course of the speech, ardently works his way up her arm. Though visibly shuddering at his touch, she does not withdraw her arm: she is bound by rules of decorum, even if he is not. Little wonder, then, that she expresses joy when he chooses wrong. Her disdain for him is deserved, and therefore the audience is inclined to forgive Portia her aversion to 'all of his complexion' (79). Indeed, the comic stereotype of a violently sexist African would seem to invite and condone a racist reponse in the audience as well.

Yet Alexander makes this gentle riddance problematic by casting a young black actor as Portia's servant Balthasar. When she dismisses everyone of a dark complexion, he flashes her a look of disapproval and mutters 'Tsk'. On the three occasions I saw this production, members of the audience responded to this moment uncomfortably, as if Balthasar were accusing them, and not just Portia, of racism. In a sense, he does. For by making us cognisant that she has openly spurned Morocco *as a black*, Balthasar forces us to recognise our own complicity too: by laughing at Morocco as a 'type' unsuitable to marry into the white world of aristocratic values, we have been guilty of a racist response. It is such complicity that makes Shylock's attack on culturally approved racism at the trial so effective. As he holds up the black attendant for all to see – 'Marry [him] to your heirs' – he does not speak in the abstract: he speaks directly to Portia and to everyone like her.

Portia, however, is blind to her own bigotry. She would no more have recognised her insensitivity to Balthasar than the xenophobia implicit in her dismissal of the suitors Nerissa lists in I.ii. That her prejudices are unconscious is revealed in the way she treats Jessica. Superficially, her *noblesse oblige* singles her out for Jessica's particular praise: 'the poor rude world/ Hath not her fellow' (III.v.70-1). Yet Portia betrays a condescension towards Jessica through tone of voice. When Jessica wishes her 'all heart's content' at the monastery, Portia replies 'I thank you for your wish, and am well pleased/ To wish it back on you' (III.iv.42-4) in the kind of patronising sing-song that one might use when speaking to a child. Unlike the Venetians, Portia *appears* to be sincere in her Christian convictions: like the rich churchgoer who heartily believes in charity for the poor but has no doubt of her own social superiority or of the value of her good works, she *means* well. Her limitations are those of the affluent bourgeoisie who advocate tolerance and open-mindedness even as they (often unawares) practise discrimination. 'No other production' of *The Merchant*, writes John Peter, 'has brought out so clearly ... this fatal schizophrenia of Western civilisation' (*Sunday Times*, 3 May 1987).

Paradoxically, Portia's ignorance of her own prejudices makes it easier to credit her sincerity and to accept the romance plot at face value. A good Catholic, she will adhere strictly to the letter of the law, and though she panics at the thought of being won by a suitor she abhors, she will not, like Joan Plowright's Portia, use guile to subvert her father's will. She plays her assigned role straight. Her voice registers a plangent fear in 'O me, the word "choose"!' (I.ii.19) yet rises to ecstatic crescendos at news that Bassanio has come to try his fortune. Credulous, dutiful, unselfconscious, she is very much a young woman in love. There is passion in her relationship with Bassanio, and the intensity of their attraction bids us to get caught up in the fiction of the three caskets and, at least for the moment, to put our moral misgivings aside – even to the point of accepting Bassanio as a suitor fully worthy of her.

Their climactic scene together does justice to the plot's fairy-tale premises by creating genuine suspense: will the handsome prince win the princess bride or be condemned forever to a life of celibacy? Bassanio comes on stage nervous with anticipation, pacing back and forth and breathing like an athlete about to run a race. His eagerness is matched by Portia's. She, now pretty in pink, enters breathlessly to him and, with comic zeal, holds him back from the caskets on the line, 'I pray you tarry' (III.ii.1); there is further laughter when she adds, 'I would detain you here some month or two' (9). And detain him she does, with her own crisis of conscience. 'I could teach you/ How to choose right' (10-11), she admits, speaking the line with gravity, as if weighing the price of sin and, suddenly ashamed of herself, opting for obedience to her father instead: 'but then I am forsworn./ So will I never be' (11-12). All the while, Bassanio grows increasingly restive, trying to sneak a look at the caskets over her shoulder.

His complaint, 'Let me choose,/ For as I am, I live upon the rack' (24-5), thus takes on a comic dimension because their youthful exuberance is working at cross-purposes: she has physically restrained him from discovering his own destiny, and hers. We momentarily forget that this Bassanio is motivated in part by desire for Portia's money and may be sexually linked to Antonio as well: here, he is simply a young man in love, vigorous and hot. When Portia tells him, 'If you do love me, you will find me out' (41), he strides downstage, 'squaring up to the caskets on which his fate depends as if to a feat of supreme athleticism', according to Stanley Wells (*Shakespeare Survey* 41 (1988) 165), the anxiety palpable as he sinks to his knees before them and flexes his arms like a wrestler.

The analogy to an athletic feat is apt. Portia, now standing with her back to Bassanio, raises her right arm when he rejects the gold and her left when he rejects the silver: together, her outstretched arms signal victory to the crowd of spectators behind her. Bassanio's exclamation when he opens the lead casket, 'What find I here?/ Fair Portia's counterfeit!' (114-15), thus provokes a trumpet fanfare and a spontaneous cheer from the crowd. Such acclaim prompts him to say that he feels like an athlete contending for a prize, who, 'Hearing applause and universal shout,/Giddy in spirit, still gaz[es] in a doubt/ Whether those peals of praise be his or no' (143-5): the staging brings Bassanio's simile to life. Portia, going to him, lays his doubt to rest, and he claims the prize with two kisses – tentative, awkward kisses that reveal his inexperience in love. In seeking a contemporary analogue for the hero and heroine of romance, therefore, Alexander happily landed on the athlete and the cheerleader. By allowing us to regard Portia and Bassanio in this way – as athletic, exuberant, and innocent – he involves us emotionally in their plot much as we might feel involved at a football match, and thereby momentarily deflects our critical judgement of their values.

Innocence characterises everything Portia does. It is especially evident in her attitudes towards marriage and money. The speech in which she offers herself to Bassanio – 'You see me, Lord Bassanio, where I stand,/ Such as I am' (149-50) – is spoken with a firm conviction that Bassanio has every right to her and her wealth, and she, no rights at all. This is an unironic Portia whose notions of women's subservience to men are deeply ingrained. Bassanio, more interested in her person than her speech, tries to stop her lips with a kiss when she exalts him as 'her lord, her governor, her king' (165), but she holds him off until she has formally relinquished all her power: 'Myself, and what is mine, to you and yours/ Is now converted' (166-7). Furthermore, she treats her inheritance as if it were play money. This is certainly the case when, on hearing that Bassanio is in debt to Antonio for three thousand ducats, she rises, smiles, then asks off-handedly, 'What, no more?' (297). Her ensuing lines betray the smug confidence of one for whom money has always been a remedy for everything: 'Pay him six thousand ... Double six thousand, and then treble that' (298-9). Her magnanimity is tinged with the superciliousness of one who has never known want.

Portia simply does not understand the nature of the bond: this becomes abundantly clear at the trial, where she matter-of-factly instructs Shylock in the need for charity, reading him a lesson as if by rote – 'The quality of mercy is not *strained*' – and naïvely assuming that he will see things her way. For such a Portia, the sentiments of this great speech are not rhapsodic – here is no music in her soul – but perfunctory, commonplace, even mundane. Her delivery, according to Maureen Paton (*Daily Express*, 29 April 1988), resembles that of a Sunday School teacher lecturing on Christian obligations to a recalcitrant pupil. If Portia honours these obligations, then so should Shylock: of this she has no doubt. Such cultural solipsism betrays the narrowness of her ideology; for however well-intentioned, she is insensible of what others feel or think. Her morality is untried in the crucible of the world. And in this, Bassanio is her match. When he offers Shylock double the money – *her* money – to let Antonio go, he demonstrates how oblivious he is to what is really at stake at the trial.

In Alexander's interpretation, then, Portia and Bassanio become the children of Thatcher's Britain and Reagan's America. Secure in their privilege and cavalier in their prejudices, they pursue material goals mindless of anything but their own desert. They are Christians in form but not in substance: charity and mercy, for them, are not spiritual duties but social obligations, manifestations of a modern *noblesse oblige*. Such, Alexander seems to suggest (with a political bias for which young RSC directors are noted), is the legacy of conservative governments: an affirmation that the monied classes may do as they please with scant regard for the rights and beliefs of those they tread on. In a significant way, his Belmontese lovers display the naïve confidence of bright young people who prospered in the 1980s, and their behaviour is made to seem excusable, even engaging, by the earnestness of their convictions.

The materialism of their marriage is brilliantly represented by the caskets themselves: gold, silver and lead boxes in the shape of miniature Palladian villas (see photograph 8). Presumably they are replicas of the 'fair mansion' in which Portia lives and which she will happily turn over to her husband: 'This house, these servants, and this same myself/ Are yours, my lord's' (170-1). These caskets, then, signify the true prize – Portia's inheritance – that inspired Bassanio's quest in the first place, a quest whose material goals Alexander has only briefly allowed us to forget. When Bassanio wins Portia, he wins the house too, and all that goes with it. Their romance is thus a means to a most material end. The exquisite little villas, strategically placed at the front of the stage, keep insisting on their own importance; in tangible terms, they promise Bassanio access to the power Portia's father once held. By visually reinforcing the ways in which money and class underpin their romance, therefore, Alexander advances a socialist interpretation of Shakespeare's text inspired by the obsessive materialism of his own society.

The three caskets, furthermore, are placed on a large crane that bears a remarkable resemblance to scales. Rising through a trap in the platform, these giant scales ask us to consider the relative value of each metal– gold, silver and lead – but here they are balanced, each casket apparently of equal weight. Metaphorically, then, these scales imply the risk of choice – of weighing options, of calculating profit and loss. They remind us of how business is done in the souk where Shylock, scales by his side, has bargained for his pound of flesh; and they anticipate the trial, where he will bring those scales to weigh Antonio's forfeiture. Scales thus become a symbol for the kindred impulses that motivate gamblers in commerce and in love, in Venice and in Belmont. They may weigh flesh or caskets: either way, they signify the means by which human beings achieve power over one another. Ultimately, they signify the scales of a dubious justice that will bring Shylock down.

With an expressive force born of great visual economy, therefore, Alexander uses stage images to symbolise the ideologies of Venice and Belmont. The Madonna icon, Bible and Prayer Book, crucifixes and chains all express the power of institutionalised religion, just as the graffito Star of David and yellow badges signify the impotence of those victimised by that religion. Miniature Palladian villas and scales represent the material world for which Venetians are willing to hazard all they have; and costuming defines characters' standing within, or without, that world. In short, Alexander uses such images to define the culturally sanctioned bigotry and violence he finds implicit in Shakespeare's text. Dominated by the Church, the playworld he creates assumes that male hegemony and class privilege are God-given rights. That world promotes material acquisition, condones anti-Semitism and other forms of racism, values women only as they provide men with access to power, and fosters homosexual cliquishness. Such a world conditions its victims to respond in understandable ways: Shylock to seek violent revenge, Jessica to crave an assimilation she cannot have, Portia and Nerissa unquestioningly to capitulate to male authority. The problem Alexander creates for his audience is how to balance a rational appraisal of this world against an affective response to those who people it.

Modern audiences, their memories of the Holocaust still fresh, are more than willing to embrace the comforting vision of Shylock as a patrician Jew established by Irving over a century ago and recently recreated by Olivier. That tradition offers us a chance to identify with an isolated and persecuted alien, to deplore the narrow-mindedness of a Venetian society that exploits and rejects him, and from a safe distance to congratulate ourselves on our own – and Shakespeare's – moral enlightenment. Such productions make bigotry a failing of individuals: the Venetians simply have made the wrong moral choices, choices we would never repeat. Alexander's *Merchant* calls precisely that conception of bigotry into question: it assumes that for all our good intentions, for all our rhetoric of tolerance, deeply ingrained and unacknowledged cultural stereo-types continue to shape our responses to racial, religious, and sexual otherness. In this production, bigotry is portrayed as an ideological system that influences people at fundamental levels, preserving cultural difference because the alien serves to define, by his very exclusion, the normalcy and homogeneity of the rest of society. To declare oneself free of the influence of ideology – a classic gesture of western humanism – is to indulge a dangerous fiction: Alexander will have none of it. By making visceral his bourgeois audience's discomfort with swarthy Semites and closet queens, he dramatises the subtle and finally violent effects of ideology and thereby denies us the smug satisfaction that moral distance would allow.

CHAPTER VII

Shylock and the pressures of history

In performance, perhaps no play by Shakespeare has been subject to the pressures of history – or, in the words of Jonathan Miller, 'held hostage to contemporary issues' (*New York Times*, 22 February 1981) – more forcibly than *The Merchant of Venice*. Particularly since Irving's landmark production of 1879, treatment of Shylock has focused the attention of western audiences on the question of whether the play is anti-Semitic. Does Shakespeare, in Shylock, promote a comic Jewish stereotype or overturn that stereotype with a broader appeal to humanist values? Does he pander to Elizabethan prejudice against Jews as bloodthirsty villains, or expose the Christians as hypocrites and the Jew as their victim? In light of these insistent questions, no production of *The Merchant* can be politically or socially disinterested. In our own century, the play has aroused more passion and prompted more theatrical extremism than any other Shakespearean comedy. Political regimes have been known to appropriate the play to further their own agendas: most notoriously, during the 1930s the Third Reich exploited it as comic propaganda against those Jews who – hook-nosed devils all, intent on bringing Germany to financial ruin – were being herded toward the Final Solution (Wulf, pp. 280-3), even as the play was staged in Palestine in 1936 by expatriate German-Jewish director Leopold Jessner to document the history of oppression against which European Jews like himself had struggled (Oz, pp. 167-71). Such extremes indicate how pervasively historical and cultural determinants have shaped the meanings of *The Merchant*.

Fear that the play might arouse anti-Semitic feeling has been especially pronounced in North America, where virtually any production may be greeted with irate letters to editors and protests by Jewish groups. The mere announcement that PBS intended to air the BBC *Merchant* in 1981 elicited calls for its cancellation. Morris Schappes, editor of *Jewish Currents*, argued that the very least PBS could do in compensation would be 'to mount swiftly an educational effort to demonstrate the evil of anti-Semitism today' (*New York Times*, 27 January 1981); and the Anti-Defamation League of the B'nai B'rith, citing a recent upsurge in anti-Semitic incidents, accused the producers of abdicating those 'social responsibilities demanded when staging a controversial presentation with an inherent potential for harm' (*New York Times*, 22 February 1981). Such protests have had long-term consequences for staging *The Merchant* in North America: seldom since the Holocaust has a production treated Shylock unsympathetically. As John Houseman admitted of his years as director of the American Shakespeare Theatre, 'we would not have had the nerve to do that play if we hadn't a completely sympathetic Shylock' (R. Cooper, pp. 46-7).

Occasionally critics have objected to a director's apparent capitulation. Michael Langham, for instance, was accused of bowing to pressure from the Canadian Jewish Congress to drop several offensive passages from his distinguished production for the Stratford, Ontario, Festival in 1989. A furore arose particularly over his excision of Shylock's forced conversion to Christianity (*The Toronto Star*, 18 May 1989). Langham, explaining that he had made the same cuts in a production for the Folger Shakespeare Library in Washington the previous year, claimed that he had omitted Shylock's conversion not because any Jewish group had pressured him to do so, but because, for modern audiences, 'this compulsory rejection of the Jewish faith takes on the odor of brutal racism'. It would, he said, have risked making Shylock 'a martyred victim', thus nullifying the impact of Portia's mercy and the Christian affirmations of Act V. Yet there is a curious paradox in Langham's self-defence: his ostensible reason for omitting Shylock's conversion – that it might draw sympathy to the Jew and away from the Christians – is antithetical to the reason directors usually give, that the conversion might provoke an anti-Semitic backlash in the audience. Reviewers were unconvinced. Some regarded Langham's cuts (which also included Portia's racist remarks about Morocco and Lancelot Gobbo's teasing Jessica about being damned as a Jew) as tantamount to 'self-censorship ... a regrettable nod in the direction of the book-burners' (*Elmira Independent*, 14 July 1989); and their complaints probably were justified, for such omissions suppress the potential of the play to confront audiences with images of racial intolerance that may be a part of their cultural history.

The controversy surrounding Langham's production brings into focus the problem of how to stage an acceptable *Merchant* for contemporary audiences. Wary, perhaps, of being accused of insensitivity to Jewish feeling, directors have frequently sanitised the text, exorcising the play's more blatant racism and offering, in place of the comic stage Jew in vogue between the wars, a Shylock more befitting a post-Holocaust sensibility. Certainly this was the case in Germany after 1945, where the play was tactfully rehabili-tated by directors – many of whom had suffered under the Third Reich – who offered a Shylock of such tragic dignity that he 'came nearer to Lessing's *Nathan* than to Shakespeare's revenge-craving usurer' and thus allowed the Nazi propaganda piece once again to enter the repertory as 'a sensitive reflector of a nation's conscious-ness of guilt' (Verch, pp. 84-8). In Israel, too, heroic portrayals of Shylock have served as touchstones in the forging of a national Jewish identity. The one attempt by an Israeli director to portray Shylock as a medievalised Jew, shrewd, grasping, and currish (Tel Aviv, 1972) was roundly attacked by the nationalistic press as a throwback to the vicious stereotype that had made 'Shylock' a household word (Oz, pp. 173-5).

The idea of interpreting *The Merchant* as a tragedy of Jewish oppression first took root in England. It was nourished by the Victorians' fascination with alien cultures and blossomed in productions by Henry Irving and his disciples. Such interpretations, despite challenges by Poel, Komisarjevsky and others to reclaim the play as comedy, lasted well into the twentieth century; and recently they have flowered again in productions which have paid homage, directly or indirectly, to their Victorian forebears. In his Berlin production of 1963, for example, Erwin Piscator deliberately recreated the contrasts of Irving's *Merchant* between a sober Renaissance Ghetto and a comically light-hearted Belmont – and, more tellingly, between a profoundly human Shylock, played by veteran Jewish tragedian Ernst Deutsch, and the frivolously amoral Christians whose discrimination against him culminated in his tragic collapse at the trial and subsequent heroic exit in the manner of Irving (Verch, p. 87). Piscator's staging anticipated Jonathan Miller's self-consciously 'Victorian' *Merchant* for the National Theatre in 1970 in which Laurence Olivier, as we have seen, played Shylock as a direct descendant of Irving and George Arliss – a very gentle Jew indeed. In America, Victorian stage traditions have been resuscitated most successfully by Morris Carnovsky, who performed the role with remarkable fidelity to Irving on several occasions, arguing that Shylock was a decent man with great nobility and loftiness of character (Carnovsky, pp. 21-8). In one notable production at Stratford, Connecticut (1957), Carnovsky allowed his bid for tragic pathos to contest the spirited comedy of Katherine Hepburn's Portia – much as Irving's had contested Ellen Terry's – even to the point of borrowing Irving's most famous melodramatic interpolation for the first-act curtain. Returing home from dining with the Christians, he spied a mask left by a reveller, grew apprehensive, then shoved it aside when he noticed that the door of his house was ajar: as he entered the house – to discover that Jessica had fled – the curtain fell (R. Cooper, p. 47). This traditional appeal for audience sympathy had been abandoned in Britain before the war; typically, in America it lingered.

Other American productions have contended with the Jewish question without resorting to such antiquated stage traditions. In a revival at Lincoln Center in 1973, director Ellis Rabb, sensitive to the risks of staging *The Merchant* before a heavily Jewish New York audience, chose to foreground modes of cultural alienation that were at once recognisable but heavily stylised. His Venice recalled the world of Fellini's *La Dolce Vita*, all cocktail bars, sunglasses, beach chairs and bikinis (*Daily News*, 5 March 1973). Belmont itself became a yacht at anchor, a pleasure-toy of the idle rich. Rabb thus created 'an atmosphere charged with languorous hedonism, decadence, and voluptuous money lust' (*Newsweek*, 19 March 1973); and contributing to that atmosphere were James Tilton's black-and-white projections of a Venice crumbling, decaying, and sinking into the sea, 'a visual metaphor for contemporary civilisation' (*After Dark*, May 1973, pp. 43-4). Such stylisation yielded a *Verfremdungseffekt* characteristic of Rabb's whole approach to the play. His actors conveyed boredom, ennui and alienation from one another and from the roles they played. The prickly homosexual relationship between Antonio and Bassanio, for example, clearly affected Bassanio's marriage to Portia who, as a sophisticated older woman, was keenly aware that her young husband was bound to another man. Even the trial was 'twisted to serve the bisexual romantic triangulation imposed on the text' (*Christian Science Monitor*, 5 March 1973). Jessica quarreled with Lorenzo, who drunkenly slapped her during the love duet opening Act V – to Clive Barnes they seemed 'more like Edward Albee haters than Shakespearean lovers' (*New York Times*, 5 March 1973); and the game of rings, which in a conventional production brings the lovers full circle, instead underscored loss, suspicion, and the unlikelihood that these marriages would last.

In striking contrast to this degenerate group, Sydney Walker's unsentimental, business-like Shylock was dignified not so much by heroic acting as by sober restraint. In a dark suit, grey gloves and Homburg, he resembled, in the eyes of one critic, Bernard Baruch (*Newsweek*, 19 March 1973); and for most, 'his sincerity, austerity, uprightness, and moral perception formed an edifying contrast to the triviality and shallowness of the Christians' (*New York Times*, 11 March 1973). The word 'edifying' alerts us to Rabb's Brechtian didacticism, and nowhere was his intention clearer than in an interpolated masque leading up to Jessica's elopement. Such masques, as we have seen, provided festive and often spectacular interludes in nineteenth-century *Merchants* – comic revelry that enhanced the pathos of Shylock's return to an empty house. Rabb, on the other hand, used his masque to illustrate the violent effects of religious persecution on minorities – Jews and women. He staged it as a Black Mass, 'a phantasmagorical, sacrilegious orgy' of men in drag during which a large cross was borne across the stage by an erotically suffering Christ. At its climax, when Jessica approached the cross to signal her conversion, 'the revelers leaped at her and tore her blouse off – presumably in order to show her, and us, just what it was she had really converted to' (*New York Times*, 11 March 1973). This atavistic attack on Jessica, a far cry from what Shakespeare's text suggests her elopement with a Christian might be, vividly demonstrates how Rabb used *The Merchant* to indict a decadent society (American, perhaps?) that would rape anyone who dared resist its pleasures.

※

Those who believe in an 'essentialist' Shakespeare – a recoverable and authoritative historical standard against which performances should be measured – may of course object that such interpolations distort the play by imposing contemporary concerns on it. Indeed, critics complained that by disparaging the Christians and ennobling the Jews, Rabb's production, like Miller's, actually reversed the sympathies Shakespeare's text cultivates. As I have tried to suggest, however, the complexities of that text, and our uncertainty of how it was originally performed, should preclude us from making any such judgements. Furthermore, events of the past century have attached new meanings to events within the play and have compelled audiences to view *The Merchant* through the lens of Jewish history. Arnold Wesker, whose anti-establishment plays such as *Chips with Everything* have won him a wide following in London and New York, posed a question that has vexed many directors: how much historical burden can Shakespeare's text be made to bear? Finding the play inescapably anti-Semitic – 'because here is a Jew who against all humanity persists in claiming his pound of flesh' (*New York Times*, 22 February 1981) – Wesker implied that productions such as Miller's and Rabb's encumbered the text with more cultural baggage than it could comfortably carry. Yet, as a Jew, he was sympathetic with their aims; recalling his response to Miller's production, he admitted that 'when Portia suddenly got to the bit about having a pound of flesh but no blood, it flashed on me that the kind of Jew I know would stand up and say "Thank God!"' (*Guardian Weekend*, 29 August 1981, p. 9). And so, like a modern-day Granville, he took it upon himself to fit the play to the temper of the times.

His adaptation, simply titled *The Merchant*, had its English-speaking première in New York in 1977. Directed by John Dexter, it featured a genially cultured Shylock (originally played by Zero Mostel, who died during the tryout) who, as a scholar, a collector of rare books, and a patron of the arts, has a humanist's faith that knowledge – the wisdom of the ancients – can save man-kind from itself: 'Knowledge, like underground springs, fresh and constant there, till one day – up! Bubbling! For dying men to drink, for survivors from dark and terrible times. I love it!' (1.7, p. 233.) Wesker's depiction of the Ghetto smells of the library. It is so doggedly authentic, so full of self-conscious references to the Venice of 1563 – to the new science, to printing presses and men of letters, to art and architecture, and to expatriate Portuguese Jews who sought refuge there – that the play at times resembles a scholarly apologia for Jewish culture with Shylock serving as Wesker's mouthpiece. In effect, Wesker revised Shakespeare's text to meet the criteria of the late-nineteenth-century naturalism that Miller had attempted to impose on it; and where Miller had found the text resistant to such imposition, Wesker skirted the problem by rewriting it as a 'problem play' in the vein of Ibsen – the play Miller perhaps wished Shakespeare had written.

The dramatic fulcrum of Wesker's *Merchant* is the relationship between Shylock and Antonio. As in Miller's production, they are two genteel old men who physically resemble one another; but where in Shakespeare they are antagonists, Wesker makes them fellows in enlightenment who cross accepted social (and Ghetto) boundaries to indulge their friendship. When Antonio needs to borrow three thousand ducats to supply an arrogant godson whom he barely knows, Shylock wants to lend them without security, as an act of friendship. Antonio, however, sensible that Jews need the protection of the law, insists on drawing up a bond; therefore Shylock – perhaps taking his lead from Olivier's Shylock, who proposed the bond not in spite but in sport – suggests that they sign an agreement so absurd that it will mock the Venetian law which refuses to sanction friendship between Jews and Christians. Shylock thus makes a political point, and Antonio concurs with it: 'the bond is their protest against the oppressive laws of Venice and, beyond that, against the whole, well-attested history of European persecution of Jews, occurring most viciously at the time of the play's action in Portugal' (Sinfield, pp. 137-8).

When the bond is forfeit, of course neither man wants to abide by its terms. Both try to raise the sum to pay it off; failing that, they may comfort themselves that the court will, if they wish, relieve them of the bond. But Wesker allows no easy solution. He creates a moral dilemma that hinges on Shylock's responsibility to (and for) the Jewish community – and, in so doing, he demonstrates an awareness that for four centuries Shylock has been made to shoulder that responsibility. In a climactic scene, Shylock's sister Rivka reminds him that there is more at stake than Antonio's friendship. As she defines his dilemma,

> To save a citizen's life the court *will* relieve you of your bond. You do *know* that don't you? ... They will even let you bend the law and lend him further ducats for repayment when the hour is passed. You do *know* that, don't you? ... More! They'll wait days, weeks, even months. But – and here your moral problem begins – not everyone in the Ghetto will agree to the bending of the law ... Some may. Some may even beg you to do that rather than have the blood of a Christian on their hands. But others will say, no! Having bent the law for us, how often will they bend it for themselves and then we'll live in even greater uncertainties than before. They'll be divided, as you are, my clever brother. Who to save – your poor people or your poor friend? You can't see that? ... It's not only your problem now, it's the community's. (2.3, pp. 242-3.)

What follows is an irony worthy of Ibsen. Irritated by Shylock's avoidance of choice, Antonio himself forces Shylock to recognise that for the sake of defending the rights of Jews – Jews who fear the consequences of legal precedent – they must hold to the terms of the bond, even though it will mean death for both of them: Antonio's at the hands of Shylock, and Shylock's at the hands of the court. Antonio affirms his understanding of Shylock's dilemma in a remarkable show of unity with him. 'Your yellow hat belongs to both of us,' he says. 'I'm party to the mockery as well' (p. 246).

This revision of the bond plot redeems Shylock from his barbaric lust for a pound of Christian flesh – a motive from which no production of Shakespeare can, according to Wesker, fully exculpate him. It dramatically fulfils the desire of many recent directors to rewrite the play as a tragedy of Jewish oppression. In his most daring appropriation of Shakespeare's text, Wesker places 'Hath not a Jew eyes' – his only direct quotation of Shakespeare – in the mouth of Lorenzo, a supercilious pedant (much like Miller's) who delivers it at the trial purportedly to defend the 'humanity' of Jews while condemning only their *practice* of usury, thereby drawing a specious distinction between doer and deed which for generations has served to mask racial prejudice. Shylock is justifiably incensed by Lorenzo's presumption: 'I will not have my humanity mocked and apologised for. If I am unexceptionally like any man then I need no exceptional portraiture. I merit no special pleas, no special cautions, no special gratitudes. My humanity is my right, not your bestowed and gracious privilege.' (2.5, p. 259)

In its context in *The Merchant of Venice*, as Alan Sinfield argues, this famous speech seems 'to manifest the transcendent humanism which is otherwise hard to find in the play' (p. 139); but Wesker's Shylock, by condemning it as a condescending plea for a humanity which should be taken for granted, reveals the tragic irony of the use to which not only the speech, but the whole of *The Merchant of Venice* has been put by ostensibly tolerant societies. Wesker glosses Shakespeare's lines as themselves a contribution to anti-Semitic mythology. By incorporating them in a new context which encourages us to hear them as such, he both acknowledges and unsettles Shakespeare's cultural authority.

✳

If Wesker, however indirectly, exposes Shakespeare's text as both a product and a cause of anti-Semitism, others have more blatantly implicated *The Merchant of Venice* in the history of Jewish oppression by calling into question the purposes for which it has been performed. German director George Tabori's production for the Stockbridge (Massachusetts) Playhouse in 1966 is a case in point. Though Tabori used Shakespeare's text, his production was even more revisionary than Wesker's: it devastatingly indicted the play as a weapon used by hegemonic societies against the Jews. Influenced by Peter Weiss's violently meta-theatrical *Marat/Sade* (1964), Tabori staged *The Merchant* as a play within a play, performed by the inmates of a German concentration camp before an audience of Nazi soldiers for whom the play presumably provided good anti-Semitic entertainment. As Shylock, Alvin Epstein wore the false nose and red beard that characterised the devilish Jew of Mystery plays and stage Shylocks of the Third Reich. According to one reviewer, however, 'the role was conceived with a double edge: on the surface, Epstein was a craven caricature of the Jew as comic villain, complete with whining accent and exaggerated hand gestures ... but just beneath the top layer of this Jewish Uncle Tom was a hostile inmate of a prison camp desperately seeking revenge' (*Judaism* 16 (1967) 463). At certain moments, Epstein would remove the nose, drop the accent, and begin in his own persona, that of inmate, to address Shakespeare's lines antagonistically to the Nazi officers who had been strategically placed on stage and among the audience. 'When it became apparent that the nameless inmate playing Shylock was ready to go at the German guards with his bare hands the rest of the acting company had to...restrain him' (*Juadism*, p. 464) – a disturbing image of Jews suppressing Jews. Such violation of theatrical decorum reached a climax during the trial scene, when Shylock, suddenly discovered to be wielding a real knife, assaulted a prison guard: in the ensuing scuffle, he was pinned down by the guards and killed – the probable fate, audiences were well aware, of all the inmates performing the play. An improvised curtain of potato sacks was then hastily drawn across the stage.

Shorn of Belmont, magic and moonlight, Tabori's *Merchant* focused exclusively on the degradation to which Jews were subjected in being forced to perform a play that, as an artifact of historical anti-Semitism, may have contributed to their present victimisation. The actors thus became victims of both Shakespeare's play and the Aryan oppressors who watched it. According to Michael Shapiro, Tabori revealed 'the potential Holocaust' which history has shown 'lurking at the heart of the play' (*Shofar*, p. 8). Shakespeare's text was viewed in light of – and was made to bear a responsibility for – historical events. By refashioning it as political theatre, Tabori eerily recalled its use in Hitler's Germany to fuel anti-Jewish sentiment.

Tabori's production imaginatively invoked and contained the most odious moment in *The Merchant*'s stage history. The Pirandellian device by which he confused the inner play – Shakespeare's play – with the outer play (the plight of the Jewish inmates) distanced the audience by fixing the historical moment of performance, but at the same time encouraged the audience to respond to *The Merchant* itself as a cultural document with political and social resonances. When Tabori restaged it in his native Germany twelve years later (1978), those resonances grew even stronger. Here, the performance venue was not a theatre but the former boiler room of the Munich Kammerspiele; the camp was identified as nearby Dachau; and the role of Shylock was shared among thirteen different inmates, who thus formed a *group* of German actors collectively 'struggling with and acting out' the guilt of Germany's anti-Semitic past (Verch, p. 89). Tabori succeeded in recreating for *The Merchant* a historical context that apparently, for German audiences, lent the play great contemporary significance. Jerome McGann has observed that the 'focus upon history as constituted in what we call "the past" only achieves its critical fulfilment when that study of the past reveals its significance in and for the present and the future' (p. 25). Tabori's Munich production, according to Maria Verch, achieved such fulfilment: of all recent stagings of *The Merchant* in Germany, it 'was the one which had moved furthest from its Shakespearean source and nearest to a psycho-analytic medium in its approach to the unresolved problems of the past' (p. 89).

One may object, of course, that a production so far removed from its Shakespearian source is no longer *The Merchant of Venice*, but the director's play. In a sense, however, isn't *any* production of *The Merchant* the director's play? Irving's, Komisarjevsky's, Miller's, Rabb's and Alexander's all have likewise been called 'unfaithful' to Shakespeare; but this, of course, begs the question of whose Shakespeare they have been unfaithful to. Because Shakespeare has traditionally, and certainly since Irving, been constructed as a purveyor of liberal humanist values, directors have resorted to the various means detailed in this volume – from cutting and updating on the one hand, to recreating what they imagine to have been the original conditions of performance on the other – to make *The*

Merchant reflect those values. They have intervened to save 'their' Shakespeare from the embarrassing stigma of anti-Semitism. Tabori, therefore, may be regarded as having simply moved further along the scale of directorial intervention; and in so far as he intervened to have Shakespeare speak to his nation's consciousness, he revitalised *The Merchant* and invested it with a topical power it otherwise might have lacked.

If such intervention allows a play to speak in new ways to its audience, would Shakespeare have complained? He knew the extent to which any successful production depends on the receptivity of audiences to the material being dramatised; as playwright, actor, and sharer, he knew that the proof of a play was in performance – what drew audiences to the theatre. And for four hundred years *The Merchant* has drawn audiences. It has worn masks in which they have seen themselves; it has spoken to them in many voices on matters of race, religion, gender and social value; it has served as a Rorschach test of cultural difference. For better and worse, it has entered our historical consciousness as no other Shakespearian comedy has, converging with the pressures of history to yield meanings Shakespeare could never have imagined. Such meanings have sometimes been said to distort the play; seldom, however, has the play suffered on that account. Its adaptability, in fact, may above all else explain why, when the fortunes of other comedies have waxed and waned, the popularity of *The Merchant* has remained constant.

BIBLIOGRAPHY

Anonymous, *Critical Notes on Shylock as Played by Sir Henry Irving*, British Theatre Museum, n.d.

Beauman, Sally, *The Royal Shakespeare Company: A History of Ten Decades*, New York, 1982.

Berry, Ralph, 'Komisarjevsky at Stratford-upon-Avon', *Shakespeare Survey* 36 (1983), 73-84.

Biggs, Murray, 'A neurotic Portia', *Shakespeare Survey* 25 (1972), 153-9.

Billington, Michael, *The Modern Actor*, London, 1973.

Booth, Michael R., 'Pictorial acting and Ellen Terry', in *Shakespeare on the Victorian Stage*, ed. Richard Foulkes, Cambridge, 1986, pp. 78-86.

Brereton, Austin, *The Life of Henry Irving*, 2 vols., London, 1908.

Brown, John Russell, ed., *The Merchant of Venice*, New Arden Series, London, 1955.

—, 'The Realization of Shylock' in *Early Shakespeare* (Stratford-upon-Avon Studies 3), London, 1961, pp. 187-209.

Bulman, James C., 'The BBC Shakespeare and "House Style"', *Shakespeare Quarterly* 35 (1984), 571-81.

Carnovsky, Morris, 'On playing the role of Shylock', in *The Merchant of Venice*, ed. Francis Fergusson, New York, 1958.

Cohen, Derek, *Shakespearean Motives*, New York, 1988.

Cohen, Walter, '"The Merchant of Venice" and the possibilities of historical criticism', *English Literary History* 49 (1982), 765-89.

Cohn, Ruby, 'Shakespeare left', *Theatre Journal* 40:1 (March 1988), 48-60.

Cooper, John R., 'Shylock's humanity', *Shakespeare Quarterly* 21 (1970), 117-24.

Cooper, Roberta Krensky, *The American Shakespeare Theatre: Stratford 1955-1985*, Washington, D.C., 1986.

Cottrell, John, *Laurence Olivier*, London, 1975.

Craig, Edward Gordon, *Henry Irving*, London, 1930.

Danson, Lawrence, *The Harmonies of 'The Merchant of Venice'*, New Haven, 1978.

Dessen, Alan C., 'The Elizabethan stage Jew and Christian example: Gerontus, Barabas, and Shylock', *Modern Language Quarterly* 35 (1974), 231-45.

Draper, John W., 'Usury in "The Merchant of Venice"', *Modern Philology* 33 (1935), 37-47.

Eagleton, Terry, *William Shakespeare*, Oxford, 1986.

Ellis, Ruth, *The Shakespeare Memorial Theatre*, London, 1948.

Fenwick, Henry, 'The production', in *The Merchant of Venice*, BBC edition, London, 1980, pp. 17-26.

Fisch, Leon, *The Dual Image: A Study of the Figure of the Jew in English Literature*, London, 1959.

Fitzgerald, Percy, *Sir Henry Irving: A Biography*, London, 1906.
Foulkes, Richard, 'Helen Faucit and Ellen Terry as Portia,' *Theatre Notebook* 31:3 (1977), 27-37.
—, 'Henry Irving and Laurence Olivier as Shylock', *Theatre Notes* 27:1 (1972), 26-35.
—, ed., *Shakespeare and the Victorian Stage*, Cambridge, 1986.
—, 'The staging of the trial scene in Irving's "The Merchant of Venice", *Educational Theatre Journal* 28 (1976), 312-17.
Fraser, William, *Disraeli and His Day*, London, 1891.
Geary, Keith, 'The nature of Portia's victory: turning to men in "The Merchant of Venice"', *Shakespeare Survey* 37 (1984), 55-68.
Girard, Rene, '"To Entrap the Wisest": a reading of "The Merchant of Venice"', in *Literature and Society, Selected Papers from the English Institute*, ed. Edward Said, Baltimore, 1980, pp. 100-19.
Glassman, Bernard, *Anti-Semitic Stereotypes Without Jews: Images of Jews in England, 1290-1700*, Detroit, 1975.
Goldberg, Jonathan, 'Textual properties', *Shakespeare Quarterly* 37:2 (Summer 1986), 213-17.
Granville-Barker, Harley, *Prefaces to Shakespeare*, Second Series, London, 1930.
Greenblatt, Stephen, 'Marlowe, Marx, and anti-Semitism', *Critical Inquiry* 5 (1978), 291-307.
Grubb, James S., 'When myths lose power: four decades of Venetian historiography', *The Journal of Modern History* 58:1 (1986), 43-94.
Hattaway, Michael, *Elizabethan Popular Theatre: Plays in Performance*, London, 1982.
Hatton, Joseph, *Henry Irving's Impressions of America*, Vol. 1, London, 1884.
Hawkins, Harriet, *The Devil's Party: Critical Counter-Interpretations of Shakespearian Drama*, Oxford, 1985.
Hiatt, Charles, *Henry Irving: A Record and Review*, London, 1899.
Hinely, Jan Lawson, 'Bond priorities in "The Merchant of Venice"', *Studies in English Literature* 20 (1980), 217-39.
Holderness, Graham, 'Radical potentiality and institutional closure: Shakespeare in film and television', in *Political Shakespeare*, ed. Jonathan Dollimore and Alan Sinfield, Manchester, 1985, pp. 182-201; rpt. in *Shakespeare on Television*, ed. J. C. Bulman and H. R. Coursen, Hanover, 1988, pp. 69-75.
Hole, Richard, 'An apology for the character and conduct of Shylock', in *Essays by A Society of Gentlemen at Exeter*, London, 1796, pp. 552-73.
Honigmann, E. A. J., *The Stability of Shakespeare's Text*, London, 1965.
Howard, Jean E., 'The difficulties of closure: an approach to the problematic in Shakespearean comedy', in *Comedy from Shakespeare to Sheridan*, ed. A. R. Braunmuller and J. C. Bulman, Newark, Delaware, 1986, pp. 113-28.
Hughes, Alun, *Henry Irving Shakespearean*, Cambridge, 1981.
—, 'Henry Irving's tragedy of Shylock', *Educational Theatre Journal* 24 (1972), 249-68.
Irving, Henry, *The Drama: Addresses by Henry Irving*, New York, 1893; rpt. 1969.
—, *Mr. Henry Irving and Miss Ellen Terry in America: Opinions of the Press*, Chicago, 1884.

—, ed., *The Merchant of Venice: As Presented at the Lyceum Theatre under the Management of Mr. Henry Irving*, London, 1879.

Irving, Laurence, *Henry Irving: The Actor and His World*, London, 1951.

James, Henry, *The Scenic Art: Notes on Acting and the Drama, 1872- 1901*, New Brunswick, 1948.

Kahn, Coppelia, 'The cuckoo's note: male friendship and cuckoldry in "The Merchant of Venice"', in *Shakespeare's 'Rough Magic': Renaissance Essays in Honor of C. L. Barber*, ed. Peter Erickson and Coppelia Kahn, Newark, Delaware, 1985, pp. 104-12.

Kemp, T. C. and J. C. Trewin, *The Stratford Festival: A History of the Shakespeare Memorial Theatre*, Birmingham, 1953.

Komisarjevsky, Theodore, *The Costume of the Theatre*, London, 1931.

—, and Lee Simonson, *Settings and Costumes of the Modern Stage*, London, 1933.

—, *The Theatre and a Changing Civilisation*, London, 1935.

Lelyveld, Toby, *Shylock on the Stage*, Cleveland, 1960.

Mahood, M. M., ed., *The Merchant of Venice*, New Cambridge Shakespeare, 1987.

Marshall, F. A., ed., *The Henry Irving Shakespeare*, Vol. 3, London, 1892.

Martin, Theodore, *Helen Faucit (Lady Martin)*, Edinburgh and London, 1900.

McGann, Jerome, *The Beauty of Inflection: Historical Method and Theory*, Oxford, 1988.

Mennen, Richard E., 'Theodore Komisarjevsky's production of "The Merchant of Venice"', *Theatre Journal* 31:3 (1979), 386-97.

Miller, Jonathan, 'Director in interview: Jonathan Miller talks to Peter Ansorge', *Plays and Players* 17:6 (1970), 52-3, 59.

—, Interview by Ann Pasternak Slater, *Quarto: The Literary Review* 10 (September 1980), 9-12.

—, *Subsequent Performances*, London, 1986.

Moisan, Thomas, '"Which is the merchant here? and which the Jew?": subversion and recuperation in "The Merchant of Venice"', in *Shakespeare Reproduced: The Text in History and Ideology*, ed. Jean E. Howard and Marion F. O'Connor, New York, 1987, pp. 188- 206.

Moore, Edward M., 'Henry Irving's Shakespearean productions', *Theatre Survey* 17:2 (1976), 195-216.

Mulryne, J. R., 'History and myth in "The Merchant of Venice"', in *L'Europe de la Renaissance: Cultures et Civilisations*, Paris, 1988, pp. 325-41.

Odell, George C. D., *Shakespeare from Betterton to Irving*, 2 vols., New York, 1920.

Olivier, Laurence, *Confessions of an Actor*, London, 1982.

—, *On Acting*, London, 1986.

Overton, Bill, *Text and Performance: The Merchant of Venice*, London, 1987.

Oz, Avraham, 'Transformations of authenticity: "The Merchant of Venice" in Israel, 1936-1980', *Jahrbuch Deutsche Shakespeare Gesellschaft West*, 1983, pp. 166-77.

Perret, Marion D., 'Shakespeare and anti-Semitism: two television versions of "The Merchant of Venice"', *Mosaic* 16:1-2 (1983), 145-63, rpt. in *Shakespeare on Television*, ed. J. C. Bulman and H. R. Coursen, Hanover, 1988, pp. 156-68.

Pullen, Brian, 'The occupations and investments of the Venetian nobility in the middle and late sixteenth century', in *Renaissance Venice*, ed. J. R. Hale, London, 1973, pp. 379-408.

Richmond, Hugh, *Richard III*, Shakespeare in Performance Series, Manchester, 1989.

Robertson, W. Graham, *Time Was*, London, 1931.

Rowe, Nicholas, *The Works of Mr. William Shakespear*, London, 1709.

Rowell, George, 'A lyceum sketchbook', *Nineteenth Century Theatre Research* 6:1 (Spring 1978), 1-23.

Sanders, Wilbur, *The Dramatist and the Received Idea: Studies in the Plays of Marlowe and Shakespeare*, Cambridge, 1968.

Schlueter, June, 'Trivial pursuit: the casket plot in the Miller/Olivier "Merchant"', in *Shakespeare on Television*, ed. J. C. Bulman and H. R. Coursen, Hanover, 1988, pp. 169-74.

Scott, Clement, *From 'The Bells' to 'King Arthur'*, London, 1897.

Shapiro, Michael, *Boy Heroines in Male Disguise*, in manuscript.

—, 'Shylock the Jew onstage: past and present', *Shofar* (Winter 1986), 1-11.

Sher, Antony, 'Shaping up to Shakespeare: Antony Sher in Interview with Mark Lawson', *Drama* 4 (1987), 27-30.

Shewring, Margaret, 'A question of balance: Shakespeare's "The Merchant of Venice" on the nineteenth and twentieth century stage', in *L'Image de Venise au Temps de la Renaissance*, ed. M-T. Jones-Davies, Paris, 1989, pp. 87-111.

Sinfield, Alan, 'Making space: appropriation and confrontation in recent British plays', in *The Shakespeare Myth*, ed. Graham Holderness, Manchester, 1988, pp. 128-44.

Sinsheimer, Hermann, *Shylock: The History of a Character or The Myth of the Jew*, London, 1947.

Slater, Ann Pasternak, *Shakespeare the Director*, Brighton, 1982.

Spencer, Christopher, ed., *Five Restoration Adaptations of Shakespeare*, Urbana, 1965.

Stewart, Patrick, 'Playing Shylock', in *Players of Shakespeare: Essays in Shakespearean Performance by Twelve Players with the Royal Shakespeare Company*, ed. Philip Brockbank, Cambridge, 1985, pp. 11-28.

Stoker, Bram, *Personal Reminiscences of Henry Irving*, 2 vols., London, 1906.

Styan, J. L., *The Shakespeare Revolution: Criticism and Performance in the Twentieth Century*, Cambridge, 1977.

Sullivan, Patrick J., 'Strumpet wind: the National Theatre's "Merchant of Venice"', *Educational Theatre Journal* 26 (1974), 31-44.

Tennenhouse, Leonard, 'The counterfeit order of "The Merchant of Venice"', in *Representing Shakespeare: New Psychoanalytic Essays*, ed. Murray Schwartz and Coppelia Kahn, Baltimore, 1980, pp. 54-69.

Terry, Ellen, *Four Lectures on Shakespeare*, ed. Christopher St John, London, 1932.

—, *Ellen Terry's Memoirs*, ed. and with additional material by Edith Craig and Christopher St John, New York, 1932.

Thomson, Peter, *Shakespeare's Theatre*, London, 1983.

Trewin, J. C., *Shakespeare and the English Stage, 1900-1964*, London, 1964.

Verch, Maria, '"The Merchant of Venice" on the German stage since 1945', *Theatre History Studies* (1985), 84-94.

Wells, Stanley, 'Television Shakespeare', *Shakespeare Quarterly* 33 (Fall,

1982), 261-77; rpt. in *Shakespeare on Television*, ed. J. C. Bulman and H. R. Coursen, Hanover, 1988, pp. 41-9.

Wesker, Arnold, *Plays, Volume 4: The Journalists, The Wedding Feast, The Merchant*, Harmondsworth, 1980.

Williams, Raymond, *Drama in a Dramatised Society*, Cambridge, 1975.

Winter, William, *Henry Irving*, New York, 1885.

Wulf, Josef, *Theater und Film im Dritten Reich*, Berlin and Vienna, 1966; rpt. 1983.

Zimbardo, Rose, 'Understanding Shakespeare in the seventeenth and eighteenth centuries', in *Comedy from Shakespeare to Sheridan*, ed. A. R. Braunmuller and J. C. Bulman, Newark, Delaware, 1986, pp. 215-28.

Zitner, Sheldon, 'Wooden O's in plastic boxes', *University of Toronto Quarterly* 51 (Fall 1981), 1-12; rpt. in *Shakespeare on Television*, ed. J. C. Bulman and H. R. Coursen, Hanover, 1988, pp. 31-41.

APPENDIX

A. Some significant twentieth-century productions of
The Merchant of Venice

1901	Frank Benson	Stratford-upon-Avon
1907	William Poel	London
1908	Herbert Beerbohm Tree	London
1921	Max Reinhardt	Berlin
1922	David Belasco	New York
1928	Winthrop Ames	London
1932	Theodore Komisarjevsky	Stratford-upon-Avon
1936	Leopold Jessner	Tel Aviv
1938	John Gielgud	London
1948	Michael Benthall	Stratford-upon-Avon
1955	Tyrone Guthrie	Stratford, Ontario
1957	Jack Landau	Stratford, Connecticut
1962	Joseph Papp, Gladys Vaughan	New York
1963	Erwin Piscator	Berlin
1967	Michael Kahn	Stratford, Connecticut
1970	Jonathan Miller	London
1971	Terry Hands	Stratford-upon-Avon
1973	Ellis Rabb	New York
1978	Georg Tabori	Munich
1978	John Barton	Stratford-upon-Avon
1980	Jack Gold	BBC Television
1987	Bill Alexander	Stratford-upon-Avon
1989	Michael Langham	Stratford, Ontario
1989	Peter Hall	London; New York

Offshoots:

Charles Marowitz, *Variations on "The Merchant of Venice"*

1977	Charles Marowitz	London

Arnold Wesker, *The Merchant*

1977	John Dexter	New York

B. Major actors and staff for productions discussed in this volume

Lyceum Theatre, London, 1 November 1879
Director: Henry Irving Designer: Hawes Craven Music: Hamilton Clarke

Shylock	Henry Irving	*Morocco*	Frank Tyars
Antonio	Henry Forrester	*Tubal*	J. Carter
Portia	Ellen Terry	*Lancelot Gobbo*	Sam Johnson
Bassanio	J. H. Barnes	*Old Gobbo*	Clifford Cooper
Gratiano	Frank Cooper	*Salanio*	Arthur Elwood
Nerissa	Florence Terry	*Salarino*	Arthur Pinero
Jessica	Alma Murray	*Duke*	A. Beaumont
Lorenzo	N. Forbes		

Shakespeare Memorial Theatre, Stratford-upon-Avon, 25 July 1932
Director and designer: Theodore Komisarjevsky

Shylock	Randle Ayrton	*Morocco*	Stanley Howlett
Antonio	Wilfrid Walter	*Arragon*	Eric Maxon
Portia	Fabia Drake	*Tubal*	Kenneth Wicksteed
Bassanio	R. Eric Lee	*Lancelot Gobbo*	Bruno Barnabe
Gratiano	Gyles Isham	*Old Gobbo*	Geoffrey Wilkinson
Nerissa	Hilda Coxhead	*Solanio*	Richard Cuthbert
Jessica	Dorothy Francis	*Salarino*	Roy Byford
Lorenzo	Ernest Hare	*Duke*	Gerald Kay Souper

American Shakespeare Festival, Stratford, Connecticut, July 1957
Director: Jack Landau Set designer: Rouben Ter-Arutunian
Costume designer: Motley Music: Virgil Thomson

Shylock	Morris Carnovsky	*Bassanio*	Donald Harron
Antonio	Richard Waring	*Nerissa*	Lois Nettleton
Portia	Katherine Hepburn	*Morocco*	Earl Hyman

National Theatre, London, 28 April 1970; adapted for television 1973
Director: Jonathan Miller Set designer: Julia Trevelyan Oman

Shylock	Laurence Olivier	*Morocco*	Tom Baker
Antonio	Anthony Nicholls	*Arragon*	Charles Kay
Portia	Joan Plowright	*Tubal*	Lewis Jones
Bassanio	Jeremy Brett	*Lancelot Gobbo*	Jim Dale
Gratiano	Derek Jacobi	*Old Gobbo*	Harry Lomax
Nerissa	Anna Carteret	*Salerio*	Richard Kay
Jessica	Jane Lapotaire	*Solanio*	Michael Barnes
Lorenzo	Malcolm Reid	*Duke*	Benjamin Whitrow

Royal Shakespeare Theatre, Stratford-upon-Avon, 30 March 1971
Director: Terry Hands Set designer: Timothy O'Brien
Costume designers: Timothy O'Brien, Tazeena Firth
Music: Guy Woolfenden

Shylock	Emrys James	*Jessica*	Alison Fiske
Antonio	Tony Church	*Lorenzo*	David Calder
Portia	Judi Dench	*Morocco*	Bernard Lloyd
Bassanio	Michael Williams	*Arragon*	Derek Godfrey
Gratiano	Geoffrey Hutchings	*Tubal*	Jeffery Dench
Nerissa	Polly James	*Lancelot Gobbo*	Peter Geddis

Old Gobbo	Sydney Bromley	*Salarino*	Miles Anderson
Salerio	Anthony Pedley	*Duke*	Peter Woodthorpe
Solanio	Alton Kumalo		

Vivian Beaumont Theater, Lincoln Center, New York, 1 March 1973
Director: Ellis Rabb   Set designer: James Tilton
Costume designer: Ann Roth

Shylock	Sidney Walker	*Jessica*	Roberta Maxwell
Antonio	Josef Sommer	*Lorenzo*	Peter Coffield
Portia	Rosemary Harris	*Morocco*	Fred Morsell
Bassanio	Christopher Walken	*Arragon*	Alan Mandell
Gratiano	Philip Bosco	*Lancelot Gobbo*	Dan Sullivan
Nerissa	Olivia Cole		

The BBC TV Shakespeare, first broadcast 1980 (UK) and 1981 (USA)
Producer: Jonathan Miller   Director: Jack Gold
Set designer: Oliver Bayldon   Costume designer: Raymond Hughes

Shylock	Warren Mitchell		
Antonio	John Franklyn-Robbins	*Morocco*	Marc Zuber
		Arragon	Peter Gale
Portia	Gemma Jones	*Tubal*	Arnold Diamond
Bassanio	John Nettles	*Lancelot Gobbo*	Enn Reitel
Gratiano	Kenneth Cranham	*Old Gobbo*	Joe Gladwin
Nerissa	Susan Jameson	*Salerio*	John Rhys-Davies
Jessica	Leslee Udwin	*Solanio*	Alan David
Lorenzo	Richard Morant	*Duke*	Douglas Wilmer

Royal Shakespeare Theatre, Stratford-upon-Avon, 23 April 1987
Director: Bill Alexander   Set designer: Kit Surrey
Costume designer: Andreane Neofitou

Shylock	Antony Sher	*Morocco*	Hakeem Kae-Kazim
Antonio	John Carlisle	*Arragon*	Richard Conway
Portia	Deborah Findlay	*Tubal*	Bill McGuirk
Bassanio	Nicholas Farrell	*Lancelot Gobbo*	Phil Daniels
Gratiano	Geoffrey Freshwater	*Old Gobbo*	Arnold Yarrow
Nerissa	Pippa Guard	*Salerio*	Michael Cadman
Jessica	Deborah Goodman	*Solanio*	Gregory Doran
Lorenzo	Paul Spence	*Duke*	Richard Conway

Festival Stage, Stratford, Ontario, 8 May 1989
Director: Michael Langham   Designer: Desmond Heeley

Shylock	Brian Bedford	*Morocco*	Hubert Baron Kelly
Antonio	Nicholas Pennell	*Arragon*	Peter Donaldson
Portia	Seana McKenna	*Tubal*	Brian Tree
Bassanio	Geraint Wyn Davies	*Lancelot Gobbo*	Eric Coates
Gratiano	Paul Boretski	*Old Gobbo*	Ian White
Nerissa	Kim Horsman	*Salerio*	John Innes
Jessica	Susannah Hoffmann	*Solanio*	Bradley C. Rudy
Lorenzo	Andrew Dolha	*Duke*	Ian White

INDEX

Albee, Edward, 147
Alexander, Bill, 117-42, 152
American Shakespeare Theater, Stratford, Connecticut, 144, 146
Ames, Withrop, 51
anonymous account of Irving's Shylock, 34-8
Ansorge, Peter, 78, 84
anti-Semitism, history of in England, 16-22; in the late nineteenth century, 31-3; in the 1930s, 68-9, 72-4; origins of modern, 76-7; contemporary analogues for, 120-1, 124-5; in North America, 144-5; contribution of *The Merchant of Venice* to, 150-3
Arendt, Hannah, 76
Aristotle, 20
Arliss, George, 51, 80, 146
Ayrton, Randle, 68-70, 74

Bancroft family, 26-7, 39, 41
Barber, John, 3
Barnabe, Bruno, 59-61
Barnes, Clive, 147
Baruch, Bernard, 147
Bateman family, 29
Bayldon, Oliver, 109
BBC Television, 101-16, 144
Beckett, Samuel, *Waiting for Godot*, 104
Benson, Frank, 53, 54, 55, 68
Berliner Ensemble, 78; and Brechtian techniques, 146-7
Betterton, Thomas, 23
Billington, Michael, 92
B'nai B'rith, Anti-Defamation League of, 144
Booth, Edwin, 26
Booth, Michael, 41-2
Bordone, 77
Botticelli, 109
Braithwaite, Lilian, 53
Brandes, Georg, 43

Brett, Jeremy, 79
Bridges-Adams, William, 53, 54, 69
British Theatre Museum, 34, 37
Brown, Ivor, 54, 57
Brown, John Russell, 25
Bryden, Ronald, 99
Burbage, Richard, 8
Burdett-Coutes, Baroness, 29

Canadian Shakespeare Festival, Stratford, Ontario, 144-5
Canaletto, 109
Carlisle, John, 126, 129
Carnovsky, Morris, 146
Castiglione, *The Courtier*, 15
Chaucer, Geoffrey, *The Prioress's Tale*, 18
Chekhov, Anton, 54
Clive, Kitty, 25, 66
Cohen, Derek, 118
Coleridge, Samuel Taylor, 25
Commedia dell'arte tradition, 58-61, 68, 70, 106
Craven, Hawes, 30
Cromwell, Oliver, and Jews, 18

Dachau, 152
Dawison, Bogumil, 55
de Primoli, Count, 77, 108
The Death of Usury, or, The Disgrace of Usurers, 20
Dench, Judi, 4-6
Deneslow, Anthony, 130
Deutsch, Ernst, 145
Dexter, John, 148
Diaghilev, Serge, 56
Discourse upon Usury, A, 20
Disraeli, Benjamin, 31, 51, 76, 80, 120
Doggett, Thomas, 24
Donat, Robert, 53
Drake, Fabia, 59, 64, 66, 69
Drury Lane Theatre, London, 25

Eagleton, Terry, 94

Edward I, and Jews, 18
Elizabeth stage conventions, 6-13
Epstein, Alvin, 151

Fagin, as Jewish type, 80
Faucit, Helen, 43, 44, 49
Fellini, *La Dolce Vita*, 146
Fenwick, Henry, 102
Findlay, Deborah, 135
Fitzgerald, Percy, 34, 45
Folger Shakespeare Library, 46, 144
Forrester, Henry, 34
Foulkes, Richard, 30
Freud, Sigmund, 91
Fuchs, Georg, 56

Gilbert, Miriam, 121
Giorgione, 77
Gold, Jack, 102-16
Grant, Steve, 128
Granville, George (Lord Lansdowne), *The Jew of Venice*, 22-4, 26, 148
Granville-Barker, Harley, 2, 39
Greer, Germaine, 127

Hall, Peter, 123
Hands, Terry, 3-6
Hardwicke, Cedrick, 53
Harron, Mary, 127
Hattaway, Michael, 7
Hazlitt, William, 26
Hepburn, Katherine, 146
Higgons, Bevill, 22
Hitler, Adolf, and anti-Semitism in the Third Reich, 72-4, 91, 133, 143, 145, 151-2
Hobson, Harold, 93
Hoffman, Dustin, 123
Holderness, Graham, 111
Houseman, John, 144
Hoyle, Martin, 127
Hugh of Lincoln, 18
Hughes, Alan, 40
Hughes, Raymond, 109
Hunt, Holman, 119

Ibsen, Henrik, 150
Irving, Henry, 27, 28-52, 53, 55, 61, 67, 70-1, 75, 76, 77, 79, 83, 84, 94-5, 100, 113, 141, 143, 145, 146, 152
Irving, Laurence, 46
Israel, theatre in, 145
Italian comedy, 9, 106

James, Emrys, 3-4
James, Henry, 43, 84

Jessner, Leopold, 143
Jordon, Thomas, 'The Forteiture', 19

Kaddish, 98
Kahn, Coppelia, 2
Kammerspiele, Munich, 152
Kean, Charles, 26, 37, 39, 45
Kean, Edmund, 25-6, 28, 46, 119
Kempe, Will, 7-8
Kerrigan, John, 112, 116
King's Men, 13
Kingston, Jeremy, 119
Kokoschka, 56
Komisarjevskaya, Vera, 53
Komisarjevsky, Theodore, 52, 53-74, 84-5, 145, 152

Lambert, J. W., 83
Langham, Michael, 144-5
Lelyveld, Toby, 26, 47
Lessing, G. E., *Nathan*, 145
Lewis, Leopold, *The Bells*, 29
Lincoln Center, 146
Lopez, Ruy, physician to Elizabeth I, 18, 19
Lord Chamberlain's Men, 13
Lyceum Theatre, London, 27, 28-52, 75
Lyly, John, 1

McGann, Jerome, 152
Macklin, Charles, 25, 28, 46, 66, 69, 119
Macready, William, 26
Mahood, Molly, 5
Marlowe, *The Jew of Malta*, 19, 105; *Tamburlaine*, 16
Marshall, F. A., 43
Martin, Theodore, 43, 44
medieval dramatic tradition, 4, 5, 7, 8, 17, 18-19, 151
Mellish, Fuller, 36, 37, 45, 50, 51
Mennen, Richard, 62, 69
Meyerhold, V. E., 53, 56
Miller, Jonathan, 6, 75-100, 101-16, 117, 134, 143, 145-6, 147-8, 148-9, 150, 152
Mitchell, Warren, 102-6
Monet, 109
Maroni, 30
Moscow Art Theatre, 56; Imperial Theatre and State Theatre, 54
Moshinsky, Elijah, 110
Mostel, Zero, 148
Mulryne, J. R., 15

Nathan, David, 130
National Theatre, 6, 75-100, 101, 106, 108, 112-13, 115, 146
Nightingale, Benedict, 81, 84, 91, 99

Old Vic, 77, 101
Olivier, Laurence, 75-100, 102, 103, 120, 141, 146
Oman, Julia Trevelyan, 77-8, 108
Otway, Thomas, *Venice Preserved*, 29
Overton, Bill, 22

Palestine, theatre in, 143
Paton, Maureen, 139
Perret, Marion, 104, 115
Peter, John, 137
Petrarch, 87, 107
Picasso, 56, 62
Piper, 109
Pirandello, Luigi, 152
Piscator, Erwin, 145
Playfair, Nigel, 53
Plowright, Joan, 84-8, 93-4, 137
Podet, Rabbi Allen, 118
Poel, William, 51, 145

Raban, Jonathan, 4
Rabb, Ellis, 146-7, 148, 152
Radin, Victoria, 133
Regisseur, 53, 67-8, 72
Rembrandt, 110
Rich, Frank, 126
Richmond, Hugh, 120
Roberts, David, 119
Robertson, Graham, 48
Rothschild family, 31, 33, 76, 77, 80, 120
Rowe, Nicholas, 24-5
Royal Shakespeare Company, 3-4, 78, 117-42
Ruskin, John, 43

Sanders, Wilbur, 19
Schappes, Morris, 144
Schlueter, June, 85
Shakespeare, William, *All's Well that Ends Well*, 110; *Antony and Cleopatra*, 109; *As You Like It*, 109; *Hamlet*, 7, 29, 75; *King Lear*, 68, 69, 90; *A Midsummer Night's Dream*, 110; *Othello*, 29, 75, 90-2; *Richard III*, 75, 120; *The Taming of the Shrew*, 61; *The Tempest*, 96; *Twelfth Night*, 58, 68

Shakespeare Memorial Theatre, Stratford-upon-Avon, 53-74
Shapiro, Michael, 10, 12, 105, 151
Shaw, Sebastian, 68
Sher, Antony, 117-42
Siddons, Sarah, 25
Sinfield, Alan, 150
Stockbridge Playhouse, Massachusetts, 151
Stoker, Bram, 30, 47
Surrey, Kit, 132, 135
Svevo, Italo, 78

Tabori, Georg, 151-3
Taylor, Paul, 127
Terry, Ellen, 29, 37, 41-51, 64, 66, 83, 87, 146
Thomson, Peter, 7
Tilton, James, 146
Tintoretto, 109
Titian, 30, 109
Tree, H. Beerbohm, 51, 55
Trewin, J. C., 53, 80
Turner, J. M. W., 109
Tynan, Kenneth, 75

Udwin, Leslee, 106-7
usury, history of in England, 19-21

Veneto, as analogue for Belmont, 15
Venice, and trade, 14-16
Verch, Maria, 152
Verdi, *Rigoletto*, 38
Vermeer, 110
Veronese, 30, 77, 109
Victorian staging, 26-7, 28-52, 63

Walker, Sydney, 147
Wardle, Irving, 80
Weiss, Peter, *Marat/Sade*, 151
Wells, Stanley, 138
Wesker, Arnold, *The Merchant*, 148-50, 151
Wilde, Oscar, 79
Wilders, John, 109
Williams, Raymond, 108
Wills, W. G., *Iolanthe*, 50
Winter, William, 29, 41
Woffington, Peg, 25

Young, B. A., 4

Zitner, Sheldon, 108